T0326394

ASIA PACIFIC HUMAN RESOURCE MANAGEMENT AND ORGANISATIONAL EFFECTIVENESS

ELSEVIER

ASIAN STUDIES SERIES

Series Editor: Professor Chris Rowley,
Cass Business School, City University, London, UK;
Institute of Hallyu Convergence Research, Korea University, Korea
Griffith Business School, Griffith University, Australia
(email: c.rowley@city.ac.uk)

Elsevier is pleased to publish this major Series of books entitled Asian Studies: Contemporary Issues and Trends. The Series Editor is Professor Chris Rowley of Cass Business School, City University, London, UK and Department of International Business and Asian Studies, Griffith University, Australia.

Asia has clearly undergone some major transformations in recent years and books in the Series examine this transformation from a number of perspectives: economic, management, social, political and cultural. We seek authors from a broad range of areas and disciplinary interests covering, for example, business/management, political science, social science, history, sociology, gender studies, ethnography, economics and international relations, etc.

Importantly, the Series examines both current developments and possible future trends. The Series is aimed at an international market of academics and professionals working in the area. The books have been specially commissioned from leading authors. The objective is to provide the reader with an authoritative view of current thinking.

New authors: we would be delighted to hear from you if you have an idea for a book. We are interested in both shorter, practically orientated publications (45,000+ words) and longer, theoretical monographs (75,000–100,000 words). Our books can be single, joint or multi-author volumes. If you have an idea for a book, please contact the publishers or Professor Chris Rowley, the Series Editor.

Dr Glyn Jones
Email: g.jones.2@elsevier.com

Professor Chris Rowley
Email: c.rowley@city.ac.uk

ASIA PACIFIC HUMAN RESOURCE MANAGEMENT AND ORGANISATIONAL EFFECTIVENESS

Impacts on Practice

Edited by

ALAN NANKERVIS

CHRIS ROWLEY

NOORZIAH MOHD SALLEH

Amsterdam • Boston • Heidelberg • London
New York • Oxford • Paris • San Diego
San Francisco • Singapore • Sydney • Tokyo
Chandos Publishing is an imprint of Elsevier

British Library Cataloguing-in-Publication Data
A catalogue record for this book is available from the British Library

Library of Congress Cataloging-in-Publication Data
A catalog record for this book is available from the Library of Congress

ISBN: 978-0-08-100643-6 (print)
ISBN: 978-0-08-100654-2 (online)

For information on all Chandos Publishing publications
visit our website at https://www.elsevier.com/

Working together
to grow libraries in
developing countries

www.elsevier.com • www.bookaid.org

Publisher: Glyn Jones
Acquisition Editor: Glyn Jones
Editorial Project Manager: Harriet Clayton
Production Project Manager: Debasish Ghosh
Designer: Maria Ines Cruz

Typeset by TNQ Books and Journals

CONTENTS

Section 2: Regional HRM perspectives

4. Where was HRM? The crisis of public confidence in Australia's banks   67

A. Montague, R. Larkin and J. Burgess

5. HRM as a strategic business partner: the contributions of strategic agility, knowledge management and management development in multinational enterprises – empirical insights from India   87

S. Ananthram

6. An exploratory study of HRM roles and competencies in Vietnam, India and Malaysia   111

V. Prikshat, N.M. Salleh and A. Nankervis

LIST OF FIGURES

LIST OF TABLES

ABOUT THE EDITORS AND AUTHORS

ABOUT THE EDITORS

A. Nankervis is a Professor of Human Resource Management in the School of Management, Curtin Business School. He was formerly the Research Director of the School (2000–6) and has worked at the University of Western Sydney and RMIT University, as well a visiting professor at York University (Canada), Strathclyde University (UK) and the Prince of Songkla University (Thailand). His current research interests include comparative Asian models of HRM, challenges of the ageing workforce, skill shortages and skill development in the Asia Pacific and talent management issues. He is the Chair of the Australian Human Resources Institute's national HRM programme accreditation committee and was recently invited to participate as a regional expert in an APEC workshop on 'HRM and Sustainable Foreign Direct Investment' in Taipei (26–30 January 2015).

C. Rowley is Professor at the Cass Business School, City University, London; at Griffith University, Australia; at the IHCR, Korea University, Korea; and at IAPS, Nottingham University, UK. He was the founding Director of the Centre for Research on Asian Management and won several grants, including an ESRC/AIM Overseas International Fellowship (2004–12), RCUK Academic Fellowship (2006–11) and British Academy awards (2004, 2004). He was twice (2006, 2011) awarded for 'Outstanding Contribution to Reputation and Impact Through Research' and has won prizes for research and publications at Cass (FT list) and internationally. He has examined over 30 PhDs internationally and has had a range of external and visiting appointments to universities globally. He is Editor of the SCI (and ABS) rated leading academic cross-disciplinary journal, *Asia Pacific Business Review* (Routledge) and also the *Journal of Chinese Human Resource Management* (Emerald) as well as Book Series Editor of *Working in Asia* (Routledge), *Asian Studies* (Elsevier) and *Asian Business and Management Studies* (World Scientific Press) in addition to serving on the editorial boards of many journals. He collaborates with a network of international colleagues and has published widely, with over 550 journal articles, books and chapters and other contributions in practitioner journals, magazines and newsletters. Professor Rowley has given briefings, talks and lectures at universities and companies nationally and internationally and has consultancy experience with unions, businesses and governments on a range of topics, including cultural awareness, diversity, leadership, knowledge management, employment and human resource management policy, and practice issues generally in Asian business. He also writes regularly for practitioners and has given comments and interviews for international radio stations, newspapers, magazines and websites.

N.M. Salleh is a Senior Lecturer at the Faculty of Business and Management, Universiti Teknologi MARA, Sabah, Malaysia. She obtained her PhD in Management at the RMIT University, Melbourne, Australia, in 2012. Noorziah's research interest focuses on management with a specific interest in strategic and human resource management. She has more than 14 years of experience in teaching and learning and has presented papers at both national and international conferences. Her written contributions have appeared in a number of journals and proceedings. She also has taught many business courses at both undergraduate and postgraduate levels and conducted training programmes on management for teachers, managers and administrators.

ABOUT THE AUTHORS

S. Ananthram is a Senior Lecturer in International Business at Curtin Business School, Curtin University. His research interests are in the areas of strategic management in Asian multinationals (FDI entry modes, strategic agility, strategic business partner roles); the managerial and organisational global mindset in Asian multinationals; the ethical practices of Asian multinationals and international human resource development in Asian multinationals.

K.Ag. Budin is currently working as a Lecturer in the Universiti Teknologi MARA (UiTM), Kota Kinabalu, Sabah. She graduated from the Universiti Malaysia Sarawak with a Bachelor of Human Resource Management. Following this, she lectured part-time at UiTM and was offered a scholarship to pursue her study. She continued her research in human resource management and received the best student award in 2010. She also has published several articles in journals and presented at several conferences.

A.M. Noor is an Executive Officer in the Administration Division, Universiti Teknologi MARA, Kota Kinabalu. After his graduation, he joined AirAsia Berhad in 2005. He has a Diploma in Business Studies, UiTM

Sabah (1999), and a Bachelor of Business Administration (Hons.) Finance, UiTM Dungun, Terengganu.

J. Burgess is a Professor of HRM in the School of Management, Curtin University. His research interests include diversity management, HRM practices of multinational enterprises, contingent employment arrangements, managing job quality development and cluster dynamics. He has extensive experience in managing large-scale research projects and has conducted contract research for the Australian government and the New South Wales government.

D.J.Q. Chen is a Senior Researcher with Research & Insights at the Human Capital Leadership Institute (HCLI). His studies on work stress and work–life intersections have been featured in publications such as the *Harvard Business Review*, *Forbes*, the *Wall Street Journal* and *The Globe and Mail*. Prior to joining HCLI, Dr Chen was a research scholar at the National University of Singapore and has worked closely with various governmental agencies on issues related to employment and employability.

J. Connell is Director, Researcher Development at the University of Technology, Sydney (UTS) and an Adjunct Professor of Management, Curtin Business School, Curtin University. Julia has published over 80 refereed journal articles, 20 book chapters and co-edited five books related to employment, change and organisational effectiveness as well as consulting to a number of public and private sector organisations on related topics.

L. Herkenhoff is currently a full Professor at the Graduate School of Business at Saint Mary's College where she teaches leadership, organisational behaviour and quantitative analysis. She serves as the Director of the Global MBA programme. She has published both theoretical and applied papers that span numerous workplace and academic issues.

J.A. Heydenfeldt specialises in neurobiological and behavioural elements of emotional health, cognitive acuity, leadership and team building. She has published numerous papers discussing the influence of new insights from interpersonal neurobiology on organisational theory. An organisational psychologist, Dr Heydenfeldt is currently a Lecturer in the School of Economics and Business at St Mary's College of California.

P. Hosie is an Associate Professor at the Curtin Graduate School of Business at Curtin University. He has taught undergraduates and graduates in most aspects of human resource management in Australia, the United Arab

Emirates, Austria, Singapore, China, Hong Kong, Taiwan and Vietnam. His distinguished academic and research track record has yielded over 110 refereed publications which are widely cited and referenced in international publications.

A.K. Rosline is currently the Rector of Universiti Teknologi MARA, Kota Kinabalu, Sabah, Malaysia and is on the Faculty of Administrative Science and Policy Studies. He teaches Human Resource Management, Organisational Learning, Organisational Behaviour, Industrial Relations and International Business. He earned a bachelor's degree in Human Resource Management at Universiti Teknologi MARA Shah Alam, Malaysia, a Master of Business Administration degree from Edith Cowan University Perth, Western Australia and a PhD in Public Management from Cardiff University Wales, UK. He has published articles and has spoken at conferences throughout the world on matters dealing with Human Resource Management, Industrial Relations, Organisational Learning and local government.

R.P.J. Kingshott is the Director of Programs in the Curtin Business School, Curtin University. He has more than 32 years of industry and university experience in a wide variety of teaching, programme management, higher degree supervision and research-related roles. He has also taught in Singapore, Hong Kong, Malaysia and New Zealand, and has extensive industry experience in developing educational programmes in the mining sector in Western Australia. Russel has published in many international academic journals.

J.K.S. Len began her involvement in research when she worked as an officer in the Institute for Development Studies, Sabah (IDS), Malaysia in 2000. She has undertaken research studies in entrepreneurship and marketing, and has published several articles and conference papers since she joined Universiti Teknologi Mara, Sabah as a Lecturer in 2005. She is currently a PhD student and her research interests include industrial relations, management, human resource management, entrepreneurship and psychology.

R. Larkin is a lecturer in Employment Relations and Human Resource Management at the University of Newcastle. Roslyn's teaching areas include advanced ER/HRM applied through Work Integrated Learning opportunities with partner organisations, International HRM and, intra-organisational knowledge management in MNEs. Current research interests are focusing on knowledge transfer in SME and ME clusters and employment in the aged care sector.

A. Montague is Lecturer in Business Management at Royal Melbourne Institute of Technology (RMIT) University. His particular research and publication areas include skill/vocational shortages, government policies relating to the links between education and industry, employment/education programme policy development and management, the ageing workforce and workforce planning.

A. Najeeb is a former member of the Employment Tribunal of the Maldives. He holds a PhD in Management from the University of Wollongong, Australia, a Master's degree in Human Resource Management from the University of Newcastle, Australia, and a Bachelor of Arts in Business Studies from the University of the South Pacific. He is a chartered professional member of Chartered Institute of Personnel and Development (CIPD) and a certified professional member of the Australian Human Resource Institute (AHRI). He is currently a senior lecturer at the Villa College, Maldives. His research interests include HRM, SHRM, IR, institutional change and employment relations in the tourism industry.

V. Prikshat has more than 17 years' academic experience, including teaching, research and programme coordination at the tertiary level, in Australian and Indian universities (RMIT University, Melbourne/Punjab Technical University, India). His key expertise is in the fields of management, human resource management, leadership, employment relations and general management. He has presented his research findings in numerous international conferences and his major areas of interest are in human resource competency frameworks and skills shortages in the Asia-Pacific region. Presently he is working as a Lecturer (management/human resource management) at the Australian Institute of Business, Adelaide.

R.U. Mohammed is a Senior Finance Lecturer and Administrator at UiTM Sabah. She has a vast experience as a professional banker, an auditor, a manager and an educator. She has worked in a well-known *Sharia* compliant bank and two prominent private colleges in Sabah. She has affiliations with various agencies of the state government, NGOs and public schools in Sabah. She has more than 50 publications in the forms of proceedings and books in various fields published by UiTM and other local universities.

A. Sharma MBA is currently the Manager of External Relations and Executive Officer to the President at the University of Wollongong in Dubai. Her research interests include strategic management, strategic marketing, human resource management and change management. Arpana has more than 18 years of work experience in different fields of management including higher education and the health sector.

W. Su-Yen is Chief Executive Officer of the Human Capital Leadership Institute (HCLI), which was established by the Ministry of Manpower, the Singapore Economic Development Board and the Singapore Management University to develop global leaders with a strong understanding of leading in Asia, as well as to build Asian leaders with the ability to lead on the global stage. She is Non-Executive Chairman of Nera Telecommunications, a global telecom and IT solutions provider that is listed on the Singapore Exchange Mainboard. Concurrently, she is an Independent Director at MediaCorp, Singapore's leading media company, and at NTUC First Campus which is the largest provider of childcare services in Singapore.

FOREWORD

Although the Asia Pacific region is being hailed as the largest and fastest developing economic theatre of the world, scholarly research in the critical area of human resource management focusing on this region has been sparse. The key question as to what extent human resource policies, practices and, most importantly, organisational cultures need to be examined not only in the industry or corporate contexts but also in the diversity of this region remains an unexplored area. Therefore it is wonderful to see three highly reputed scholars from Australia, Malaysia and the UK bring together this edited volume titled *Asia Pacific Human Resource Management and Organisational Effectiveness*. To their credit, the editors have assembled a number of experts from the Asia Pacific region with deep understanding and informed thinking.

Some four decades ago Japanese culture-bound human resource practices drew global attention. More recently, new models of human resource management have been taking shape in China and India. It is therefore highly timely to take a fresh look at the human resource underpinnings of organisational effectiveness in the Asia Pacific region. This volume opens up a potential due both to its scholarly tone and meaningful practical insights. Unless the mainstream conceptual foundations of the disciplines of human resources and organisational effectiveness, including the challenges facing human capital management in closing the gap in traditions and historical practices and aligning with the divergent context of the Asia Pacific region, they will be rendered irrelevant both to academics and practitioners. The current volume most certainly adds to this far-reaching imperative in a commendable way.

The book is organised into three parts, namely Contextual Frameworks, Regional HRM Perspectives, and Employment Relations and Islamic Perspectives, and contains eleven chapters. The themes emphasised in the book are the policies and practices of HRM as well as distinctive features of organisational effectiveness in the Asia-Pacific region. The most important research issues are balanced in terms of their conceptual and empirical as well as practical implications. Interestingly, the synergies generated in the overall contributions from both new researchers as well as experienced scholars have been remarkably impactful. Countries under focus in this book include Australia, the UK, Singapore, Malaysia, India, Vietnam and the

Maldives, and it is interesting to note the underlying thematic connections in their micro foundations of ideas.

The editors deserve to be commended for bringing together such an impressive volume. I hope this effort will serve the purpose of fostering new research interest on the region and spark fresh thinking by opening up of new frontiers in the discipline of human resources studies.

Emeritus Professor Samir Ranjan Chatterjee
Asia Business Centre – Curtin University

Asia Pacific Human Resource Management and Organization Effectiveness
Alan Nankervis, Chris Rowley and Noorziah Mohd Salleh

Preview by Dave Ulrich

What a delight to preview this edited book of thoughtful essays on why and how HR practices will deliver organization effectiveness in Asian settings.

Nankervis, Rowley and Salleh do an outstanding job synthesizing and weaving together the themes of the insightful essays in both the introductory and conclusion chapters, so I will not repeat their observations.

The reason I like this book so much is that it addresses some of the major issues in the HR profession in rigorous and creative ways.

1. How does HR add value?

The profession of HR has evolved from creating value primarily through administrative efficiencies embedded in policies and practices. The field has pivoted to also delivering value through talent (more competent and committed employees) and culture (more robust and defined organization capabilities) that not only cedes strategy, but builds confidence in customers and investors. The essays in this book show the value of HR to important organizational outcomes. HR is not about HR per se, but about how HR can help the organization better deliver to customers and investors through talent and culture. These essays also point out that defining the organizational outcomes of HR is still a work in progress. The variety of approaches and analyses continues to show that HR impact on organization effectiveness is possible and gaining momentum.

2. How does HR vary by geography?

Anyone who has visited multiple countries recognizes both similarities and differences across country boundaries. This multicultural view has been documented by thoughtful colleagues who show differences in values and practices. Most also recognize the enormous rise of the Asian region. But fewer appreciate some of the subtle differences between Asian countries. The essays in this anthology do a wonderful job of looking at subtle, but important, differences among HR practices and approaches in Australia, Brunei Darusallam, India, Indonesia, Malaysia, the Maldives, Singapore and Vietnam. What a delight to peek inside these countries to see meaningful differences that show how HR can adapt to cultural settings. By recognizing geographic differences within Asia, HR thought leaders can begin to become more granular in their recommendations for HR investments.

3. What does it take to be an effective HR professional?

Every HR professional association wants to codify, certify and improve HR professionals. There are many approaches to doing so. The divergence of this approaches is a strength of our field as we learn what it means to be an effective HR professional. These essays contribute to these important conversations. HR professionals have to know themselves and to know how to build relationships with others so that they can positively impact their organization.

In brief, this delightful book offers insights on the HR profession's definition of value, geographic granularity and personal HR competencies that will keep HR central to important business discussions.

Asia Pacific Human Resource Management and Organizational Effectiveness
Alan Nankervis, Chris Rowley and Noorziah Mohd Salleh
Publisher: Elsevier, 2016
Expert Testimonial (Recommendation)

Nankervis, Rowley and Salleh are well-established and well-recognized authors who have written an invaluable book that describes the relationships among human resource management policies and practices and organizational effectiveness in the Asia Pacific region of the world. As they note, there have been many studies that have investigated these relationships, but they have been largely conducted in large organizations headquartered in Western countries, in particular North America and Europe. The authors provide an excellent framework on human resource management and organizational effectiveness and then allow their contributing authors the freedom to utilize that framework and focus on aspects of it that are most interesting and relevant within their countries. As a consequence the reader is provided with a variety of topics on specific aspects of human resource management and organizational effectiveness within several countries in Asia, namely India, Vietnam, Malaysia, the Maldives and Australia. Each contributing author is a country expert and has deep knowledge of the country being described. In addition to these five country chapters, there is a chapter that discusses human resource management and organizational effectiveness from a union perspective, and a chapter that explores organizational effectiveness from an Islamic perspective. Nankervis, Rowley and Salleh do an excellent job in their concluding chapter, as well as the introductory chapter. Overall, the reader, whether academic or HR professional, will find the book to be filled with very interesting information and insights into the relationships between human resource management and organizational effectiveness regarding specific aspects of human resource management, all of which make for a valuable contribution to the field.

Randall S. Schuler, Distinguished Professor of Strategic International Human Resource Management, Rutgers University, New Brunswick, New Jersey, USA

Samir Ranjan Chatterjee
Emeritus Professor Samir Ranjan Chatterjee, Asia Business Centre – Curtin University, Australia

Although the Asia Pacific region is being hailed as the largest and fastest developing economic theatre of the world, scholarly research in the critical area of human resource management focussing on this region has been sparse. The key question as to what extent human resource policies, practices and most importantly, organisational cultures, need to be examined not only in the industry or corporate contexts but also in the diversity of this region remains an unexplored area. Therefore it is wonderful to see three highly reputed scholars from Australia, Malaysia and UK bring together this edited volume titled, *Asia Pacific Human Resource Management and Organisational Effectiveness: Impacts on Practice*. To their credit, the editors have assembled a number of experts from the Asia-Pacific region with deep understanding and informed thinking.

Some four decades ago Japanese culture-bound human resource practices drew global attention. More recently, new models of human resource management have been taking shape in China and India. It is therefore highly timely to take a fresh look at the human resource underpinnings of organisational effectiveness in the Asia-Pacific region. This volume opens up a potential both due to its scholarly tone and meaningful practical insights. Unless the mainstream conceptual foundations of the disciplines of human resources and organisational effectiveness, including the challenges facing human capital management in closing the gap in traditions and historical practices and aligning with the divergent context of the Asia-Pacific region, they will be rendered irrelevant both to academics and practitioners. The current volume most certainly adds to this far reaching imperative in a commendable way.

The book is organised into three sections, namely, contextual frameworks, regional HRM practices and employment relations & Islamic perspectives and contains eleven chapters. The themes emphasised in the book are the policies and practices of HRM as well as distinctive features of organisational effectiveness in the Asia-Pacific region. The most important research issues are balanced in terms of their conceptual and empirical as well as practical implications. Interestingly, the synergies generated in the overall contributions from both new researchers as well as experienced scholars have been remarkably impactful. Countries under focus in this book include Australia, UK, Singapore, Malaysia, India, Vietnam and the Maldives, and it is interesting to note the underlying thematic connections in their micro foundations of ideas.

The editors deserve to be commended for bringing together such an impressive volume. I hope this effort will serve the purpose of fostering new research interest on the region and spark fresh thinking by opening up of new frontiers in the discipline of human resources studies.

CHAPTER 1

Introduction: human resource management and organisational effectiveness – an overview and synthesis

A. Nankervis, C. Rowley, N.M. Salleh

INTRODUCTION

An important major challenge for human resource (HR) professionals and for HR management (HRM) research and the associated literature has been to establish clear, robust evidence concerning the relationships between the contributions of HRM systems, processes and functions to organisational effectiveness. While strategic HRM (SHRM) theory proposes and promotes these linkages as a key foundation, supportive empirical work has been limited and largely confined to small-scale studies conducted in the West, most commonly in particular sectors or large organisations. Few such studies have been undertaken in the Asia Pacific region. Our book presents contemporary research from this region to explore the relationship between HRM systems and practices and organisational effectiveness both conceptually and empirically through an Asia Pacific contextual lens. Accordingly, our book adds to both the existing literature on this issue and aims to encourage further research on such aspects as differences and similarities between these linkages in Asian and Western contexts, diverse sectors, local and multinational companies (MNCs) and organisations and larger versus smaller organisational types.

This chapter first briefly explores the theory on HRM and organisational effectiveness and the proposed conceptual links between them. We then explain the rationale, sequence and content of each chapter and conclude with a discussion of their overall implications for researchers, HR professionals and organisational managers who have an interest or an investment in the Asia Pacific region.

Asia Pacific Human Resource Management
and Organisational Effectiveness
ISBN 978-0-08-100643-6

CONCEPTS OF HUMAN RESOURCE MANAGEMENT

HRM for some commentators emerged with the greater individualism post–1980s, although the management of people is not new. Indeed, writing on the area dates back to at least the first century, with Columella, a Roman farmer whose *De Rustica* featured one of the earliest tracts on people management. Two or three millennia ago Chinese and Indians wrote manuals on how to effectively manage people. Sun Tzu and *The Art of War* has been revived in the West but his work and that of the unknown authors of the '36 Strategies' remain in use in Asian management. The Indian *Bhagavad Gita* has been a basis for managing in South Asia, even when the Hindu origins of the advice is no longer considered.

HRM itself has been defined in many different ways and from diverse perspectives. In its most basic sense the term describes the primary functions of HR professionals, such as resourcing, rewards, development and employee relations (Rowley, 2003; Dessler et al., 2005; Rowley and Jackson, 2011; Nankervis et al., 2013). Broader definitions consider HRM to be 'a pattern of shared basic assumptions' which is disseminated throughout the organisation in order to ensure the 'external adaptation' of organisations to their industries and markets on the one hand, and to assure the 'internal integration' of all institutional HRM systems, processes and practices in order to progress organisational goals and desired outcomes on the other. This is also referred to as external and internal 'fit' (Wright and Snell, 1998), which emphasises the importance of the horizontal integration of all HRM activities with each other and the vertical alignment of these with an organisation's business strategy.

For Fitz-enz (2000) HRM combines the knowledge, skills and attitudes of employees with other factors, such as the diverse information possessed by employees and their willingness to share it with, and for, their organisations. The concept of human capital management encapsulates these ideas, linking data, people and organisational effectiveness (Cascio, 1989; Fitz-enz, 2000). Other authors have attempted to determine the nature of this relationship between employee and organisational performance (Delaney and Huselid, 1996; Dessler et al., 2005; Nankervis et al., 2013). From these perspectives, employee performance is enhanced through greater efficiency and effectiveness in such HRM functional areas as job design, recruitment and selection, learning and development, and performance review, together with dynamic employment relationships in response to both internal and external environmental triggers (Delaney and Huselid, 1996; Dessler et al., 2005; Nankervis et al., 2014).

Theoretically, for some commentators the key objective of HRM is to support organisations in achieving their objectives by developing and implementing HR strategies that are integrated with business strategy to contribute to the development of a high-performance culture in order to ensure that the organisation has the talented skilled and engaged people it needs and to create a positive employment relationship between management and employees (Armstrong and Taylor, 2014). Thus the aims of HRM, at one level, are to enhance employees' skills and increase employee engagement levels, which may then lead to increased organisational efficiency (Lepak and Snell, 2002). To achieve those aims, Renwick (2003) suggested three HR manager roles: 'Policy-Makers', 'Advice Providers' and 'Administrators'. Subsequently, Crouse, Doyle and Young (2011: 39) asserted that functional HRM roles have been 'supplanted by a more strategic role' with different levels of competencies. According to Nankervis et al. (2014), these new competencies include business, change management, data collection and analysis, consulting, programme evaluation and accountability skills. Ulrich's studies used large global samples to support an HR competency model of: 'Strategic Positioner', 'Capability Builder', 'Change Champion', 'Technology Proponent', 'HR Innovator and Integrator' and 'Credible Activist' (Ulrich et al., 2013: 24). Lawler (2005: 167) endorsed the crucial business partner role of effective HRM professionals. He argues that HRM 'needs to move beyond ... traditional personnel functions ... *to adding value through directly improving the performance of the business*' (our italics). It can do this by effective talent management, helping with change management, influencing business strategy, and a host of other high-value-added activities that impact organizational effectiveness (OE).

Finally, the different challenges and influences of national cultures on HRM roles and the consequent ways in which organisational effectiveness is achieved is a key research focus. Authors such as Rowley (1997a, 1997b), Rowley and Benson (2002, 2003a, 2003b), Rowley et al. (2004), Rowley and Warner (2008), Chatterjee and Nankervis (2007), Nankervis et al. (2006, 2013) and Yeung et al. (2008), among others, have discussed the case for the 'convergence', 'divergence' or even 'cross-vergence' of HRM systems and practices, especially in the Asia Pacific region. They have also researched the distinctive cultural characteristics of countries such as South Korea (Rowley and Bae, 2003), China, India, Vietnam, Taiwan, Indonesia, Singapore, Malaysia and Thailand, which may influence HRM and organisational effectiveness and the links between them. Some of these cultural features include more paternalistic management styles, respect (and sometimes reverence) in relationships between management and employees, acceptance of authority, eagerness to work for organisations which share similar values, employee loyalty and demands for ongoing learning and development opportunities. Based on such cultural values, Rowley et al. (2004) and Yeung et al. (2008) suggested that an esoteric 'Asian model' of HRM is in evolution, based on their studies of Japan, China and South Korea, while Chatterjee and Nankervis (2007) and Nankervis et al. (2013) proposed a 'new HRM model' for Indian and Chinese organisations.

HRM AND ORGANISATIONAL EFFECTIVENESS

Like HRM itself, organisational effectiveness can be considered from different perspectives. Traditionally, 'effectiveness' was largely equated with quantitative objectives, such as financial performance and hence HRM imperatives centred on cost containment or cost reduction in functions such as staffing, training, and the rewards and benefits systems. Narrow organisational performance measures, such as balance sheets, return on investment, shareholder value, profitability levels and comparative competitive statistics influenced the levels of recruitment and the amount of employee training or management development, with emphases on greater productivity per employee.

More recent perspectives have adopted a multi-stakeholder model of effectiveness, a broader concept than performance. As Schuler and Jackson (2014: 40) explained: 'Today's more comprehensive model of HRM and OE includes elements of the external global environment, the internal organisational environment, the HRM system and multiple stakeholders.' Expanding on these themes that effectiveness involves multiple stakeholders and qualitative as well a quantitative measures, Brewster et al. (2000) identified the broad benefits or contributions of SHRM. These include contributions to: the goal accomplishment and survival of the company; successful implementation of business strategies; enhancing competitive advantage, responsiveness and innovation; and competitive advantage, as part of HRM's 'Strategic Business Partner' (SBP) role. Others have suggested that the future of HRM lies in 'understanding and supporting activities that create sustainable capability and external shareholder value' (Donaldson, 2006: 1) and improving both employee and shareholder satisfaction; and that 'organisational capabilities, such as talent, speed, collaboration, accountability, shared mindset, learning and leadership are the deliverables of HR ... [which] contribute to an organisation's market value' (Kramar, 2006: 7).

In short, some argue that the relationship between HRM and organisational effectiveness is one of the key outcomes of SHRM. The moderator between SHRM and organisational effectiveness is employee performance and consequently HRM's role is to increase both employee performance and organisational effectiveness. For Ulrich (1997) HRM can deliver business effectiveness in four ways. This involves HR professionals who should:

- be closely involved in the execution of business strategy;
- provide expertise in work performance issues, including cost-reductions and quality;
- represent employee concerns and enhance competence and engagement;
- drive change management processes and enhance its organisational capacities here.

In summary, while there is a growing body of theory and empirical evidence that HRM strategies, policies and practices influence organisational effectiveness, there is a need for further studies which identify the associated relationships and specific variables. In our book, organisational effectiveness is considered as a broader concept than mere organisational performance and includes a range of quantitative and qualitative dimensions. These dimensions encompass specific business outcomes, shareholder value perceptions, competitive capabilities, employee satisfaction and engagement and long-term sustainability. Our next section explores the particular contextual challenges posed for HRM researchers and professionals in the Asia Pacific region.

HRM AND ORGANISATIONAL EFFECTIVENESS RESEARCH IN THE ASIA PACIFIC

Some Asia Pacific HRM studies have attempted to determine whether competitive advantage can be achieved through people and leads to organisational effectiveness (Long and Wan Ismail, 2008). Some authors have concluded that HRM do have positive causal effects on organisational effectiveness (Hoe, 2013). In particular, the notion of 'best practice' in HRM has received considerable attention, even in Asia (Kwon et al., 2010; Lawler et al., 2011; Lin et al., 2014). Although the adoption of contemporary HRM systems is reportedly slow and cautious in many Asia Pacific countries (Cheah-Liaw et al., 2003), some studies have shown that effectiveness in managing HR may also lead to improved business performance and overall organisational effectiveness (Armstrong and Baron, 2002; Zheng et al., 2006;

Singh, 2004) and if neglected might have detrimental impacts. As an illustration of this, one study found a strong positive relationship between HRM practices and labour productivity mediated by HR outcomes in manufacturing small and medium-size enterprises (SMEs) in Japan, where many firms had gone out of business and new firm entry rate had a downward trend (Gamage, 2015). According to some, one of the reasons for high rates of business failures here is the lack of attention to the human side of their businesses.

Other regional studies have also shown a positive effect between HR practices and improved organisational performance and effectiveness. In Malaysia, for example, one study of particular HRM functions – training, employee participation, performance appraisal and job descriptions – found that in combination they can have a significant impact on organisational effectiveness (Tahsildari and Shahnaei, 2015). Another Malaysian study, using data from CEOs/managing directors, reported that they had specific expectations regarding the forms of HRM practice that should be developed by their HR professionals (Othman et al., 2001). These expectations were that HR managers needed to be competent in the main elements of HRM practices and use innovative techniques, such as developing employee participation, teamwork and productivity improvement, important capabilities that were considered to be largely lacking in their HR professionals. Yang and Lin (2014: 61) concluded with regard to Taiwan that 'HRM effectiveness, including the delivery of high quality technical HRM and strategic HRM in a complementary manner, will result in positive firm-level outcomes.' A further Malaysian research project found the HR 'business partner role is positively related with HRM effectiveness' (Yusoff, 2012: 1).

Studies on the Asia Pacific largely suggest that an organisation's chosen 'bundle of HR practices' affects overall business performance and effectiveness (Osman et al., 2011; Tahsildari and Shahnaei, 2015). As well as these HRM practices, employees' perceptions also play an important role in the prediction of organisational commitment, which also may contribute to organisational performance. However, it is argued that these perceptions are partially mediated by procedural justice expectations (Chang, 2005). Employees' knowledge, skills and acquisition of expertise and employees' satisfaction have also been seen to be associated with organisational effectiveness. In Chang's (2005) study, organisational effectiveness was measured by assessing the satisfaction and commitment level of employees and customers. Satisfaction and commitment, in turn, were measured by already established tools. Correlation techniques showed that human capital development had a strong significant positive relation with the satisfaction levels of the employees and customers and which would eventually lead to increased organisational effectiveness. At a broader level, Ulrich and Sutton (2010) explored the nature of Asian leadership styles into the future and concluded that they will need to be transformed in order to better drive organisational effectiveness within Asia's increasingly competitive and dynamic environments, while Rowley and Ulrich (2014) distinguish the importance of effective leadership in Asia and organisational performance.

The findings of many studies in both Western and Asian contexts have shown the importance of HRM practices for organisational effectiveness. However, the cause-effect nature of the relationship is still unclear and there is a dearth of empirical evidence which sheds light on the variables in this relationship. Nevertheless, the primary objectives of SHRM for many are to contribute to a profitable and sustainable organisation, increase workforce competency and engagement, develop excellence in HR management and create a dynamic and productive work environment.

Our book contributes to helping us understand this ongoing conundrum better by presenting a collection of research on the Asia Pacific region. The following section summarises the ideas on this key HRM challenge within the relatively unexplored regional context of Asia.

STRUCTURE AND CONTENT

The Asia Pacific countries considered in this volume are Australia, Brunei Darusallam, India, Indonesia, Malaysia, the Maldives, Singapore and Vietnam, with further broad discussion of the present and future roles of the Association of South East Asian Nations (ASEAN). Many of the chapters were originally prepared as papers presented at the First HRM and Organisational Effectiveness Conference, co-hosted by Curtin University and Universiti Technologi Mara (Sabah) at Kota Kinabalu, Sabah, in December 2014.

The chapters are divided into three parts. The first part contains two conceptual chapters which explore broad contextual issues likely to have an impact on the relationship between HRM and organisational effectiveness in different regions and in particular organisations. The second part includes five chapters which present empirical research on HRM roles and competencies and their relationship to organisational effectiveness in Asia Pacific countries – specifically, India, Vietnam, Malaysia, the Maldives and Australia. The final part of the book contains two complementary chapters which analyse the influences of Asian employee relations systems and Islamic traditions on the HRM–organisational effectiveness relationship. The final chapter then revisits the content and details the types of HR practitioner literature to place current debates in conetext, and summarises the overall contributions of the book together with some discussion of their implications for both senior and HR managers and researchers.

In Part 1, we start with Chen and Wong's chapter as it provides a useful contemporary overview of the challenges and opportunities associated with the formation of the new Asian Economic Community (AEC) in 2015, including the likely 'winner' and 'loser' countries. In particular, it reveals that Singapore has significant talent attraction and retention opportunities relative to Malaysia, Thailand, Indonesia and the Phillipines, but may struggle to retain its competitive advantage in competition with Australia and New Zealand due to their more attractive employment conditions and lifestyle issues. Given the immense projected increase in HR mobility envisaged by the AEC, the relationship between HRM and organisational effectiveness may well become a crucial factor in such developments.

The third chapter, by Hosie et al., presents an entirely different macro-perspective on the nexus between HRM and organisational effectiveness. An intra-psychic lens is used to explore the transference of Western theories of emotional intelligence, mindfulness and neurobiological science to Asian cultures and their HRM practices, given the significant cultural differences in emotional expression between them. They consider the applications of these concepts to management practices of teamwork, job performance, productivity and leadership and overall organisational performance. It concludes that a better understanding of HRM practice in Asian cultures of self-reflection, contemplative practice and meditation can also be valuable in Western contexts.

In Part two, in contrast, Chapter 4 analyses the unethical practices of two major Australian banks during and after the global financial crisis. Given that HR professionals are often charged with maintaining ethical standards and codes of conduct in organisations, Montague et al. investigate the rhetoric and realities of corporate social responsibility and moral principles within the banking sector and explain how unethical behaviours may erode stakeholders' (employees' and customers') commitment and engagement, with serious consequences for both perceived and actual organisational effectiveness. It also suggests how various HRM practices can be enhanced through careful attention to the inclusion of ethical behaviours and their reinforcement in all organisations.

The following three chapters focus on the relationships between HRM roles and competencies and organisational effectiveness in five different Asia Pacific countries. First, in Chapter 5 Ananthram's research on the HRM 'SBP' role in Indian MNCs evaluates effective HRM roles from the perspective of CEOs and managing directors. The findings suggest that SHRM is most productive for corporations when it encompasses three key components: 'Strategic Agility' (external fit), 'Knowledge Management' and 'Management Development' (internal fit). It concludes that the SBP role of HRM is especially critical for MNCs operating in complex and dynamic business environments focused on competitive advantage, especially in the Asia Pacific region.

Chapter 6 reports the findings of Prikshat et al.'s three-country study which aimed to ascertain their relative stages of HRM development from an administrative to a more SHRM role and their associated contributions to organisational effectiveness. Using a new 'Model of (HRM) Excellence' developed by the Australian HR Institute in conjunction with the University of Michigan, data was collected from HR and non-HR managers in Vietnam, Malaysia and India. The study found that while there are differences in the forms and applications of SHRM across diverse ownership and industry types, overall most HR roles in all three countries were still primarily that of functional expert, having progressed from purely administrative roles but not yet developed fully as SBPs. It identifies some differences between countries, industry sectors and organisational types, but concludes that HRM in these three countries was in a transitional phase, moving inexorably from an administrative to a more strategic role.

The following Chapter 7 analyses the application of concepts of social capital and HRM devolution to the links between HRM, line managers and organisational effectiveness. This uses a sample of hospitality resorts in the Maldives. Najeeb used interviews with resort managers, field observations and analysis of secondary sources to explore how these managerial relationships enhanced HRM practices and organisational effectiveness within a dynamic and higly competitive industry environment. The findings suggest that there is an 'interaction effect' between HR professionals and line managers as they contest and reconcile their interests and roles. Productive synthesis of these inherent conflicts in organisations may contribute to enhanced organisational effectiveness.

Chapter 8, in contrast, focuses on the relationships between SHRM and work quality in nine Australian case study organisations by Connell and Burgess. They developed a four-dimensional analytical framework based on the 2012 Eurofound survey – job prospects, intrinsic job quality, extrinsic job quality and working time quality – to explore practical HRM applications in a variety of states and sectors. Demonstrating that organisational effectiveness has both qualitative as well as quantitative components, it associates work quality with well-being from the employees' perspective. The findings suggest that good work quality (on all four dimensions) is highly likely to result in higher productivity and enhanced organisational effectiveness, evidenced by lower rates of employee turnover, absenteeism and tardiness on the one hand and improved employee well-being on the other.

Part three of the book contains two chapters with quite diverse perspectives on the linkages between HRM and organisational effectiveness. The first, Chapter 9, provides an interesting insight into developing trade union relationships with their members and the government in Malaysia. Salleh et al. analyse the effectiveness of unions in the manufacturing sector in relation to their representation of the collective 'voice' of members' needs, particularly with respect to negotiations over salary, security and safety and whether they assist in the satisfaction of employees' self-esteem and self-actualisation needs. In an era of significant price rises and a decline in union influence on governments, the study questions whether unions can be strengthened through the facilitation of expressions of member 'voice'.

Chapter 10, in contrast, provides a fascinating conceptual framework for the analysis of employee job satisfaction from an Islamic perspective. Asmad et al. use traditional Western notions of extrinsic and intrinsic job satisfaction determinants as their basis to explore how they are applied in Islamic organisations in Malaysia, Indonesia and Brunei Darussalam. The chapter employs specific examples of Islamic concepts and principles in order to demonstrate the differences (and similarities) between these organisations and their Western counterparts, within and outside these countries. The conclusion is that Islamic organisations are more likely to favour intrinsic rather than extrinsic approaches towards employee job satisfaction, with emphases on religious values, personal goals and community service. It may be inferred from this that qualitative HRM contributions, as well as quantitative components, are required to ensure effectiveness in such organisations.

Finally, Rowley et al. in Chapter 11 summarises the overall content and themes of the chapters included and grounds them in the context of HR professionals and their different roles and development. It provides some constructive implications and applications for all senior and HR managers and researchers in the Asia Pacific region.

CONCLUSION

The research presented in various chapters of this volume encompasses many diverse Asia Pacific countries, together with both macro- and micro-HRM roles, systems and processes. The influences of different contextual frameworks and diverse perspectives are considered and compared with their Western counterparts. Limitations with respect to the coverage of HRM functions, Asia Pacific countries and industry sectors are acknowledged.

Our collection provides a valuable addition to the ongoing debate about the relationships between HRM and organisational effectiveness by including contemporary conceptual and empirical research on the issue in the Asia Pacific region and some less covered countries. The underlying assumptions of the book are that HRM and the associated roles and competencies of its HR professionals are major drivers of organisational performance and effectiveness and that organisational effectiveness blends both traditional quantitative measures, such as profitability, return on investment and competitiveness, with more qualitative measures, such as employee engagement, job satisfaction, corporate propriety and perceptions of overall stakeholder value.

We hope that the following chapters will serve to stimulate future discussion and argument on the conundrum of the relationship between organisational effectiveness and HRM and further to encourage researchers to broaden and deepen our understanding of them. This can be seen within the Asia Pacific region and beyond.

REFERENCES

Armstrong, M., Baron, A., 2002. Strategic HRM: The Key to Improved Business Performance. CIPD Publishing, London.

Armstrong, M., Taylor, S., 2014. Armstrong's Handbook of Human Resource Management Practice. Kogan Page, London.

Brewster, C., Mayrhofer, W., Morley, M. (Eds.), 2000. New challenges for European HRM. Macmillan, Basingstoke.

Cascio, W., 1989. Managing HR: Productivity, Quality of Work, Life, Profits, second ed. McGraw-Hill, New York.

Chang, E., 2005. Employees' overall perception of HRM effectiveness. Human Relations 58 (4), 523–544.

Chatterjee, S., Nankervis, A., 2007. Asian Management in Transition: Emerging Themes. Palgrave UK, Basingstoke.

Cheah-Liaw, G., Petzall, S., Selvarajah, C., 2003. The role of human resource management (HRM) in Australian-Malaysian joint ventures. Journal of European Industrial Training 27, 244–262.

Crouse, P., Doyle, W., Young, J.D., 2011. Workplace learning strategies, barriers, facilitators and outcomes: A qualitative study among human resource management practitioners. Human Resource Development International 14 (1), 39–55.

Delaney, J., Huselid, M.A., 1996. The impact of human resource management practices on perceptions of organizational performance. Academy of Management Journal 39, 949–969.

Dessler, G., Sutherland, G., Cole, N.D., 2005. Human Resources Management In Canada. Pearson Education Canada, Toronto.

Donaldson, C., 2006. Intangibles crucial to HR's future. Human Resources 107 (27), 1.

Fitz-enz, J., 2000. ROI of Human Capital: Measuring the Economic Value of Employee Performance. Amacom, Division of American Management Association, New York.

Gamage, A.S., 2015. The role of HRM in improving labour productivity: an analysis of manufacturing SMEs in Japan. Sri Lankan Journal of Human Resource Management 5 (1).

Hoe, P.T., 2013. Human Resource Management in the Transitional Economy in Vietnam Unpublished Master's thesis. University of Applied Sciences, Helsinki, Finland.

Kramar, R., 2006. Cranet-Macquarie Survey on International HRM: Report on the Australian Findings. Macquarie University, Sydney, p. 7.

Kwon, K., Bae, J., Lawler, J., 2010. High commitment HR practices and top performers: impacts on organizational commitment. Management International Review 50 (1), 57–80.

Lawler, E.E., 2005. From human resource management to organisational effectiveness. HRM 44 (2), 165–169.

Lawler, J., Chen, S.-J., Wu, P.-C., Bae, J., Bai, B., 2011. High performance work systems in foreign subsidiaries of American multinationals: an institutional model. Journal of International Business Studies 42, 202–220.

Lepak, D.P., Snell, S.A., 2002. Examining the human resource architecture: the relationships among human capital, employment, and human resource configurations. Journal of Management 28, 517–543.

Lin, L.-S., Chen, S.-J., Huang, P.-C., Lu, C.-M., 2014. High commitment HR practices in Taiwanese service industry: demographic and functional diversity. Asia Pacific Journal of Human Resources 52, 443–459.

Long, C.S., Wan Ismail, W., 2008. Human resource competencies: a study of the HR professionals in manufacturing firms in Malaysia. International Management Review 4, 65–76.

Nankervis, A., Baird, M., Coffey, J., Shields, J., 2014. Human Resource Management: Strategies and Processes, 8th edn. Cengage, Melbourne.

Nankervis, A., Chatterjee, S., Coffey, J., 2006. Perspectives of Human Resource Management in the Asia Pacific. Pearson Education, Sydney.

Nankervis, A., Chatterjee, S., Cooke, F., Warner, M., 2013. New Models of HRM in China and India. Routledge, London and New York.

Osman, I., Ho, T.C., Galang, M., 2011. The relationship between human resource practices and firm performance: an empirical assessment of firms in Malaysia. Business Strategy Series 12, 41–48.

Othman, R., Abdul-Ghani, R., Arshad, R., 2001. Great expectations – CEOs' perception of the performance gap of the HRM function in the Malaysian manufacturing sector. Personnel Review 30, 61–80.

Renwick, D., 2003. Line manager involvement in HRM: an inside view. Employee Relations 25, 262–280.

Rowley, C., 1997a. Reassessing HRM's convergence. Asia Pacific Business Review 3 (4), 198–211.

Rowley, C., 1997b. Comparisons and perspectives on HRM in the Asia Pacific. Asia Pacific Business Review 3 (4), 1–18.

Rowley, C., 2003. The Management of People: HRM in Context. Chandos/Spiro, Oxford.

Rowley, C., Bae, J., 2003. Changes and continuities in Korean HRM. Asia Pacific Business Review 9 (4), 76–105.

Rowley, C., Benson, J., 2002. Convergence and divergence in Asian HRM. California Management Review 44 (2), 90–109.

Rowley, C., Benson, J., 2003a. Changes in Asian HRM. Asia Pacific Business Review 9 (4), 186–195.

Rowley, C., Benson, J., 2003b. Changes and continuities in Asian HRM. Asia Pacific Business Review 9 (4), 1–14.

Rowley, C., Jackson, K., 2011. HRM: The Key Concepts. Routledge, London.

Rowley, C., Ulrich, D., 2014. Leadership in the Asia Pacific: A Global Research Perspective. Routledge, London.

Rowley, C., Warner, M., 2008. Globalizing International Human Resource Management. Routledge, Oxford.

Rowley, C., Benson, J., Warner, M., 2004. Towards an Asian model of human resource management? A comparative analysis of Japan and Korea. International Journal of Human Resource Management 15 (4–5), 917–933.

Schuler, R., Jackson, S.E., 2014. Human resource management and organisational effectiveness: yesterday and today. Journal of Organisational Effectiveness: People and Performance 1 (1), 40.

Singh, K., 2004. Impact of HR practices on perceived firm performance in India. Asia Pacific Journal of Human Resources 42, 301–317.

Snell, S., Morris, S., Bohlander, G., 2015. Managing Human Resources. Cengage Learning, Philadelphia.

Tahsildari, A., Shahnaei, S., 2015. Enhancing organizational effectiveness by performance appraisal, training, employee participation, and job definition. European Journal of Business and Management 7, 56–63.

Ulrich, D., 1997. Human Resource Champions: The Next Agenda for Adding Value to HR Practices. Harvard Business School Press, Boston.

Ulrich, D., Sutton, R., 2010. Asian Leadership: What Works. McGraw-Hill, Singapore.

Ulrich, D., Brockbank, W., Younger, J., Ulrich, M., 2013. Global HR Competencies: Mastering Competitive Value from the Outside In. McGraw-Hill, New York.

Wright, P.M., Snell, S.A., 1998. Toward a unifying framework for exploring fit and flexibility in strategic human resource management. Academy of Management Review 23, 756–772.

Yang, C.-C., Lin, Y.Y., 2014. Does technical or strategic HRM provide a better explanation of organisational performance? Business 6, 61.

Yeung, A., Warner, M., Rowley, C., 2008. Guest editors' introduction: growth and globalization – evolution of HRM practices in Asia. HRM 47 (1), 1–13.

Yusoff, Y.M., Abdullah, H.S., Baharom, A., 2012. HRM effectiveness within the role of the HRM department in large Malaysian companies. International Journal of Business and Management Science 3 (1), 1.

Zheng, C., Morrison, M., O'Neill, G., 2006. An empirical study of high performance HRM practices in Chinese SMES. International Journal of Human Resource Management 17, 1772–1803.

SECTION 1

Contextual frameworks

CHAPTER 2

ASEAN and the AEC: challenges and opportunities for human resource management

D.J.Q. Chen, W. Su-Yen

INTRODUCTION

In the 1997 ASEAN Leaders' Summit, the 10 member countries of the Association of South East Asian Nations (ASEAN) collectively agreed to adopt Vision 2020 – a vision to transform ASEAN into an economically stable, prosperous and highly competitive region with equitable development, anchored in the principles of achieving regional prosperity. The commitment to integrate and transform ASEAN into an economic regional bloc was reaffirmed subsequently during similar summits in 2003 and 2006 with the collective agreement to advance ASEAN's interest by creating the ASEAN Economic Community (or AEC for short) by the end of 2015 (ASEAN, 2008). The following section summarises the key characteristics and objectives of ASEAN.

ASSOCIATION OF SOUTH EAST ASIAN NATIONS

The Association of Southeast Asian Nations, or ASEAN for short, was founded on 8 August 1967 with the signing of the ASEAN Declaration in Bangkok, Thailand. Since its inception with five founding member states (Indonesia, Malaysia, the Philippines, Singapore and Thailand), ASEAN now comprises all countries in South East Asia, with its latest member, Cambodia, joining the Association on 30 April 1999 (ASEAN, 2008).

Broadly, the ASEAN was set up with the objectives to:
- accelerate economic growth, social progress and cultural development in the region;
- promote regional peace and stability;
- foster collaboration and mutual assistance on issues that are of common interest to the region;

Asia Pacific Human Resource Management and Organisational Effectiveness
ISBN 978-0-08-100643-6

- assist member states in training and research facilities in education, professional, technical, scientific and administrative fields;
- more effectively utilise agriculture and industries to improve the living standards of the region;
- promote South East Asia studies; and
- maintain and foster beneficial cooperation with other international and regional organisations with similar aims and purposes.

As a regional entity, ASEAN has signed several Free Trade Agreements (FTAs) and comprehensive economic partnership agreements with major economic players, such as Australia, China, India, Japan and the United States.

Collectively, ASEAN has a total population of approximately 625 million, a combined nominal GDP (2013) of USD 2.4 trillion and foreign direct investment of USD 12 billion in 2013 (ASEAN, 2014b). The Organisation for Economic Cooperation and Development (OECD) estimates that ASEAN will experience a steady year-on-year economic growth rate of approximately 5 per cent over the next decade (OECD, 2015). If growth in the region continues at a fixed rate of 5 per cent, the Asian Development Bank projects that ASEAN will be the fourth largest market in the world after the European Union, United States and China by 2050 (ADB, 2015).

In this Chapter, we will discuss:

- the key push and pull factors of talent in ASEAN and how these factors might lead to winners and losers among ASEAN countries in the war for talent;
- how the free movement of talent in the AEC will lead to both opportunities and challenges on three levels – national, business and individual PME (professionals, managers and executives). In particular, we will address how these opportunities and challenges will impact the way human resources management (HRM) practitioners manage human capital in the increasingly dynamic ASEAN environment.

THE ASEAN ECONOMIC COMMUNITY

Similar in spirit to the formation of a common market in the European Union (EU), the AEC is envisaged to deepen and broaden ASEAN's economic integration through four main pillars (ASEAN 2014b):

1. to achieve a single market production base;
2. to build a competitive economic region;
3. to have equitable economic development;
4. to attain closer integration with the global economy.

In support of establishing a single market and production base, and with specific reference to the responsibilities and contributions towards the development of a strategic regional human capital and HRM road-map member countries of ASEAN have agreed to:

- recognise professional qualifications from member countries in order to achieve free flow of services;
- standardise the issuance of employment passes across member countries to facilitate the free flow of skilled labour; and
- foster greater economic integration by eliminating tariffs and barriers to trade, harmonising capital market standards and creating customised integration with other regional economic blocs.

Although AEC is unlikely to fully meet all its objectives by its original target of 2015, the ambitious target serves as an important planning parameter that sets the wheels in motion for greater regional collaboration. To date, much has been achieved to support the formation of the AEC.

For example, to support the single market production base pillar, the ASEAN Trade in Goods Agreement has been in force since 2010 to ensure free flow of goods within the AEC by eliminating 99.2 per cent of the tariff line for six ASEAN member states (Brunei Darussalam, Indonesia, Malaysia, the Philippines, Singapore and Thailand); also, the ASEAN Framework Agreement on Services has been implemented to eliminate restrictions on trade services in 80 sub-sectors to allow foreign ownership in these sectors. To build the competitive economic region pillar, ASEAN countries have, for example, committed to pass competition policies and laws to offer cross-border protection of consumers' interest and intellectual property. Importantly, the ASEAN Open Sky Policy will enhance the connectivity of passengers and cargo in the region, enabling greater movement of people, goods and services.

To ensure that the formation of the AEC will lead to equitable economic development across ASEAN, the ASEAN Framework for Equitable Economic Development was implemented to narrow the development gaps among members so as to achieve inclusive and sustainable growth that alleviates poverty. To better integrate ASEAN with the global economy, a number of Free Trade Agreements (FTA) have been signed with other countries or regional groups to strengthen trade links and to create business opportunities. These will be complemented by the projected Trans Pacific Partnership (TPP). ASEAN is currently in the process of negotiating a Regional Comprehensive Economic Partnership with its six FTA partners to create a mega trade bloc that has a combined GDP of USD 21.2 trillion (approximately 30 per cent of total global GDP) and a population of 3.4 billion people (approximately 48 per cent of the world's population). Once concluded, the trade bloc will be the largest of its kind in the world.

From a policy standpoint, much has been implemented to ensure that the AEC is on track to meet its economic objectives. One aspect of the AEC that seems rather ambiguous at the current moment is how movement of talent will be managed and how talent mobility will affect the talent profile of individual ASEAN countries- and by implications, HR policies of companies operating in these countries.

THE AEC, TALENT AND MOBILITY IN ASEAN

Despite the fact that the ASEAN Agreement on the Movement of Natural Persons was enacted to provide the legal framework to regulate cross-border movements of people and the Mutual Recognition Agreement was intended to facilitate cross-recognition of eight professional qualifications, there has been much disquiet on the grounds of the impact that the free movement of professionals and skilled labour will have on individual ASEAN countries (Promchertchoo, 2015).

With unequal economic and infrastructural development, divergent political systems and beliefs, differences in labour and talent attractiveness, and dissimilar financial and capital market structures, it is difficult to ignore scenarios where the AEC might lead to disproportionate benefits for some ASEAN member states while impoverishing others.

Talent development and attraction in ASEAN

To understand what might influence the development and attraction of talent in ASEAN, we turn to the 2014-2015 data of the Global Talent Competitiveness Index (GTCI). The GTCI is an annual index published by INSEAD and its research partners that maps the relationships between economics and social policies with talent growth and countries' competitiveness. In its 2014-2015 edition, the GTCI provides talent competitiveness benchmarks for 103 countries based on 50 variables grouped into two main parameters of Input (*Talent Enablers*, *Attract*, *Grow* and *Retain* sub-pillars) and Output (*Labour and Vocational Skills* and *Global Knowledge Skills* sub-pillars) (see Table 2.1).

Using GTCI data from 2014-2015 we examined the correlation between the Input and Output parameters from countries in ASEAN and compared them with the correlation of the same variables from the global

Table 2.1 The GTCI 2014-2015 model

Global Talent Competitiveness Index (GTCI)

Enablers	Input			Output	
	Attract	Grow	Retain	Labour and vocational skills	Global knowledge skills
Regulatory landscape	External openness	Formal education	Sustainability	Employable skills	Higher skills and competencies
Market landscape	Internal openness	Lifelong learning	Lifestyle	Labour productivity	Talent impact
Business landscape		Access to growth opportunities			

Source: Lavin and Evans (2014).

index. While the correlations are not definitive indices that explain causal relationships between the Input and Output parameters, they nonetheless provide an indication about the important potential drivers of in-country talent development and the pull factors that are deemed attractive to talent in ASEAN, as well as how such pull factors in ASEAN countries might differ from countries in the overall GTCI index.

By correlating the four Input sub-pillars (*Enablers, Attract, Grow* and *Retain*) with the two Output sub-pillars (*Labour and Vocational Skills* and *Global Knowledge Skills*), we found that the *Enablers* Input sub-pillar has the strongest relationship with the *Labour and Vocational Skills* Output sub-pillar and the *Grow* Input sub-pillar has the strongest relationship with the *Global Knowledge Skills* Output sub-pillar. This set of two correlational relationships is stronger among ASEAN countries than countries in the overall GTCI index. What these results suggest is that any variations in the *Enablers* and *Grow* sub-pillars would bring about larger variations in the Output parameters among countries in ASEAN than similar correlations of countries in the overall GTCI index.

Looking at how specific indicators of *Enablers* and *Grow* sub-pillars affect Output parameters in ASEAN, we are keen to understand which factors among *Enablers* and *Grow* sub-pillars have the strongest impact on the development of talent in ASEAN, and which specific aspects of *Enablers* and *Grow* sub-pillars would attract mobile talent to a particular ASEAN country.

Labour and Vocational Skills

Table 2.2 reveals that in the overall GTCI index, *Labour and Vocational Skills* are related to several different *Enablers* indicators. In the ASEAN sub-sample, however, the relationships between *Enablers* indicators and *Labour and Vocational Skills* are more well-defined and can be distilled into three factors: business–government relationships, ICT access and research and development (R&D) expenditure.

Juxtaposing these findings against the current talent landscape in ASEAN, it is not surprising to find Singapore, which has invested heavily in its ICT infrastructure, to be highly attractive to professionals, managers and executives (PMEs) from the region, especially PMEs from high value-added service industries such as software engineering, precision manufacturing, banking and finance.

Since the 1980s, the Singapore government has invested aggressively in the ICT sector and ICT infrastructure. Being a key driver of Singapore's

Table 2.2 Labour and vocational skills indicators, overall GTCI and ASEAN sub-samples

Labour and vocational Skills indicators	Overall GTCI index	ASEAN Sub-Sample
Secondary educational workforce	Ease of starting foreign business	Business–government relations
Secondary educational population	Ease of starting foreign business	Business–government relations
Technicians and associate population	ICT access	ICT access and R&D expenditure
Labour productivity	ICT access	ICT access and R&D expenditure
Pay to productivity	Labour–employer relationship	ICT access and R&D expenditure
Vocational skill intensive export	Intensity of local competition	Business–government relations

growth, the ICT sector has generated approximately USD 22.44 billion (MTI, 2012) in revenue in 2010 and Singapore has continued to invest heavily in ICT. For example, in 2015 alone, Singapore has committed to invest approximately USD 1.8 billion (Mokhtar, 2015) to realise its 'Smart Nation' vision. Comparatively, Malaysia, despite being significantly geographically larger than Singapore, is projected to have a governmental spending of approximately USD 1.34 billion on ICT development (Economic News Update, 2014) during the same time period. Similarly, other ASEAN countries such as the Philippines (USD 1.6 billion in 2015 – Casayuran, 2015) are spending comparatively less amounts of money to develop their ICT infrastructure vis-à-vis Singapore. Given that the growth and attraction of PMEs, productivity and pay to productivity ratios among ASEAN countries are most closely related to ICT access, it is highly plausible that Singapore will continue to attract talent in high value-added industries from its neighbouring countries given its proportionally higher emphasis on ensuring that the nation continues to be one of the best wired in ASEAN.

Based on the 2014–2015 GTCI index, R&D was another important *Enablers* indicator that is closely related to the development and attraction of PMEs and growth in productivity indices. Compared to other countries in ASEAN, Singapore is known to be aggressive in courting multinational corporations to set up their regional headquarters and research laboratories in the country. In recent years, a large number of international corporations have set up research and development facilities in Singapore. For example,

DSM Nutritional Production has opened its Asia Pacific Nutrition Innovation Centre in Singapore. Similarly, Rolls-Royce, in partnership with the Singapore government, has set up the Advanced Technology Centre that is developing the next generation of environmentally friendly engines. Also, Lucasfilm was courted to set up one of its largest operations outside the United States in Singapore. To continue to boost Singapore's status as an R&D hub, the Singapore government, in its Research Innovation Enterprise 2020 Plan (RIE2020) will commit SGD19 billion dollars to support the development of Singapore into an innovation-driven economy by 2020 (Loke and Kek, 2016).

These concerted efforts by the Singapore government to establish the country as a R&D hub and its strategy to constantly develop clusters in new industrial frontiers such as biochemical and life sciences, pharmaceuticals, digital media and more recently space technologies have well-positioned Singapore as a talent magnet and hub that will continue to attract the best and brightest in the region. In 2013 alone, 2,200 new R&D jobs were created and this figure is expected to be higher in 2015 (A*STAR, 2013). With many new jobs created in emerging industries, Singapore is likely to experience net immigration of talent from the rest of ASEAN, and perhaps even from the rest of the world.

Compared to Western economies where governments and businesses may not necessarily always enjoy amicable relationships, governments in ASEAN, have in general recognised the importance of being pro-business. In the *World's Easiest Place to do Business* index published by the World Bank Group (World Bank Group, 2014), Singapore is ranked first in the index, Malaysia came in at 18th, Thailand at 26th and Vietnam at 78th. In a related rating, Singapore was ranked by *The Economist* Intelligence Unit in 2014 as having the most conducive environment for business (EIU, 2014) and was rated by IMD as being the least bureaucratic in Asia to do business (IMD, 2013). The pro-business environment of Singapore and the generally positive relationship between the Singapore government and businesses continues to attract multinationals to set up their regional headquarters, once again making Singapore a highly attractive location for talent in the region.

These impressive achievements provide attractive country-level prerequisites that Singapore-based organisations and their HRM professionals could capitalise on in order to attract the best talent from across the region. At the same time, Singapore being the only matured economy in ASEAN, would mean that companies operating in Singapore will have to grapple with increased human capital cost, especially in remuneration and training & development cost. For neighbouring countries such as Malaysia,

Indonesia, Thailand, Vietnam and even Australia, the challenge for HR is, quite obviously, one of attraction and retention - How can companies-based in these seemingly less attractive countries continue to attract and retain their best talent in respond to a strong talent magnet? Perhaps, the solution lies in their abilities to offer a more varied career track in a wider range of industries than Singapore could.

Global Knowledge Skills

We now examine which specific indicators of *Grow* are most strongly correlated with individual indicators of *Global Knowledge Skills* in ASEAN. Two indicators that stand out clearly for ASEAN are *University Ranking* and *Quality of Management Schools*. In the ASEAN sub-sample, *University Ranking* is highly correlated with six out of seven indicators in the *Higher Skills and Competencies* sub-pillar of *Global Knowledge Skills*, and *Quality of Management School* is highly correlated with five out of seven indicators in the same sub-pillar. Both *University Ranking* and *Quality of Management School* are also highly correlated with three out of four indicators in the *Talent Impact* sub-factor of *Global Knowledge Skills*. These results seem to confirm the emphasis placed on education in Asian societies and favour countries such as Singapore and Australia that have strong tertiary education structures. Conversely, these results also suggest that companies operating in emerging ASEAN countries such as Malaysia, Indonesia, Thailand, and Vietnam would experience difficulties in procuring highly-skilled labour to support activities at the top of the value chain. In order to support those activities.

In the QS World University Ranking (QS University Ranking 2015) and Times Higher Education World University Ranking (Times Higher Education, 2015), tertiary institutions in Singapore are constantly ranked as among the best in the world while tertiary institutions of their counterparts in ASEAN were, typically, not featured in either of these rankings, although in some cases their systems are in a rapid development phase. Given that the quality of tertiary institutions is one of the most significant drivers that help ASEAN countries deepen and attract their talent pool, it is highly plausible that Singapore will continue its upwards trajectory in attracting young talent in the region who were seeking out high-quality tertiary education.

WINNERS AND LOSERS IN TALENT MOBILITY IN ASEAN/AEC

Correlational analyses based on 2014-2015 GTCI data suggest several key indicators that are closely related to talent development and attraction in ASEAN. Although these key indicators may seem similar to those that drive talent development and attraction elsewhere in the world, further analyses show that there is a pattern of relationship that reflects distinct characteristics of ASEAN. For example, compared to the correlations in the overall GTIC index, the stronger correlations between the quality of tertiary educational institutions and *Global Knowledge Skills* in the ASEAN sub-sample underline Asia's traditional emphasis on academic pursuit. Similarly, the strong association between government–business relationships and *Labour and Vocational Skills* among ASEAN countries suggests that government-led growth, which has characterised much of Asia's economic progress since the Second World War, is likely to continue to have a strong influence on the development of *Labour and Vocational Skills* among ASEAN countries, especially in Singapore (and to a lesser extent, Australia) where the government has traditionally played an active role in shaping the country's economy and labour profile.

Our initial discussion of 2014-2015 GTCI's findings seem to indicate that Singapore is the clear winner in the war for talent and is likely to benefit from a net brain gain from the region due to its continued emphasis on ICT and R&D investments, pro-business climate and strong tertiary institutions. Actual talent migration from other ASEAN countries to Singapore, however, is unlikely to be unfettered. In fact, Singapore's attractiveness as a talent hub has in recent years faced strong competition from its neighbouring countries which is likely to intensify when talent is completely mobile in the AEC.

From a political perspective, Singapore's liberal talent policy has, in recent years, been put under increasing pressure from its electorates. Since 2011, the Singapore government has tightened its immigration policies, mandating stronger employment criteria for foreigners who intend to work in Singapore (Yeoh and Lin, 2012). As a result, the growth of the non-resident population and foreign employment in Singapore slowed to 2.9 per cent and 3 per cent in 2014 respectively, from 4 per cent and 5.9 per cent in 2013 (World Bank Group, 2015), the slowest rate in recent years. From an economic standpoint, due to a lacklustre global economy and fall in consumption demands among its trading partners, Singapore's economy in 2014 registered a growth rate of 2.9 per cent – the lowest since 2008. This rate of growth is the second lowest in ASEAN after Thailand (0.7 per cent) – a country mired in political quagmire since two of its most recent former prime ministers were removed from office. Indonesia, Malaysia and Vietnam have fared better, but still suffer from both political and economic concerns.

The tightening of immigration policies and low economic growth is a constraint to Singapore's ambitions to attract talent. Although Singapore will continue to remain a highly attractive location for talent, tighter immigration policies would mean that talent from the region is more likely to also explore migrating to other emerging economies in the region that offer similar career opportunities. For instance, although the Philippines and Indonesia are traditionally regarded as less attractive to talent in ASEAN, these countries have, in recent years, been seen as viable alternatives to Singapore due to their strong economic growth and career opportunities. In 2014, the Philippines and Indonesia experienced growth of 6.9 per cent and 5 per cent respectively (World Bank Group, 2015). Their continued strong economic growth, large domestic markets, extensive hinterland, and relative political stability in recent years have made these countries important markets for multinationals and have helped attract investment and talent from the region. For example, Singapore's annual direct investment in the Philippines and Indonesia has increased exponentially by 177 per cent and 330 per cent respectively since 2004. Specifically, in the past decade, Singapore's investments in both countries have risen from SGD 2.93 billion and SGD 11.2 billion in 2004 to SGD 5.20 billion and SGD 39.5 billion in 2013 (SingStats, 2013). Together with the increased investments is a corresponding increase in the number of Singaporeans working in these countries.

Malaysia, Singapore's closest neighbouring country, has moved up five spots in the 2015-2016 GTCI index (from 35th in 2014-2015 to 30th in 2015-2016), firmly securing it as the second most attractive country in ASEAN for talent. Immigration data from Malaysia suggest that, as of 2013, there are approximately four million foreign workers in Malaysia. Although a majority of these foreign workers are unskilled and semi-skilled workers from Bangladesh and Sri Lanka, there is an uptrend of skilled workers from Cambodia, Thailand, Vietnam and the Philippines immigrating to Malaysia for short-term employment. This trend can be attributed to several factors but most importantly to the rapid urbanisation and industrialisation of Malaysia, which led to an increased quality of life and job opportunities (Ministry of Human Resources, Malaysia, 2013). The increasing attraction of Malaysia as a job location has inevitably taken some of the gleam off Singapore as the talent hub of ASEAN. Malaysia's long-term attractiveness as a talent hub may be harmed by current political issues.

It is worth noting that Singapore, despite being rated highly as a talent magnet, has also experienced a brain drain to countries in the Asia Pacific region such as China, Australia and New Zealand. Being well educated, multi-lingual and internationally mobile, Singaporean talent is well sought after in the larger Asia Pacific region. In the past decade, Singapore has experienced a 33 per cent increase in the number of Singaporeans working and living abroad. As of 2014, there are 212,000 overseas Singaporeans, making up about 6 per cent of Singapore's citizen population (NPTD, 2014). In China alone, there are more than 20,000 Singaporeans working in major cities, many of whom are in managerial positions of multinationals or home-grown Chinese companies.

Given Singapore's small citizen population base, the number of Singaporeans emigrating and working abroad is sizeable; in fact, Singapore's Prime Minister has publicly voiced concerns about the upward trend of young talented Singaporeans leaving the country and not coming back (Lee, 2015). If Singapore is deemed to be highly attractive to talent from the rest of ASEAN, why are young talented Singaporeans choosing to live and work overseas? Anecdotal evidence suggests that young talented Singaporeans are emigrating out from Singapore for both economic and lifestyle reasons. For example, several young Singaporeans who left Singapore for the United States were quoted as saying that the main impetus for their emigration was the fast-paced lifestyle in Singapore and their yearning for a slower pace of life. Others have commented that countries such as Australia and New Zealand have a more conducive and supportive work environment (Lee, 2015).

PUSH AND PULL FACTORS IN TALENT MOBILITY IN ASEAN/AEC

Putting this anecdotal evidence to one side, the findings from the GTCI index seem to suggest two sets of distinct push and pull factors that may possibly explain talent movement in ASEAN/AEC. First, talent is drawn to countries that provide them with better economic opportunities than their home countries. These pull economic factors are best illustrated by Singapore's status as the financial and business hub of ASEAN – despite its slower growth – and the continued commitment from the Singapore government to transform the nation's economy. These factors are deemed to be highly attractive to mobile ASEAN talent who are in search of better job opportunities.

Second, push factors are often a combination of economic, social and lifestyle factors that provide talent with the impetus to leave their home countries in search of greener pastures. Although we have used Singapore's experience to explain why young talent is leaving the country in search of a slower pace of life, the desire to move to another part of the world for social and lifestyle reasons is not unique to Singaporeans. For example, the affirmative policies that Malaysia put in place to safeguard the rights of their indigenous majority (*bumiputera*) have led to some adverse impacts that curtail the educational and economic rights of non-*bumiputera*, including ethnic minorities of Chinese and Indians. In a highly interconnected world, such policies have pushed a large number of highly educated and skilled Malaysian Chinese and Indians, who have cited 'social injustice' in Malaysia as the key reason why they left their home country, to live and work in countries such as Singapore, the United Kingdom and Australia (The Economist, 2014). This affirmative action policy has led to a significant and accelerating rate of brain drain in Malaysia despite it being the second most attractive country for talent in ASEAN after Singapore.

Given that the migration of talent in ASEAN is likely to be complex and rooted in both economic and socio-political factors, a related question to ask at this point in time is what can ASEAN countries – and HRM professionals in particular – do to manage talent since the AEC will lead to a more rapid flow of talent in the region?

One obvious measure that countries can take is to invest in and improve on indicators that are most highly correlated with talent competitiveness. Based on the GTCI data, countries aiming to develop and attract talent with *Labour and Vocation Skills* ought to invest in providing infrastructure that facilitates ICT access and the establishment of R&D centres. At the same time, countries should foster close government–business relationships that encourage businesses to set up their regional headquarters in their countries, thereby initiating a process of vocational skill transfer. Similarly, countries that are keen to build their *Global Knowledge Skills* talent pool ought to invest heavily in their tertiary educational institutions to uplift the overall quality of the workforce and to attract young talent in pursuit of quality education to the country, and through that process initiate a positive spiral of developing domestic talent and attracting talent from abroad.

In addition, HRM professionals can redesign their jobs, to capitalise on the regional common market for talent. For example, the removal of visa requirements and bureaucracies associated with mobility will enable organisations to build in short rotational stint for their Hi-Po in different business functions located in different geographies of the region so as to develop them to take on regional or global roles more effectively.

Beyond economic measures, infrastructural improvements and HRM strategies, policy-makers need to be cognisant that a brain drain can and will occur due to socio-political reasons. In the case of countries, such as Malaysia, Indonesia and Brunei Darussalam, where affirmative action policies are implemented for the indigenous majority, careful plans must be put in place to reduce incidences of adverse impact and 'social injustice' that pushes well-educated and skilled ethnic minorities to leave the country. Institutional HRM policies and systems that emphasise merit and equity can also have beneficial outcomes in this regard. From the perspective of countries such as the Philippines and Singapore that have a significant number of citizens working overseas, policy-makers ought to continue implement plans to attract the diaspora population back to their home countries as these returnees would bring with them a distinct and important combination of overseas work experience and strong local knowledge.

THE AEC – CHALLENGES AND OPPORTUNITIES FOR TALENT MOBILITY

The formation of the AEC and the implementation of free movement of skilled labour within ASEAN have led to apprehensions among different quarters. While there are obvious advantages when member countries remove barriers that restrict the flow of skilled talent, countries also need to manage the possible downsides that might occur when talent is completely mobile. In this section, we discuss how the free movement of talent in the AEC will lead to both opportunities and challenges at three levels – national, business and individual PME.

National-level opportunities

One of the clearest opportunities that ASEAN countries have when talent is completely mobile is greater access to a skilled labour pool and diaspora-financed growth.

Having access to a regional pool of talent has significant implications for countries such as Brunei Darussalam that is struggling to move away from an economy that is fuelled by the export of its oil and gas. In Brunei Darussalam, the challenge of an economic crisis is real. Since the discovery of commercially exploitable oil and gas in the 1980s, the economy of the country has been centred squarely on the export of these commodities. Although it is currently one of the world's largest exporters of oil and gas, its wells are estimated to run dry in 22 years' time and the country has made very little progress in diversifying its economy (Vanderklippe, 2015). With weak secondary and tertiary industries and limited expansion into the hydrocarbon sector, the access to a deep and vast pool of talent from ASEAN may help Brunei Darussalam bring in different skill sets from the region that will be necessary to help the country diversify its economy beyond its current dependence on the oil and gas sector.

The growth of the Philippines is closely intertwined with its diaspora. In 2014, the Philippines received USD 3.7 billion of remittances from 2.3 million overseas Filipinos (PSA, 2014). The Philippines' diaspora-fuelled growth is often regarded as a unique growth model in ASEAN where a sizeable proportion of its citizens are working outside the country and transferring their earned income back to the Philippines on a regular basis. Other than remittances, other positive contributions of the diaspora include helping the country strengthen its network with the rest of the world, direct investments in the Philippines from diaspora who have succeeded elsewhere and skilled returnees from overseas assignments who in turn will elevate the talent profile of the country. The diaspora effect has an important impact on international 'brain circulation'. With the formation of the AEC and the free movement of labour, emerging economies in ASEAN such as Myanmar, Laos, Cambodia and Vietnam could possibly benefit from the diaspora effect and experience brain circulation when a larger proportion of their citizens venture out of their own countries to work as semi-skilled or skilled labour in the rest of ASEAN.

National-level challenges

The biggest challenge that ASEAN countries face when dealing with the free movement of talent is managing the flow and quality of talent. To manage the flow of talent, the Movement of Natural Persons framework was adopted to standardise the issuance of employment passes and the Mutual Recognition Agreement was established to facilitate cross-recognition of eight professional qualifications across ASEAN.

Although these frameworks are meant to ease the difficulties of managing the movement of talent and to facilitate the recognition of professional qualifications, the efficacy of reaching those goals is called into question. The fact that different ASEAN countries have varying economic structures and possess different attitudes towards talent migration will impose practical limitations on the implementation of these frameworks, especially from a HR recruitment and selection perspective.

For example, although Singapore has had a relatively liberal attitude towards talent migration, it has very clear guidelines on the issuance of employment passes and proactively evaluates its workforce composition on a regular basis. At the other end of the spectrum is Myanmar. As an emerging economy with less established institutional controls, Myanmar's guidelines on the issuance of employment passes are less stringent than those of Singapore and its government's stance towards talent migration is more restrictive than that of Singapore due to the country's political structure.

With Singapore and Myanmar occupying opposite ends of the spectrum, the rest of the ASEAN countries fall somewhere in between these two countries in their attitudes towards talent migration and the clarity of guidelines on employment passes. When there is such a diverse range of policy positions regarding talent migration across the different ASEAN countries, any frameworks imposed under the AEC must necessarily be broad lest they become needlessly restrictive (or liberal) in some countries. It is not hard to imagine a country like Singapore resisting the implementation of a common set of ASEAN employment pass guidelines that it deems to be too ambiguous and liberal or Myanmar actively opposing guidelines that are different from the political position of its government.

The only possible solution to such a problem is to adopt a set of broad employment pass guidelines that allow ASEAN members leeway for interpretation without being subjected to strict implementation processes. Such a system would, however, run the risk of ASEAN member countries reverting back to their current existing employment pass frameworks since such broad guidelines are non-binding. This problem is reflected in the current implementation of the Movement of Natural Persons framework. To date, the framework has made limited headway in standardising and harmonising the issuance of employment passes in ASEAN.

The Mutual Recognition Agreement is likely to be hamstrung by a similar set of problems that plague the Movement of Natural Persons framework. Although the Mutual Recognition Agreement was designed to facilitate the recognition of professional qualifications across ASEAN, it allows each individual ASEAN country to assess the quality of the candidates recognised under the agreement via assessment tests (ASEAN, 2009, 2014a). While such safeguards are necessary to ensure that potential job applicants indeed possess the requisite skill set, it will inadvertently render the agreement redundant since each ASEAN country will continue to assess each job candidate based on the existing assessment tests rather than a set of regionally recognised skills frameworks.

From a HRM perspective, although the implementation of a common talent market will, theoretically, grant organisations access to a geographical talent pool, actual access to regional talent might remain somewhat restricted due to the inability of ASEAN countries to adopt a unified work pass framework.

Business-level opportunities

The AEC will provide an immense amount of opportunities to businesses in the region. Beyond greater economic integration and commercial prospects, the AEC would allow businesses to tap into the regional talent pool to drive their growth, both domestically and regionally. Taking the example of emerging economies such as Cambodia, Vietnam, Laos, and Myanmar, businesses operating in those countries could tap into the managerial expertise from PMEs based in more mature ASEAN economies, such as Singapore, Malaysia, Indonesia, the Philippines and Thailand. Businesses in mature ASEAN economies, on the other hand, will have access to a larger pool of managerial talents armed with domestic knowledge when they decide to expand their scope of operations to other countries in the region.

Aside from the teething problems of regulating employment passes and creating a common yardstick to evaluate professional qualifications, the AEC would in the long run, enable businesses to operate more effectively in the region. Organisations and their HRM professionals need to be cognisant of both the problems associated with diverse legal regulations on these issues and the development of effective practical strategies to address them.

Business-level challenges

With ASEAN becoming a single production base and being more closely integrated with the world's economy, there is a strong impetus for businesses, especially home-grown companies, in ASEAN countries to expand the scope of their businesses beyond their home countries and into the region. To compete effectively with MNCs, which are operating in the region, as well as domestic firms in individual ASEAN countries, companies with regional business ambitions need to accelerate the development of talent with regional and global outlooks, as well as the need to develop executives with the ability to navigate the increased volatility, uncertainty, complexity and ambiguity (VUCA) of doing business in the integrated bloc. Most importantly, companies which wish to expand their geographical scope of operations to the rest of ASEAN must grow a pool of executives who are willing to move beyond their domestic markets to take up a regional role. Achieving these objectives would require HRM professionals in local businesses to redesign jobs to accelerate the development of talent with a regional view, to adopt a focused selection process that recruits employees with learning agility and an inherent interest to operate beyond domestic markets, to enhance training and development systems at all levels to tap on the wider regional market, and to offer attractive career development programmes that offers opportunities for multi-lateral movements across different geographies.

Developing such a pool of regionally mobile talent can be extremely challenging for ASEAN home-grown businesses. As opposed to multinationals which always have the option (albeit an expensive one) of deploying a globally mobile talent from elsewhere to the region, ASEAN home-grown businesses often do not have that luxury but have to groom a regional talent from their existing pool of local talent. In HCLI's qualitative research in ASEAN, chief HR officers of MNCs in the region commonly lamented that talent in the region is less mobile than their counterparts elsewhere and are often less willing to take up positions and postings beyond their home country. A large part of this can be attributed to the fact that Asians, in general, are very rooted in their family and are deeply embedded in their social network (HCLI, 2014a). Although an overseas job posting may greatly enhance an individual's career trajectory, they are often less willing to relocate, even within the geographical region of ASEAN. For home-grown ASEAN companies that are looking at expansion to the region, the lack of talent mobility can potentially hamper that ambition. HR professionals, would therefore, need to think out of the box and implement suitable human capital strategies to support the organisation's growth plan. One potential strategy is to make use of the region's transportation interconnectivity by instituting multiple short overseas stints to build regional capabilities. This, based on HCLI's interviews with chief HR officers, is one of the most effective way to circumvent mobility issues among ASEAN talents.

Individual PME-level opportunities

For highly mobile talent in ASEAN, the formation of the AEC will be greeted with much delight. To a pool of qualified, experienced and globally proficient talent, the AEC is yet another stepping stone that helps them open the doors to a protean and boundary less career. Compared to the past where immigration rules and employment pass restrictions might have impeded the career choices of such employees, the AEC opens the doors to greater job opportunities in the region by removing employment barriers that would have otherwise limited the options of PMEs. Considering that

ASEAN countries are located no more than 4.5 hours by air from each other, ASEAN is indeed highly attractive for highly mobile talent.

Individual PME-level challenges

In HCLI's research on how the leadership landscape varies across Asia, we found that executives often have distinctive weaknesses that pose challenges when operating in an environment that is different from their domestic country. For example, executives from Singapore are superb administrators but are uncomfortable with operating in a volatile, uncertain, complex and ambiguous environment (HCLI, 2014b). Executives from Indonesia, on the other hand, are good collaborators but are not tough drivers of performance (HCLI, 2014c).

While remaining as an in-country leader for one's entire career was once a viable option, the AEC is a game changer – companies are now more likely than before to seek out and promote employees who have regional experience and have the ability to operate across multiple ASEAN countries. The challenge for employees is to develop distinct skill sets that enable them to operate in the region. As part of the development process, PMEs need to develop cultural meta-cognition that will enable them to collaborate and interact across different cultures. Again, the responsibility of HRM professionals here is to provide appropriate levels of training, development and ongoing support in order to attract, develop and retain PMEs with regional management skill sets and global mindsets.

CONCLUSION

The formation of the AEC is highly anticipated and ASEAN countries have shown strong commitment to its development. From a talent management perspective, the prospect of free movement of labour is highly attractive, yet incredibly challenging.

While it is commonly believed that the AEC will lead to clear winners and losers in that some countries will inadvertently lose their top talent to others, this chapter highlights that it is more complex than merely people moving across geographies for economic reasons – political climate and social reasons such as lifestyle choices will also affect the talent migration process. It is therefore important for countries to proactively manage their economic, political and social policies in order to continue to be attractive and relevant to highly mobile talent.

The AEC is currently still work in progress and will continue to be so for the next few years to come. While it certainly has brought about some challenges to countries, businesses and individuals, it has also opened new doors and opportunities to a larger playing field.

REFERENCES

A*STAR, 2013. National Survey of Research and Development in Singapore. Agency for Science, Technology and Research, Singapore.

ADB, 2015. ASEAN Economic Community: 12 Things to Know. Asian Development Bank. Retrieved from: *http://www.adb.org/features/asean-economic-community-12-things-know.* 5th September, 2015.

ASEAN, 2008. ASEAN Economic Community Blueprint. ASEAN Secretariat.

ASEAN, 2009. Roadmap for an ASEAN Community. ASEAN Secretariat.

ASEAN, 2014a. Key Basic ASEAN Indicators. Retrieved from: *http://www.asean.org/asean/ about-asean/overview.*

ASEAN, 2014b. Thinking Globally, Prospering Regionally: ASEAN Economic Community 2015. ASEAN Secretariat.

Casayuran, M.B., 2015. POE seeks review of spending on ICT, slow internet speed. Manila Bulletin.

Economic News Update, 2014. Budget Boost for Malaysia's ICT sector. Oxford Business Group. Retrieved from: *http://www.oxfordbusinessgroup.com/news/budget-boost-malaysia's-ict-sector.*

EIU, 2014. Business Environment Ranking. Economist Intelligence Unit.

HCLI, 2014a. Leadership Mosaics Across Asia. Human Capital Leadership Institute.

HCLI, 2014b. Building Global Leaders in Asia: A Focus on Singapore Talent. Human Capital Leadership Institute.

HCLI, 2014c. Leadership Mosaics Across Asia: For Indonesia, from Indonesia. Human Capital Leadership Institute.

IMD, 2013. World Competitiveness Yearbook. International Institute for Management Development (IMD).

Lavin, B., Evans, P., 2014. The Global Talent Competitiveness Index: Growing Talent for Today and Tomorrow. INSEAD, Human Capital Leadership Institute & Adecco Group.

Lee, A., 2015. More Singaporeans overseas, but brain drain concerns dissipate. Today.

Loke, K.F., Kek, X., 2016. Govt commits S$19b to new 5-year plan for R&D initiatives RIE2020. Retrieved from: http://www.channelnewsasia.com/news/business/singapore/govt-commits-s-19b-to-new/2409426.html.

Ministry of Human Resources, Malaysia, 2013. Immigration in Malaysia: Assessment of Its Economic Effects, and a Review of the Policy and System. Human Development Social Protection and Labour Unit East Asia and Pacific Region, World Bank.

Mokhtar, F., 2015. Government to launch S$2.2n in ICT tenders to realize Smart Nation Vision. Channel News Asia. Retrieved from: *http://www.channelnewsasia.com/news/ business/government-to-launch-s-2/1874506.html.*

MTI, 2012. Singapore 2012: The Living Digital Lab. Economic Review Committee, ICT Working Group, Ministry of Trade and Industry. Retrieved from: *http://www.mti.gov.sg/ researchroom/documents/app.mti.gov.sg/data/pages/507/doc/erc_svs_ict_mainreport.pdf.*

NPTD, 2014. 2014 Population in Brief (Singapore). National Population and Talent Division, Singapore.

OECD, 2015. Economic Outlook for Southeast Asia, China, and India 2015: Strengthening Institutional Capacity. OECD Publishing, Paris.

Promchertchoo, P., 2015. Free labour movement could pose big problem for ASEAN Economic Community. Channel News Asia. Retrieved from: *http://www.channelnewsasia.com/news/asiapacific/free-labour-movement/1950482.html.*

PSA, 2014. Statistics on Overseas Filipino Workers. Philippine Statistics Authority. Retrieved from: *https://psa.gov.ph/tags/overseas-filipinos.*

QS University Ranking, 2015. QS University Rankings: Asia. QS Top Universities.

SingStats, 2013. Singapore's Direct Investment Abroad by Country/Region, 2004–2013. Department of Statistics Singapore. Retrieved from: *http://www.singstat.gov.sg/statistics/browse-by-theme/investment.*

The Economist, 27th April, 2013. A never ending policy'. The Economist 40 (8833) 26.

Times Higher Education, 2015. World University Rankings 2015–2016: Results Announced. Times Higher Education World University Ranking. Retrieved from: *https://www.timeshighereducation.com/news/world-university-rankings-2015-2016-results-announced.*

Vanderklippe, N., 2015. Brunei's oil-fuelled economy running on empty. Globe and Mail, 2 February. Retrieved from: *http://www.theglobeandmail.com/report-on-business/international-business.*

World Bank Group, 2014. Doing Business. Retrieved from: *http://www.doingbusiness.org/rankings.*

World Bank Group, 2015. GDP Growth (Annual %). Retrieved from: *http://www.data.worldbank.org/indicator/NY.GDP.MKTP.KD.ZG.*

Yeoh, B., Lin, W., 2012. Rapid Growth in Singapore's Immigrant Population Brings Policy Challenges. Migration Policy Institute, Singapore.

CHAPTER 3

Emerging HRM perspectives on emotional intelligence, mindfulness and neurobiological science on organisational effectiveness

P. Hosie, A. Sharma, L. Herkenhoff, J.A. Heydenfeldt, R.P.J. Kingshott

INTRODUCTION

Since the 'time of awakening', Star Trek Vulcans have followed Surak's philosophy of embracing logic and suppressing all emotions (Daugherty, 1969). For eons, emotions, if ever discussed in work contexts, were mainly considered in relation to interpersonal disagreements and the interference with sensible 'rationale' decision-making. Conversely, human emotional states are no longer regarded as merely illogical responses to events in the workplace (Nicholson, 2000). As Damasio (1994: xii) observed 'reason may not be as pure as most of us think it is or wish it were, that emotion and feelings may not be intruders in the bastion of reason at all: they may be enmeshed in its networks for worse and for better.'

Thus far, the overwhelming majority of research in the workplace has been focused on the measurement of tangible elements of organisational progress, with little attention paid to less readily measurable factors like 'emotional intelligence' (EI) (Salovey and Mayer 1989–90) or 'socio-emotional' elements (Bales, 1950) and 'human relations skills' (Whyte, 1955; Likert, 1967). Such paucity of research is even more noticeable within Eastern workplaces, where ironically the practice of controlling one's emotions, through meditation and other forms of self-reflection, has been practised for centuries. Research to support the emotional influence on behaviour and decision-making has emerged (largely in Western contexts) from a variety of academic disciplines including psychology (Lewis and Haviland-Jones,

Asia Pacific Human Resource Management and Organisational Effectiveness
ISBN 978-0-08-100643-6

2000), organisational behaviour (Martin et al., 1998; Aschcroft and Humphrey, 1995), sociology (Ollilainen, 2000), anthropology (Levy, 1984) and most recently neuroscience (Damasio, 1994; Waldman et al., 2011). Unfortunately, investigating individual affective states and emotions in organisational settings has largely been avoided due to the difficulties of empirically investigating the phenomena (Turnball, 1999).

Indeed, the debate over EI has been a relatively easy sell to the general public and business world but a much tougher deal to make within the vestibules of academia. A fascinating tension is noticeable between EI scholars and commercially orientated researchers and consultants. Scholars are typically more conservative in the claims about the potential managerial benefits of EI. For example, Mayer (1999: 50) typifies this cautious approach in noting that 'the popular literature's implication – that highly emotionally intelligent people possess an unqualified advantage in life – appears overly enthusiastic at present and unsubstantiated by reasonable scientific standards.' In contrast, those supporting the 'commercial' approach tend to make expansive claims, exemplified by Goleman, on the applied value of EI within a work setting. Much of Goleman's assertions about EI in the workplace remains speculative and still requires empirical verification to provide substantial evidence and clarification of the relationship of EI to enhanced organisational functioning (Goyal and Akhilesh, 2007).

Despite known impediments to measuring EI, academic and lay interest in the human affect and emotions in the workplace intensified during the 1990s and beyond (Izard, 2002). The overwhelming focus of research has been conducted within the Western world but emotions are common human traits and universal in nature. Thus looking to the Eastern world for guidance in relation to 'controlling' emotions offers great potential to explore how to best optimise individual performance and overall organisational productivity. Researchers continue to show interest in the impact of emotions in organisational contexts (Ashkanasy et al., 1998; Fisher and Ashkanasy, 2000; Walter et al., 2011) but given the transnational nature of business future empirical studies related to the construct need to ruminate on both Western and Eastern work contexts. Despite the current contextual limitations of exploring this EI domain, the literature suggests there is merit for organisations that make investments in improving their employees EI within the workplace. There is, however, a lack of theoretical clarity surrounding the concept of EI and its measurement.

This chapter therefore aims to provide a sharper insight into the conceptual underpinnings of EI with a view to paving the way for more focused and robust empirical studies. The discussion that follows begins by defining what is meant by the EI construct. A synthesis of the literature reveals a number of clear themes in relation to the construct, used here to craft two related propositions that help to contextualise EI within the work setting. Our analysis and synthesis of the scholarly literature underpins the main tenets of these propositions: (1) employees with heightened EI work better in groups; and (2) there is a positive relationship between EI and job performance. Also, we examine literature in the domains of mindfulness, meditation and advances in neurobiological science to better understand EI in employee behaviour and through this discuss its potential in light of our two propositions.

LITERATURE REVIEW

Controversial debate has endured regarding the definition, nature, measurement and application of EI in the workplace (Spector, 2005; Walter et al., 2011). Different approaches to conceiving EI have inevitably resulted in varied methods to measuring this construct in work settings (Mayer et al., 2000b; Dulewicz and Higgs, 2000). Salovey and Mayer (1989–90) originally conceived EI in terms of an individual's ability to perceive emotion in the self and others, to understand emotion and subsequently to manage these emotions. Following on from this, Mayer and Salovey (1997: 5) distinguished EI from the notion of social intelligence, defining it as the 'ability to perceive emotions; to access and generate emotions so as to assist thought; to understand emotions and emotional knowledge; and to reflectively regulate emotions so as to promote emotional and intellectual growth'. Mayer and Salovey (1993) do, however, stress the value of considering emotional self-management as a key aspect of EI. They initially defined the construct as a 'subset of social intelligence that involves the ability to monitor one's own and others' feelings and emotions, to discriminate among them and to use this information to guide one's thinking and actions' (Salovey and Mayer, 1989–90: 189). Later, Mayer and Salovey (2000a) argue EI is essentially about emotions, founded in the modern understanding of the role of emotional circuits ('hot intelligences') within the human brain. They refine this EI conceptualisation into four themes: (1) perception of emotion (in self and others); (2) assimilation of emotion to facilitate thought; (3) understanding of emotion; and (4) managing and regulating emotion in the self and others.

Clearly, emotions are internalised human traits that do not (and cannot) exist without context and consequence. In the workplace, for example, emotions potentially shape individual behaviour therefore have important organisational ramifications. In Eastern cultures, the practice of meditation and inner reflection improves an individual's self-restraint through emotional control. If managers are able to exploit such emotion-laden control over behaviour they can potentially imbue employee deeds with positive organisational consequences. EI has many varied definitions, but Boyatzis and Sala's definition of EI provides an important link with job-related performance 'an emotional intelligence competency is considered the ability to recognize, understand, and use emotional information about oneself or others that leads to or causes effective or superior performance' is useful when considering any link to job-related performance. Perhaps EI is best conceived in terms of abilities concerning the recognition and regulation of emotion in the self and others (Ashkanasy and Daus 2005). Through this conceptualisation, a clue to how organisational decision-makers can harness its potential is offered. This is best seen through the lens of Boyatzis and Sala's definition, in which EI can be characterised as comprising two broad groups, namely the Ability (Humphrey et al., 2008; Ashkanasy and Daus, 2005) and Mixed models (Goleman, 1995; Bar-On, 1997a). This chapter favours the Ability model approaches to conceptualise EI.

Ashkanasy and Daus (2003: 69) were forthright about the merits (and limitations) of these two groups of models: 'Let us first begin by making one point "crystal clear" – we do not endorse a Goleman (1995) or Bar-On (1997b) type of approach to studying emotional intelligence . . . we also feel that to an extent, they have done much more harm than good regarding establishing emotional intelligence as a legitimate, empirical construct.' Ashkanasy and Daus (2003: 69) go on to state: 'These models may indeed be useful for organisational development and interventions, but they are much too broad in scope, and do not appear to markedly differ from traditional personality models or competency models.' Others, like Antonakis (2003: 359), are more strident about the veracity of the supporting empirical evidence on the relevance of EI to leaders, claiming it 'is non-existent or very weak at best or contradictory at worst.' Antagonists of EI, such as Locke (2005), have proclaimed EI an 'invalid concept' as it is simply not intelligence. This position is artfully repudiated by Ashkanasy and Daus (2005) who, like Walter et al. (2011), have refined and categorised research and measures of EI inquiry into three main streams:

- *Stream one* is an Ability-based model of a set of interrelated emotional abilities. An individual's capacity to solve abstract emotional problems is measured based on the four-branch abilities model of EI.

- *Stream two* is specifically based on the four-branch model. Self or peer-report of complex social behaviours is inherent to this approach and also based on Mayer and Salovey's (1997) representation of EI.
- *Stream three* comprises a Mixed model take on emotional and different dispositional competencies, including everything except cognitive ability. This model incorporates self-report as the primary means of assessment.

Curiously, there is little dispute in the literature with respect to the prevalence of EI. This is a distinctive human trait (or traits) and therefore has an inevitable presence within the workplace. The main contention lies in what specific role, if any, the EI construct can play in relation to employee and subsequent organisational effectiveness. In order to address the point, this chapter has synthesised existing scholarly literature in relation to EI to reveal two main themes identified earlier. For clarity of discussion, these themes are articulated as two propositions with the aim of taking stock of the extant debate at this particular juncture in time. From this, a number of research avenues are discussed that it is proposed are helpful in further advancing scholarly understanding of the role EI can play within organisations. Our attention now turns to each of the two propositions derived from the literature.

RESEARCH THEMES

Proposition 1: Team members with high EI increase team productivity

EI has been shown to be a predictor of individual job performance in some contexts. A considerable range of literature supports the positive influence of EI on exceptional job performance within organisations and the subsequent impact on workplace climate (O'Boyle et al., 2011). Group-level performance has been shown to be more a function of emotional than intellectual intelligence (Jordan and Troth, 2004; Offermann et al., 2004). Elfenbein and Ambady (2003) suggest EI can benefit the performance of work groups but the actual role of EI within teams is complicated and not fully understood. An effective team needs both EI and expertise so that teamwork becomes greater than the whole (McCallin and Bamford, 2007). A summary of research work and major themes in the domain of groups and EI is provided in Table 3.1.

Although limited, empirical studies on EI suggest that collective EI may be positively associated with group satisfaction and group performance (Jordan and Troth, 2004; Offermann et al., 2004). Ashkanasy and Daus (2005) draw on Mayer and Salovey's (1997) EI definition to develop a

Table 3.1 Overview of major themes related to EI and groups

Scholars	Research focus
Ashkanasy and Daus (2005)	Workgroup EI profile (WEIP)
Barzdil and Slaski (2003); Ashkanasy and Daus (2005)	EI team work productivity
Cote et al. (2010)	Leadership and EI
Druskat and Wolff (2001)	Emotions and group norms
Elfenbein and Ambady (2003)	Negative emotions and group morale
Finucane et al. (2003); Loewenstein et al. (2001)	EI, cognitive intelligence and team performance
Jordan and Troth (2004); Offermann et al. (2004)	EI and group satisfaction
Mayer and Salovey (1993)	Emotional self-management
McCallin and Bamford (2007)	EI and group performance
Pescosolido (2002)	Group emotions and organisational culture

'Workgroup EI Profile (WEIP),' which has shown promising results on the role of EI in group performance. Teams were coached in WEIP goal-setting and interpersonal skills. Initially those low performing teams were also shown to be low on EI but after coaching were able to improve their performance, equivalent to teams exhibiting high EI.

The concept of Emotionally Competent Group Norms developed by Druskat and Wolff (2001) has been related to the positive role of emotions in both group work and successful resolution of conflict (Romero and Pescosolido, 2008). A conceptual model testing the correlation between the cognitive, emotional and social competencies provided evidence of their interplay impacting on the general ability of team performance. However, there is limited support for the correlation between the complimentary relationship between EI and cognitive intelligence. These are considered to be a cornerstone of teamwork performance (Finucane et al., 2003; Loewenstein et al., 2001).

Mayer and Salovey (1993) have stressed the value of emotional self-management. Sometimes, the best way for a person to manage emotions is simply not to express any negative emotions. This is because the accurate communication of negative emotions can be damaging to group morale and effectiveness (Elfenbein and Ambady, 2003). However, Pescosolido (2002) asserts that common emotional understanding within a workgroup setting produces strong positive and long-lasting organisational culture. More recent studies (e.g. Cote et al., 2010) have focused on the emergence of leadership and EI demonstrating that the EI dimension, the ability to understand emotions, is most consistently associated with the emergence of leadership in small groups. Overall, EI has also been shown to increase productive team work (Barzdil and Slaski, 2003; Ashkanasy and Daus, 2005).

Proposition 2: There is a positive relationship between EI and job performance

Job performance impacts organsational effectivess. Goleman (1998: 5) asserts: 'IQ takes second position to EI in determining outstanding job performance.' This assertion means employees with elevated EI are more effective, particularly in discretionary performance. Boyatzis et al. (2000) argue that 'emotional competencies' (i.e. self-awareness, self-discipline, persistence and empathy) have greater implications for job-related performance than intelligence and training. Some argue convincingly that emotional mixed-mode competencies are not the same construct as EI (Ashkanasy and Daus, 2005). A summary of the research work and the major themes in the domain of performance and EI is provided in Table 3.2.

Organisational researchers investigating emotions have often neglected to include job performance as part of 'behaviors or actions that are relevant to the goals of the organization in question' (McCoy et al., 1994: 493). For example, Arvey and Murphy (1998) suggest EI facilitates better individual performance and organisational outcomes. EI is potentially relevant to contextual performance, specifically leadership and management in general (Motowidlo and Van Scotter, 1994). Goleman (1999) also argued strongly that the higher the level of management, the more vital all aspects of EI become. Employees with well-developed EI are likely to be more effective in jobs requiring extensive contextual performance, as required in managerial and executive roles (Borman and Motowidlo, 1997).

Further, Goleman (1995) proposed 25 emotional competencies encompassing five elements as the underlying principles of gaining expertise in relation to one's: (1) self-motivation, (2) self-awareness, (3) self-regulation, (4) empathy for others and (5) adeptness in establishing and maintaining interpersonal relationships. Goleman (1999) argues these social and emotional characteristics are linked to successful job performance in the workplace. Goleman (1999: 21) later asserts 'As more companies put a premium

Table 3.2 Overview of major themes related to performance and EI

Scholars	Research focus
Arvey and Murphy (1998)	EI, individual performance and organisational outcomes
Borman and Motowidlo (1997)	EI and job effectiveness
Boyatzis et al. (2000)	Emotional competencies and job performance
Boyatzis and Sala (2004)	Empathy, emotional self-awareness and performance
Cherniss (2010)	EI, work context and performance
Cropanzano et al. (1993); Hosie and Sevastos (2009); Staw and Barsade (1993); Wright and Staw (1999a, 1999b); Wright and Cropanzano (2000)	Emotions and job performance
Goleman (1995)	Emotional competencies
Goleman (1998); Van Rooy and Viswesvaran (2004)	EI and job performance
Goleman (1999); Boyatzis et al. (2000)	Emotional control
Joseph and Newman (2010); Newman et al. (2010)	Mixed EI and performance
Motowidlo and Van Scotter (1994)	EI and contextual performance
Newman et al. (2010)	Emotional labour levels and performance
Spector (2005)	Emotional dissonance and performance

on people who can lead, the ability to influence is one of the competencies at a premium.' How well employees handle themselves and each other emotionally, are as important as the intelligence or expertise possessed (Goleman, 1999; Boyatzis et al., 2000).

As Goleman's (1998: 34) argument goes, apart from intelligence, the single most important factor distinguishing 'star performers' from the 'also rans' is EI. As with many of Goleman's assertions about EI this is yet to be empirically verified. Goleman's (1995) view that emotions play an important role in business decision-making – the more important the decision, the stronger the influence – is, however, supported by a seven-year longitudinal study conducted by Dulewicz and Higgs (2000). A meta-analysis by Van Rooy and Viswesvaran (2004) also found that EI predicts workplace performance but to a much lesser degree than other proponents suggest (Van Rooy and Viswesvaran, 2004). This is consistent with Joseph and

Newman's (2010) finding that EI only explains incremental validity over cognition and personality for employee performance.

Reports from a study conducted by Barzdil and Slaski (2003) showed employee's concerns for the quality of products and services to be positively correlated with the EI competencies of empathy and self-regulation. Self-awareness and self-regulation are positively linked with problem-solving capabilities associated with subordinate conflict situations (Morehouse, 2007). Further, empathy and emotional self-awareness has been found to predict successful work performance (Boyatzis and Sala, 2004). A link has also been made between work performance and self-awareness, emotional resilience and motivation (Barzdil and Slaski, 2003).

A number of the elements such as empathy towards employees, genuine concern, self-management and suitable leadership style are important in reducing obstacles to help ensure effective job performance. Boyatzis and Sala (2004) demonstrated that EI is linked to workplace performance across a range of organisational contexts. Specifically, employee EI has been positively linked with health, teamwork, productivity and profit. Aspects of EI have been shown by qualitative and qualitative investigations to be critical for effective job performance and the prevention of negative job stress (Offermann et al., 2004; Daus et al., 2004). Jordan et al. (2002) argue that employees with high levels of EI have the ability to identify and proactively manage work-related stress and emotional outcomes of work insecurity, leading to successful job performance outcomes. EI has emerged as an important construct in relation to job performance (Lopes et al., 2005). The emotion–performance link has been explored in general (Bar-On et al., 2005) and more specifically in relation to managers (Caruso and Salovey, 2004). Studies using a variety of methods and samples have also shown a positive relationship between some forms of emotion and job performance (Cropanzano et al., 1993; Hosie and Sevastos, 2009; Staw and Barsade, 1993; Wright and Staw, 1999a,b; Wright and Cropanzano, 2000). Poor discriminant validity, however, exists between some EI and Big Five personality dimensions (Barrick et al., 2001).

From the perspective of the Ability model, EI does indicate discriminant validity with the Big Five (Daus and Ashkanasy, 2005). Of note are extensive meta-analyses by O'Boyle et al. (2011) and Joseph and Newman (2010). A meta-analysis extension of a previous meta-analysis, using dominance analysis, by O'Boyle et al. (2011: 788) determined that 'all three streams of EI measures [self- and peer-report measures and mixed models] exhibited substantial relative importance in the presence of Five Factor Model and intelligence when predicting job performance.' Although in this research EI accounts for the unique variance in predicting job performance other studies indicate otherwise.

In contrast, Joseph and Newman (2010) concluded that, overall, job performance measures added no incremental predictability over cognitive ability and the Five Factor Personality Model. A progressive model of EI developed by Joseph and Newman (2010) empirically confirmed meta-analytic data to test a 'cascading model' of ability-based EI facets. Emotional regulation was identified as a key dimension of EI that influences job performance. Job role context was shown to be critical for jobs requiring high emotional labour (Joseph and Newman, 2010; Newman et al., 2010). EI positively predicted performance on jobs with high emotional labour but exhibited no relationship for low emotional labour jobs as would be expected (Newman et al., 2010). In contrast, 'emotional dissonance' increases employee tension, thus negatively impacting their performance (Spector, 2005).

Work by Cherniss (2010) acknowledged that EI is positively associated with performance, suggesting that context does makes a difference. For example, a positive relationship between EI and job performance is noticeable for jobs that would be expected to require high levels of EI (Daus et al., 2004; Cage et al., 2004). Emotion perception was found in this model to causally precede emotion understanding. Subsequently, this was found to precede conscious emotion regulation and job performance. Mixed-based measures of EI seemingly explained variance in job performance beyond cognitive ability and personality. Links to the ability-based EI and job performance was inconsistent. Mixed-based EI have been found to be empirically stronger (although theoretically weaker) predictors of job performance than ability-based EI (Joseph and Newman, 2010; Newman et al., 2010).

POTENTIAL AVENUES FOR FUTURE RESEARCH

Our synthesis of relevant literature indicates that if EI is conceptualised as an ability and thus provides incremental validity for predicting socially relevant outcomes (Mayer et al., 2008: 503) then empirical support is tantamount. This means specific empirical field investigations must also explore the wider variety of workplaces to establish the generalisability of the construct on performance. Scholars can look to Eastern contexts for inspiration and direction. As indicated, the widely used practice of controlling the mind in many Eastern cultures as a means of governing one's emotions and subsequent behaviour provides general face validity that emotions (and similarly EI) potentially impact behaviour. Western organisations are increasingly supporting the practice of mindfulness in the workplace (Hyland et al., 2015). A vast and growing literature on the topic is emerging in both Eastern and Western contexts. Such individual and group behaviour, if positive, will inevitably contribute to positive organisational outcomes.

To date, literature in the Eastern context on this particular point is scant, as is the paucity of investigations linking EI to *actual* job performance as a variable criterion (Joseph and Newman, 2010). Evidence in the Western literature does, however, indicate an increasing awareness of the emotion–performance nexus (Hosie et al., 2012). The perplexing question facing scholars is not whether EI and individual (and by default organisational) performance exists, but rather how managers can best enrich an individual's EI with a view to influencing individual and group behaviour. Employees need the ability to persuade and influence emotions in a work context because strong emotions have an encouraging or harmful impact on performance. Extending the scope of studies into Eastern realms, where self-reflection (such as concern for giving and receiving 'face') and contemplation moderate individual behaviour, offers great potential to unlock this secret and warrants further examination.

Concerns about operational definitions of EI still exist and need addressing if the robustness and acceptance of the construct (and its impact within organisations) is to become mainstream. EI should be distinguishable from conceptualisations and measurement of individual personality traits. In order to address these two issues concurrently, Cole and Humphrey (2011: 52) depict three broad research domains that need pursuing in order to further develop and explore the EI–leadership nexus, namely: '(1) more rigorous methodologies; (2) examination of more comprehensive theoretical models; and (3) pursuit of innovative research areas'. The first two areas pertain to more arduous scholarly activity and the last relates to specific work-related contexts of potential research. Collectively these will contribute towards a much clearer understanding and significance of EI within organisations.

In addressing the first two research domains, when measuring EI it is critical to ensure that the construct is distinct from others. Some commentators suggest that EI or ESC (emotional social competencies) measures simply do not predict important outcomes very well, especially when personality and cognitive ability are taken into account. Much of this difficulty is due to small sample sizes, lack of validation and poorly designed studies that do not take into account the breadth and structure of both personality and ability studies (Harms and Credé, 2007). Clearly caution is necessary when generalising these findings. Nevertheless, the results in the literature to date still have important implications for organisations. This conceptual clarity between constructs is particularly important when developing measures to be used across multicultural contexts because conceptual domains and associated measures often have different meanings across different contexts (Brislin, 1970; Douglas and Craig, 2007). If future studies are to draw upon and learn from widely used 'mind control' practices within Eastern contexts, then it is imperative that ways of capturing and measuring these concepts, especially mindfulness, are methodologically sound.

A number of specific areas need to be addressed. First, studies of EI and leadership while controlling for cognitive ability, personality, functional skills and specific cultural dimensions (Antonakis, 2003; Walter et al., 2011) would be particularly beneficial. In light of this, more effective measures to determine EI organisational outcomes are also required. Second, while the influence of EI on team effectiveness is in its infancy, the construct still requires further substantive quantitative results (Ashkanasy and Daus, 2002; Elfenbein and Ambady, 2002; Druskat and Wolff, 2001; Jordan and Ashkanasy, 2006). The third area involves investigating the nexus between leaders' cognitive and emotive states. On this point, new medical science research is now revealing how parts of the brain explain the interconnections between emotive and rational based behaviours (Walter et al., 2011) and, when coupled with the psychological and sociological domains, potentially further explain aspects of leadership (Waldman et al., 2011). Overall, 'hard' scientific methodologies in this emerging research in the domain of brain science have the potential to reconsider existing and develop new theories, as well as test new and existing constructs.

INTERPERSONAL NEUROBIOLOGY

One area worth exploring in relation to EI is the interdisciplinary field of interpersonal neurobiology. Research in this domain focuses on how the brain and extended nervous system interact with the minds of others in an 'embodied relational process that regulates the flow of energy and information' (Siegel, 2012: xxvi) to create responses and reactions in the social and physical environment. The goal of interpersonal neurobiology is to contribute to healthy minds, integrated brains and empathic relationships (Siegel,

2012). Interpersonal neurobiology rose to prominence in the 1990s, the 'decade of the brain' (Siegel, 2007). Based on neuroscience, these studies recorded behavioural changes based on self-report data-gathering instruments, such as the Profile of Moods Questionnaire and Quality of Life Inventory (Baer et al., 2006). However, the recent discovery of neuroplasticity – the capacity of the brain to change and improve throughout life – and the use of advances such as the Computer-Aided Tomography (CAT) and Positron Emission Tomography (PET) scans to map accompanying changes in the brain's neural structure are yielding perspectives that augment EI research.

Mindful awareness or 'attention to intention' research is based on the neurobiological scientific mechanism underlying EI and ESC. Mindfulness has been defined differently across disciplines but converges in relation to three elements: (1) awareness (2) of present experience (3) with acceptance (Black, 2011). Mindfulness or mindful awareness is operationally defined by Brown et al. (2007: 212) as

> as a receptive state of mind wherein attention is kept to a bare registering of the facts observed . . . permitting the individual to 'be present' to reality as it is rather than react to it or habitually process it through conceptual filters . . . Without the overlay of discriminatory, categorical, and habitual thought, consciousness takes on a clarity and freshness that permits more objectively informed psychological and behavioural responses.

In common with EI and ESC research exploring mindfulness is concerned with understanding and constructing adaptive outcomes in social relations as well as crafting human mental and physical well-being. Therefore, mindfulness research investigates variables that are complementary and content that is overlapping with EI (Siegel, 2007, 2010; Mayer et al., 2008). Scientific advances such as CAT and PET scans enable researchers to map neurological changes in the brain that can be attributed to mindful awareness practice (Begley, 2007; Doidge, 2007; Siegel, 2007). Increasingly, it has become evident that mindful awareness is not only a corrective treatment for disorders and a component of health and well-being; it also contributes to optimal mental functioning (Siegel, 2012) which can have positive work consequences for employees learning to increase organisational effectiveness. When people are introduced to EI or ESC they generally expect to develop insights to better understand their own and other's behaviour, thus leading to improved relationship management and goal achievement. This 'good behaviour' in organisations has been described as 'how to play nice, share candy and not bite their co-workers' (Tan, 2012: 17).

In contrast, interpersonal neurobiology focuses primarily on expanding the range and depth of people's emotional abilities so that people can be free from the emotional compulsion to react in one way or another. Therefore, employees develop skills that enable them to respond in more adaptive, creative and rational ways that are best for themselves and everybody else (Tan, 2012). From an organisational view point, this means individuals can learn how to be more cognisant of how they are thinking and reacting emotionally and responding in ways that serve them well. Mindful awareness research that encapsulates this realm is closely connected to neuroscience by psychiatrists and neuroscientists (Siegel, 2007) and others such as Begley (2007), Doidge (2007), Langer (1997) and Wallace (2006). This stream of scholarly activity continues to bridge the gap between the 'soft' sociological sciences, such as EI and ESI and 'hard' cognitive behavioural scientific research. Mindfulness research cited here is scientifically validated suggesting this stream of research can potentially provide another clue to help optimise organisational performance.

Greeson's (2009) review of the extant mindfulness research examined the effects of mindfulness on the human mind, body and behaviour and revealed interesting insights for organisational scholars and practitioners alike. This review indicates mindfulness has a greater association with having a positive state of mind, the net effect being a beneficial influence on the brain, the autonomic nervous system, stress hormones, the immune system and healthy behaviours in areas that include eating, sleeping and substance abuse. Other researchers have demonstrated that mindfulness practice can influence areas of the brain involved in regulating attention, awareness and emotion and thereby significantly improve the efficiency of executive attention (Lutz et al., 2008; Tang et al., 2007). There are other methods developed in the East such as yoga, tai chi, contemplative prayer and meditation that promote this way of thinking/being. However, mindfulness and/or mindsight is discussed here from the perspective of scholarly literature related to neuroscientific research and is not implicitly based or grounded in religious or martial arts practice.

Mindful awareness training has been demonstrated to improve performance in tasks that require skills in sustained attention, switching, inhibition of elaborative processing and adopting a wider perspective to contribute to greater mental acuity (Bishop et al., 2004). For example, a study by Jha et al. (2007) examined whether or not meditation through mindfulness training could modify the three subcomponents of attention, namely the ability to:

(1) prioritize and manage tasks and goals; (2) voluntarily focus on specific information; and (3) stay alert to the environment. Such training included 30 minutes of daily mindful awareness meditation for eight weeks to see if this enhanced performance and the ability to focus attention (Jha et al., 2007). This research supports earlier studies demonstrating that the practice of intentional focus on sensory experience results in synaptic changes that restructure the brain. From an organisational perspective, the real question is whether such training has long-term consequences on both individual performance and organisational productivity. If mindful awareness practice for neurological fitness can be compared to the effects of physical exercise to build strength and endurance (Greeson, 2009) to broaden and build mental traits (Compton, 2005).

There are important lessons to be learnt from current applications of 'exercising and controlling the mind' across a wide variety of Eastern cultures that we currently draw on for scholarly and practitioner guidance. For example, during the past 20 years, Jon Kabat-Zinn and colleagues (2005) have experimented with a form of Buddhist meditation juxtaposed with mainstream medicine. This particular meditation is referred to as Mindfulness-Based Stress Reduction Training (MBSRT), a discipline aimed at developing the ability to: (1) pay attention utilising mindfulness qualities and affective qualities such as generosity, empathy, gratitude, gentleness and loving kindness; and (2) pay attention within a systems perspective to the simultaneous consciousness of being a whole and being part of a larger whole (Shapiro and Schwartz, 2000). The ability to self-regulate, focus attention and manage stress is valuable in business environments. Organisations such as Green Mountain Coffee in Vermont (Stanley and Jha, 2009) and Google's Silicon Valley operation (Tan, 2012), among others, support employee mindful awareness programmes. Mindfulness protocols continue to be refined to reduce stress and suffering through increased self-awareness. These practices are gaining widespread support in universities (for example, Stanford in the United States and Monash, Queensland University of Technology and Curtin in Australia) for both students and staff as well as being integrated into university courses.

Interest in nurturing the capacity for self-regulating skills such as mindfulness continues to grow exponentially (Kabat-Zinn, 2005; Stanley and Jha, 2009; Greeson, 2009; Brown et al., 2007) because the constantly changing business environment requires employees to make intelligent decisions efficiently and to manage relationships wisely. Developing self-awareness is a highly disciplined skill that requires longer training to acquire than similar skills (Needleman, 1975). Professional training programmes offering evidence-based practicums for those interested in teaching MBSR are becoming available worldwide. In the business environment, specific ways to achieve this unique quality of consciousness through mindfulness training is becoming increasingly mainstream (Brown et al., 2007; Greeson, 2009). This particular stream of practitioner activity and scholarly research along with other domains cited here, represents exciting prospects for developing the type of individual mindsets capable of increasing productivity in the workplace. They do, however, represent an equal array of challenges and complexities that need to be addressed if we are to fully appreciate the value of an individual's EI within organisations. Humans tend to be bad at focusing on the good and very good at focusing on the bad or the mistakes they make (Hanson, 2013). We struggle to survive and therefore notice when something is wrong, is a mistake or is out of the ordinary more readily than we do when things are good.

'Taking in the Good' requires paying attention to purpose with a different nerve pathway than the one stimulated by error (Dane, 2011). Recent developments in neurobiological research and practice have been translated effectively into new approaches to wellness programmes, motivation and leadership. For example, frontier work by Hanson (2013) at the Wellspring Institute for Neuroscience and Contemplative Wisdom indicated that 'people who completed the Taking in the Good Course experienced significantly less anxiety and depression, and significantly greater self-control, savouring, compassion, love, contentment, joy, gratitude, self-esteem, self-compassion, satisfaction with life, and overall happiness.' Results from this work suggest that it is possible to for people to learn how to make 'good stronger than bad'.

Another salient finding of neuroscience is a reaffirmation of what has been often affirmed in the past but too often overlooked when pressure, haste and goal achievement become paramount. In these circumstances, human beings are more likely to behave adaptively and intelligently and to thrive in environments where authentic or genuine relationships with trusted colleagues are valued. When humans feel safe energy can be directed toward creativity, cooperative problem-solving and inspired goal achievement rather than defensiveness. Debilitating emotions, such as fear and anger, arise in a more accessible neurological process than friendly, loving and cooperative feelings. This is the survival instinct. To counteract this instinct, effective team building, leadership and managerial training can mindfully nurture behaviours, processes and practices that produce safety and avoid focusing on negative behaviour (Siegel, 2007, 2010; Doidge, 2007; Begley, 2007; Langer, 1997; Wallace, 2006)

Overcoming unproductive mindsets is important to organisational agility. Dweck (2006) describes 'growth' versus 'fixed' mindsets. She points out that when we have learned what to expect through training or experience we are very good at producing the status quo because we correct to what we think we know and miss opportunities for creative or growth mindsets. It takes effort and attention to intention or mindfulness to consciously choose to be innovative. Nobel Prize winner Daniel Kahneman (2011) points out that most of our thinking is reactive not creative – fast. To be responsive, creative and innovative rather than reactive in an environment that is constantly disrupted with radical change requires mindful attention and deliberate effort – slow. Concerns about human survival in an increasingly global and complex environment are addressed in interpersonal neurobiology research since human reactions to threat or safety are explored. Increasingly corporations are realising that new formulas for leadership and human interaction must be carefully crafted.

CONCLUSION

Despite the plethora of publications about emotions in the various literatures to date, the study of EI is still in its infancy and not without criticism. This permeates across scholarly and practitioner realms. Typically, Goleman's musing about EI has been extensively criticised in the academic press for a lack of coherence and conceptual clarity. Admittedly, many of Goleman's (and supporters') statements have not been substantiated through empirical research but his ideas should, at the very least, be characterised as early attempts at valuable theory building in this domain. Goleman is not the intellectual heretic some academics would suggest but one of the forerunners in an exciting field of organisational research. Moreover, Goleman has been successful in bringing this interesting – and useful idea – to public prominence.

Clearly, EI transcends theory to become an accepted aspect of job-related performance, attracting continual interest from both scholars and practitioners. Of course the important questioning about the validity of this construct, including its measurement, still remain. Despite limited generalisable empirical research to support the assertions of EI proponents, the literature has on balance proved more useful than harmful in understanding the potential application of EI in the organisation. Although opinion about EI may seem to be polarised at this point in time, given that the parallel domain of IQ has been scrutinised by academics for more than 90 years, it is clearly going to take some time for EI to gain traction (or be repudiated) and maturity in academia.

Unfortunately, Goleman and other researchers do not always help with respect to their depictions of EI, particularly within the work setting. Those supporting the 'commercial' approach on the applied value of EI have tended to make expansive and faddish claims (Murphy and Sideman, 2006), typified by Goleman, on the applied value of EI within organisational settings. Assertions by Goleman and like-minded commentators about the impact of EI in the workplace still remain largely speculative and require empirical verification to provide evidence and clarification of the relation of EI to organisation functioning (Goyal and Akhilesh, 2007). However, as Landy (2005) observed, despite the many academic detractors, there is strong and continuing support for the EI idea, with concomitant instruments and interventions, in the lay business community. Lopes et al.'s (2005) research suggested that assisting employees to develop emotional skills may yield organisational benefit and, despite the many criticisms, EI is still worthy of further empirical exploration.

Ashkanasy and Daus (2005) posit that EI will continue to be a construct of interest in research on organisation behaviour. They consider EI to be another tool for researchers and psychologist alike to help better understand human behaviour and not a substitute or a new form of social or intellectual aptitude. These authors argue EI is positively linked to other forms of intelligence but retains its distinctive identity, varies from individual to individual, develops from childhood but can be learned and enhanced through training, and contributes partly to a person's abilities to effectively and successfully recognise, perceive (self and others), understand and manage emotions. As organisational focus shifts from individual to high-performance work-team systems, intangible assets like socio-emotional competencies, knowledge, cognitive competencies and innovativeness are likely to be integral to high-quality job performance. Leaders therefore need to recognise the influence of employee emotions in determining team design (teamwork) or work outcomes (productivity and profit). Emotions and behaviours like fear, conflict, ego, anger, anxiety and so on can be detrimental to job performance. The question of how much EI translates into those competencies that yield successful performance at work needs addressing. The literature indicates such competencies are now likely to be as important for successful workplace performance as is other individual traits but generalisable empirical models to support this position are still scant.

Typically, EI potentially enables employees to assess and moderate the impact of external and internal contingencies while making decisions within an organisational framework and bureaucracy. Overreacting to situations and fuelled by 'uncontrollable' emotions can negatively impact effective decision-making and performance. Possessing EI allows individuals to relate emotionally and intellectually to other people at work, encouraging positive self-expression and communication. Indeed, Nelis et al. (2009) confirm that EI can be learnt and therefore may lead to improved job performance outcomes in the workplace. Individuals high on EI are able to remain calm and avoid being impulsive and not lose control in stressful situations, which can be very important to successfully performing front-line jobs (Barry and Fulmer, 2004) and/or managerial and executive roles.

EI has the potential to explain behavioural variance not accounted for by general mental ability or personality. Further investigation in needed to establish EI's contribution to predicting effective work outcomes for cognitive skills and personality dimensions (Salovey and Grewal, 2005). Despite the paucity of empirical research on EI, the overarching theme in the literature supports the notion that EI competence can dictate the capacity of leaders and managers to further develop their own EI, as well as that of their employees – leading to positive team and organisational outcomes. There is evidence to suggest that an individual's EI awareness and development can be improved through training and development (McEnrue et al., 2010) but it is necessary to determine how important EI is to employees' job performance before determining whether it makes sense to invest resources into improving specific employee EI. To this effect, Ashkanasy and Daus (2005) propose five guidelines for the effective emotional management of employees:

1. Job design should include emotional aspects of jobs.
2. A positive emotional work climate should be created.
3. The employee selection process should include consideration of past records of emotional attitudes and contributions.
4. Employees should demonstrate positive and friendly emotional skills which should be encouraged through rewards.
5. Training in EI skills should be institutionalised within organisations.

On a final note, the latest neuroscientific research is yielding new information about the way emotions affect the brain's executive functions, decision-making and attentional focus. Interpersonal neurobiology scholars are now studying various interactions between and within individuals and the environmental (intrapersonal), individuals and community groups. This strand of research is helping the understanding of how these interactions shape the brain or mind's capacity to react or respond either adaptively or destructively. Scholars in this domain are beginning to learn how to better shape habitual emotional experience and behaviour in individuals and groups. These topics are closely related to EI and may offer perspectives on useful human resource practices that will impact organisational effectiveness. Perhaps the academically rigorous research based on neurobiological science can be blended with useful, practical approaches in the social sciences with regard to EI and ESC. This could be a useful approach to help promote growth and well-being at the same time as yielding new insights into the nature of human experience and interpersonal interactions (Siegel, 2012). Perhaps a better understanding of well-founded practice in Asian and Eastern cultures of self-reflection, contemplative practice and meditation can be advanced in Western contexts through scholarly examination of the impact of emotions on employees and organisations.

REFERENCES

Antonakis, J., 2003. Why "emotional intelligence" does not predict leadership effectiveness: a comment on Prati, Douglas, Ferris, Ammeter, and Buckley (2003). International Journal of Organizational Analysis 11 (4), 355–361.

Arvey, R.D., Murphy, K.R., 1998. Performance evaluation in work settings. Annual Review of Psychology 49, 141–168.

Aschcroft, B.E., Humphrey, R.H., 1995. Emotion in the workplace: a reappraisal. Human Relations 48 (2), 97–125.

Ashkanasy, N.M., Daus, C.S., 2005. Rumors of the death of emotional intelligence in organizational behavior are vastly exaggerated. Journal of Organizational Behavior 26 (4), 441–451.

Ashkanasy, N.M., Daus, C.S., 2002. Emotion in the workplace: the new challenge for managers. Academy of Management Executive 16 (1), 23–45.

Ashkanasy, N.M., Hartel, C.E., Fischer, C., Ashforth, B., 1998. A Research Program to investigate the Causes and Consequences of Emotional Experience at Work. In Annual Meeting of the Australasian Society Psychologists. Christchurch, New Zealand.

Baer, R.A., Smith, G.T., Hopkins, J., Krietemeyer, J., Toney, L., 2006. Using self-report assessment methods to explore facets of mindfulness. Assessment 13 (1), 27–45.

Bales, R.F., 1950. Interaction Process Analysis. Addison-Wesley, Cambridge, MA.

Bar-On, R., 1997a. Bar-On Emotional Quotient Inventory, Technical Manual (EQ-i). Multi-Health Systems, Toronto.

Bar-On, R., 1997b. The Emotional Intelligence Inventory (EQ-I): technical manual. Toronto, Canada: Multi-Health Systems.

Bar-On, R., Handley, R., Fund, S., 2005. The Impact of Emotional Intelligence on Performance, Linking Emotional Intelligence and Performance at Work: Current Research Evidence with Individuals and Groups. Lawrence Erlbaum Associates, Mahwah, NJ.

Barrick, M.R., Mount, M.K., Judge, T.A., 2001. Personality and job performance at the beginning of the new millennium: what do we know and where do we go next? International Journal of Selection and Assessment 9, 9–30.

Barry, B., Fulmer, I., 2004. The smart negotiator: cognitive ability and emotional intelligence in negotiation. International Jounal of Conflict Management 15 (3), 245–272.

Barzdil, P., Slaski, M., 2003. Emotional Intelligence: fundamental competencies for enhanced service provision. Managing Service Quality 13 (2), 97–104.

Begley, S., 2007. Train Your Mind, Change Your Brain: How a New Science Reveals Our Extraordinary Potential to Transform Ourselves. Ballantine Books, New York.

Bishop, S., Lau, M., Shapiro, S., Carlson, N., 2004. Mindfulness: a proposed operational definition. Clinical Psychology: Science and Practice 11 (3), 230–241.

Black, D.S., 2011. A brief definition of mindfulness. Mindfulness Research Guide. Available at: http://www.mindfulexperience.org (accessed 8 January, 2016).

Borman, W.C., Motowidlo, S.J., 1997. Task performance and contextual performance: the meaning for personnel selection research. Human Performance 10 (2), 99–109.

Boyatzis, R.E., Sala, F., 2004. The emotional competence inventory (ECI). In: Geher, G. (Ed.), Measuring Emotional Intelligence. Nova Science, Hauppauge, New York. pp. 147–180.

Boyatzis, R.E., Goleman, D., Rhee, K., 2000. Clustering competence in emotional intelligence: insights from the Emotional Competence Inventory. In: Bar-On, R., Parker, J.D.A. (Eds.), Handbook of Emotional Intelligence. Jossey-Bass, San Francisco, pp. 343–362.

Brislin, R.W., 1970. Back-translation for cross-cultural research. Journal of Cross-Cultural Psychology 1 (3), 185–216.

Brown, K.W., Ryan, R.M., Creswell, J.D., 2007. Mindfulness: theoretical foundations and evidence for its salutary effects. Psychological Inquiry: An International Journal for the Advancement of Psychological Theory 18 (4), 211–237.

Cage, T., Daus, C.S., Saul, K., 2004. An Examination of Emotional Skill, Job Satisfaction, and Retail Performance. In Paper submitted to the 19th Annual Society for Industrial/Organizational Psychology, as part of the symposium.

Caruso, D.R., Salovey, P., 2004. The Emotionally Intelligent Manager: How to Develop and Use the Four Key Emotional Skills of Leadership. Jossey-Bass, San Francisco.

Cherniss, C., 2010. Emotional Intelligence: toward clarification of a concept. Industrial and Organizational Psychology 3, 110–126.

Compton, W., 2005. An Introduction to Positive Psychology. Thompson-Wadsworth, New York.

Cote, S., Lopes, P.N., Salovey, P., Miners, C.T., 2010. Emotional intelligence and leadership emergence in small groups. Leadership Quarterly 21 (3), 496–508.

Cropanzano, R.S., James, K., Konovsky, M.A., 1993. Dispositional affectivity as a predictor of work attitudes and job performance. Journal of Organizational Behavior 14 (6), 595–606.

Damasio, A.R., 1994. Descartes' Error: Emotion, Reason, and the Human Brain. Grosset/Putnam, New York.

Dane, E., 2011. Paying attention to mindfulness and its effects on task performance in the workplace. Journal of Management 37 (4), 997–1018.

Daugherty, H., 1969. Star Trek [Television]. Paramount Television, Hollywood.

Daus, C.S., Ashkanasy, N.M., 2003. Will the real emotional intelligence please stand up? On deconstructing the emotional intelligence "debate". Industrial and Organizational Psychologist 41 (2), 69–72.

Daus, C.S., Ashkanasy, N.M., 2005. The case for the ability-based model of emotional intelligence in organizational behavior. Journal of Organizational Behavior 26 (4), 453–466.

Daus, C.S., Rubin, R.S., Smith, R.K., Cage, T., 2004. Police Performance: Do Emotional Skills Matter? In Paper submitted to the 19th Annual Meeting of the Society for Industrial and Organizational Psychologists, as part of the symposium, "Book 'em Danno".

Doidge, N., 2007. The Brain That Changes Itself: Stories of Personal Triumph from the Frontiers of Brain Science. Penguin Group, New York.

Douglas, S., Craig, C., 2007. Collaborative and iterative translation: an alternative approach to back translation. Journal of International Marketing 15 (1), 30–43.

Druskat, V.U., Wolff, S.B., 2001. Group emotional competence and its influence on group effectiveness. In: Cherniss, C., Goleman, D. (Eds.), The Emotionally Intelligent Workplace. Jossey-Bass, San Francisco, pp. 132–155.

Dulewicz, V.P., Higgs, M.J., 2000. Emotional Intelligence: a review and evaluation study. Journal of Managerial Psychology 15 (4), 341–372.

Dweck, C., 2006. Mindset The New Psychology of Success. Ballantine Books, New York.

Elfenbein, H.A., Ambady, N., 2002. Is there an in-group advantage in emotion recognition? Psychological Bulletin 128 (2): 243–249.

Elfenbein, H.A., Ambady, N., 2003. Predicting workplace outcomes from the ability to eavesdrop on feelings. Journal of Applied Psychology 87 (5), 963–975.

Finucane, M.L., Peters, E., Slovic, P., 2003. Judgment and decision making: the dance of affect and reason. In: Schneider, S.L., Shanteau, J. (Eds.), Emerging Perspectives on Judgment and Decision Research. Cambridge University Press, New York, pp. 327–364.

Fisher, C.D., Ashkanasy, N.M., 2000. The emerging role of emotions in work life: an introduction. Journal of Organizational Behavior 21 (2), 123–129.

Goleman, D., 1995. Emotional Intelligence: Why It Can Matter More than IQ. Bantam Books, New York.

Goleman, D., 1998. What makes a leader? Harvard Business Review 76, 93–115.

Goleman, D., 1999. Working with Emotional Intelligence. Bantam Books, London.

Goyal, A., Akhilesh, K., 2007. Interplay among innovativeness, cognitive intelligence and social capital of work teams. Team Performance Management 13 (7/8), 206–226.

Greeson, J.M., 2009. Mindfulness research update. Complementary Health Practice Review 14 (1), 10–18.

Hanson, R., 2013. Hardwiring Happiness. Harmony Crown, New York.

Harms, P.D., Credé, M., 2007. Emotional intelligence and transformational and transactional leadership: a meta-analysis. Journal of Research in Personality 41, 1107–1117.

Hosie, P., Sevastos, P., 2009. Does the "happy-performing managers" proposition apply to managers? International Journal of Workplace Health 2 (2), 131–160.

Hosie, P., Sevastos, P., Willemyns, M., 2012. The impact of happiness on managers' contextual and task performance. Asia Pacific Journal of Human Resources 50 (3), 268–287.

Humphrey, R.H., Pollack, J.M., Hawver, T., 2008. Leading with emotional labor. Journal of Managerial Psychology 23 (2), 151–168.

Hyland, P.K., Andrew Lee, R., Mills, M.J., 2015. Mindfulness at work: a new approach to improving individual and organizational performance. Industrial and Organizational Psychology 1, 8(4), 576–602.

Izard, C., 2002. Translating emotion theory and research into preventative interventions. Psychological Bulletin 128 (5), 796–824.

Jha, A.P., Krompinger, J., Baime, M.J., 2007. Mindfulness training modifies subsystems of attention. Cognitive, Affective, and Behavioral Neuroscience 7 (2), 109–119.

Jordan, P.J., Ashkanasy, N.M., 2006. Emotional intelligence, emotional self-awareness, and team effectiveness. In: Druskat, V.U., Sala, F., Mount, G.J. (Eds.), Linking Emotional Intelligence and Performance at Work: Current research evidence with individuals and groups. Jossey-Bass, San Francisco. pp. 145–163.

Jordan, P.J., Troth, A.C., 2004. Managing emotions during team problem solving: emotional intelligence and conflict resolution. Human Performance 17, 195–218.

Jordan, P.J., Ashkanasy, N.M., Hartel, C.E.J., Hooper, G.S., 2002. Workgroup emotional intelligence: scale development and relationship to team process effectiveness and goal focus. Human Resource Management Review 12 (2), 195–214.

Joseph, D.L., Newman, D.A., 2010. Emotional intelligence: an integrative meta-analysis and cascading model. Journal of Applied Psychology 95 (1), 54–58.

Kabat-Zinn, J., 2005. Coming to Our Senses: Healing Ourselves and the world Through Mindfulness. Hyperion Press, New York.

Kahneman, D., 2011. Thinking Fast and Slow. Farrar, Strauss & Giroux, New York.

Landy, F.J., 2005. Some historical and scientific issues related to research on emotional intelligence. Journal of Organizational Behavior 26 (4), 411–424.

Langer, E., 1997. The Power of Mindful Learning. Perseus, Cambridge, MA.

Levy, R.I., 1984. The emotions in comparative perspective. In: Scherer, K.R., Ekman, P. (Eds.), Approachs to Emotion. Erlbaum, Hillsdale, NY, pp. 397–410.

Lewis, M., Haviland-Jones, J.M. (Eds.), 2000. Handbook of Emotions, 2nd edn. Guilford Press, New York.

Likert, R., 1967. The Human Organization. McGraw-Hill, New York.

Locke, E.A., 2005. Why emotional intelligence is an invalid concept. Journal of Organisational Behaviour 26 (4), 425–431.

Loewenstein, G.F., Weber, E.U., Hsee, C.K., Welch, N., 2001. Risk as feelings. Psychological Bulletin 127 (2), 267–286.

Lopes, P.N., Côté, S., Salovey, P., 2005. An ability model of emotional intelligence: implications for assessment and training. In: Druskat, V.U., Sala, F., Mount, G. (Eds.), Linking Emotional Intelligence and Performance at Work: Current Research Evidence. Erlbaum, Mahwah, NJ, pp. 53–80.

Lutz, A., Slagter, H.A., Dunne, J.D., Davidson, R.J., 2008. Attention regulation and monitoring in meditation. Trends in Cognitive Sciences 12 (4), 163–169.

McCallin, A., Bamford, A., 2007. Interdisciplinary teamwork: is the influence of emotional intelligence fully appreciated? Journal of Nursing Management 15, 386–391.

McCoy, R.A., Campbell, J.P., Cudeck, R., 1994. A confirmatory test of a model of performance determinants. Journal of Applied Psychology 79 (4), 493–504.

McEnrue, M., Groves, K., Shen, W., 2010. Emotional intelligence training: evidence regarding its efficacy for developing leaders. Leadership Review 10, 1–26.

Martin, J., Knopoff, K., Beckman, C., 1998. An alternative to bureaucratic impersonality and emotional labor: bounded emotionality at The Body Shop. Administrative Science Quarterly 43 (2), 429–469.

Mayer, J.D., 1999. Emotional intelligence: popular or scientific psychology? APA Monitor 30, 50.

Mayer, J.D., Salovey, P., 1993. The intelligence of emotional intelligence. Intelligence 17 (4), 433–442.

Mayer, J.D., Salovey, P., 1997. What is emotional intelligence? In: Salovey, P., Sluyter, D. (Eds.), Emotional Development and Emotional Intelligence: Implications for Educators. Basic Books, New York, pp. 3–31.

Mayer, J.D., Caruso, D.R., Salovey, P., 2000a. Selecting a measure of emotional intelligence: the case for ability scales. In: Bar-On, R., Parker, J.D.A. (Eds.), The Handbook of Emotional Intelligence. Jossey-Bass, San Francisco, pp. 320–342.

Mayer, J.D., Salovey, P., Caruso, D.R., 2000b. Models of emotional intelligence. In: Sternberg, R.J. (Ed.), Handbook of Human Intelligence, 2nd edn. Cambridge University Press, New York, pp. 396–420.

Mayer, J.D., Salovey, P., Caruso, D.R., 2008. Emotional intelligence: new ability or eclectic traits? American Psychologist 63 (6), 503–517.

Morehouse, M.M., 2007. An exploration of emotional intelligence across career arenas. Leadership and Organisation Development Journal 28 (4), 296–307.

Motowidlo, S.J., Van Scotter, J.R., 1994. Evidence that task performance should be distinguished from contextual performance. Journal of Applied Psychology 79 (4), 475–480.

Murphy, K.R., Sideman, L., 2006. The two EIs. In: Murphy, K.R. (Ed.), A Critique of Emotional Intelligence. Erlbaum, Mahwah, NJ, pp. 37–58.

Needleman, J., 1975. A Sense of the Cosmos: The Encounter of Modern Science and Ancient Truth. Garden City, N.Y.: Doubleday.

Nelis, D., Quoidbach, J., Mikolajczak, M., Hansenne, M., 2009. Increasing emotional intelligence: (how) is it possible? Personality and Individual Differences 47, 36–41.

Newman, D.A., Joseph, D.L., MacCann, C., 2010. Emotional intelligence and job performance: the importance of emotion regulation and emotional labor context. Industrial and Organizational Psychology 3 (2), 159–164.

Nicholson, N., 2000. Managing the Human Animal. Crown, New York.

O'Boyle, E.H., Humphrey, R.H., Pollack, J.M., Hawver, T.H., Story, P.A., 2011. The relation between emotional intelligence and job performance: a meta-analysis. Journal of Organizational Behavior 32, 788–818.

Offermann, L.R., Bailey, J.R., Vasilopoulos, N.L., Seal, C., Sass, M., 2004. The relative contribution of emotional competence and cognitive ability to individual and team performance. Human Performance 17, 219–243.

Ollilainen, M., 2000. Gendering emotions, gendering teams: construction of emotions in self-managing teamwork. In: Ashkanasy, N.M., Härtel, C.E.J., Zerbe, W.J. (Eds.), Emotions in the Workplace. Quorum, Westport, CT, pp. 3–18.

Pescosolido, A.T., 2002. Emergent leaders as managers of group emotion. Leadership Quarterly 13 (5), 583–599.

Romero, E.J., Pescosolido, A.T., 2008. Humor and group effectiveness. Human Relations 61 (3), 395–418.

Salovey, P., Grewal, D., 2005. The science of emotional intelligence. Current Directions in Psychological Science 14 (6), 281–285.

Salovey, P., Mayer, J.D., 1989–90. Emotional intelligence. Imagination, Cognition and Personality 9 (3), 185–211.

Shapiro, S.L., Schwartz, G.E., 2000. The role of intention in self regulation: toward intentional systematic mindfulness. In: Boekaerts, M., Pintrich, P.R., Zeidner, M. (Eds.), Handbook of Self-Regulation. Academic Press, San Diego, CA, pp. 253–273.

Siegel, D.J., 2007. The Mindful Brain. W.W. Norton, New York.

Siegel, D.J., 2010. Mindsight. Bantam Books, New York.

Siegel, D.J., 2012. Pocket Guide to Interpersonal Neurobiology. W.W. Norton, New York.

Spector, P.E., 2005. Introduction: emotional intelligence. Journal of Organisational Behaviour 26 (4), 409–410.

Stanley, E., Jha, A.P., 2009. Mind fitness: increasing operational effectiveness and building warrior resilience. Joint Forces Quarterly 55, 144–151.

Staw, B.M., Barsade, S.G., 1993. Affect and managerial performance: a test of the sadder-but-wiser vs. happier-and-smarter hypotheses. Administrative Science Quarterly 38 (2), 304–331.

Tan, C.-M., 2012. Search Inside Yourself: The Unexpected Path to Achieving Success, Happiness (and World Peace). HarperCollins, New York.

Tang, Y.-Y., Ma, Y., Wang, J., Fan, Y., Feng, S., Lu, Q., Yu, Q., Sui, D., Rothbart, M.R., Fan, M., Posner, M.I., 2007. Short-term meditation training improves attention and self-regulation. Proceedings of the National Academy of Science 104 (43), 17152–17156.

Turnball, S., 1999. Emotional labour in corporate change programmes: the effects of organisational feeling rules on middle managers. Human Resource Development International 2 (2), 125–146.

Van Rooy, D.L., Viswesvaran, C., 2004. Emotional intelligence: a meta-analytic investigation of predictive validity and nomological net. Journal of Vocational Behavior 65 (1), 81–95.

Waldman, D.A., Balthazard, P.A., Peterson, S.J., 2011. Leadership and neuroscience: can we revolutionize the way that inspirational leaders are identified and developed? Academy of Management Perspectives 25 (1), 60–74.

Wallace, A., 2006. The Attention Revolution. Wisdomm, Somerville, MA.

Walter, F.H., Cole, M.S., Humphrey, R.H., 2011. Emotional intelligence: sine qua non of leadership or folderol? Academy of Management Perspectives 25 (1), 45–59.

Whyte, W.F., 1955. Street Corner Society: The Social Structure of an Italian Slum. University of Chicago Press, Chicago.

Wright, T.A., Cropanzano, R.S., 2000. Psychological well-being and job satisfaction as predictors of job performance. Journal of Occupational and Health Psychology 5 (1), 84–94.

Wright, T.A., Staw, B.M., 1999a. Affect and favorable work outcomes: two longitudinal tests of the happy-productive worker thesis. Journal of Organizational Behavior 20 (1), 1–23.

Wright, T.A., Staw, B.M., 1999b. Further thoughts on the happy-productive worker. Journal of Organizational Behavior 20 (1), 31–34.

Regional HRM perspectives

CHAPTER 4

Where was HRM? The crisis of public confidence in Australia's banks

A. Montague, R. Larkin, J. Burgess

INTRODUCTION

Pre- and post–global financial crisis (GFC), Australian banks have been subject to ongoing public scrutiny regarding their advice to clients and their treatment of them, the effectiveness of their training programmes and the efficacy of their governance systems, and the fees charged (and profits earned) in a regulated oligopoly market. The recent scandals and allegations have been so serious that Senate inquiries (Senate Economics References Committee, 2014, 2015a, 2015b) were conducted and considerable media commentary followed that indicated a culture of unacceptable behaviour regarding advice and regulatory activities across the banking sector. Thousands of clients appeared to have been given unreliable advice and consequently lost millions of dollars in assets and savings, generating personal and community hardship that in many cases is subject to ongoing litigation. Behind these events is a systems failure where the bank's financial and human resource management (HRM) systems and programmes allowed such practices to proceed largely unchecked. The banks operated with a code of ethical and professional practice that was not met by some of its employees, nor was it enforced by the bank. If the HRM systems had been operationally effective then many of the practices outlined would have been prevented or dealt with expeditiously.

In this chapter, we examine the HRM practices of two of the large Australian banks involved in the ongoing public scandal and litigation. The banks not identified specifically are referred to as Bank A and Bank B in this chapter as there are ongoing processes including court cases, internal organisational inquiries, a Federal Senate inquiry, the payment of compensation to aggrieved clients and the sacking of staff deemed to have been engaged in unethical business practices.

*Asia Pacific Human Resource Management
and Organisational Effectiveness*
ISBN 978-0-08-100643-6

Internationally, the banking and finance system has been accused of unethical, reckless and even criminal behaviour in the run-up to the GFC. The list of allegations, fines and failures is extensive: 'Barclays has been handed the biggest UK bank fine in history as six banks were ordered to pay $6bn (£3.9bn) over manipulating the foreign exchange markets' (Makin, 2015: 2). Barclays was ordered to pay £284.4m by the Financial Conduct Authority as a proportion of the British bank's £1.5bn settlement with the 'City watchdog' as well as four US regulators. It was reported that JP Morgan, Royal Bank of Scotland , Citigroup, UBS and Bank of America were fined as well by the Federal Reserve, with only the Bank of America avoiding being forced to 'plead guilty to criminal charges and being penalised by the Department of Justice based in the United States (Makin, 2015: 2). The reports by regulators outlined that financial traders within these banks referred to themselves with names such as 'The Cartel' and 'colluded to rig euro-dollar currency benchmarks, profiting at the expense of customers' (Makin, 2015: 2).

In the aftermath of the GFC in the United States, the consequence of bank failures, mortgage foreclosures and falling housing prices saw depressed economic conditions that resulted in 26 million unemployed and unable to locate full-time work (Financial Crisis Inquiry Commission (FCIC), 2011). Approximately 'four million families have lost their homes to foreclosure and another four and a half million have slipped into the foreclosure process or are seriously behind on their mortgage payments. Nearly, $11 trillion in household wealth has vanished, with retirement accounts and life savings swept away. Businesses, large and small, have felt the sting of a deep recession' (FCIC, 2011: xv). The angst this has caused in the United States has been felt in many other parts of the world and people are justifiably angered (FCIC, 2011). Ireland, for example, with around four million people now had a crippling debt: '. . . the economic crisis that downed Ireland's once-vibrant "Celtic Tiger" economy forced Dublin to agree to an 85 billion euro ($A116.4 billion) bailout with the European Union and International Monetary Fund last November [2010]' (FCIC, 2011). This is an example of the significant economic pain and resulted in a change of government due to the angst of the population (Ritchie, 2011). Innocent people who had adhered to the fundamental rules now found themselves unemployed, disenfranchised and without a job (FCIC, 2011).

The global banking system has been embroiled in a series of scandals including collusion, rigging markets, defrauding clients, tax evasion, money laundering and fraud. This all occurred in the context of an elaborate system of national and international financial regulation designed to support the stability of the financial systems. It is not only the practices and conduct of individual banks that have been questioned, but it is also the failure of the regulatory systems around the banking system that has been questioned (Verick and Islam, 2010). However, the reputation and probity of the banking sector was questioned well before the GFC. There have been some outstanding instances where greed appears to have distorted corporate social responsibility. As illustrative examples, in 1998 the Swiss banks were shamed into settling a 'holocaust accord'. After protracted legal challenges and resistance from the banks, 'representatives of Swiss commercial banks and Holocaust survivors announced a settlement yesterday in which the banks agreed to pay $1.25 billion in restitution to victims of the Nazi era' (Fried, 1998: webpage). Then, on 15 September 2008 – 'Dark Monday' –

> the world witnessed a radical reshaping of Wall Street. Lehman Brothers fell toward bankruptcy; Merrill Lynch was sold to its rival, Bank of America; and AIG pleaded for $40 billion in government relief. Those calamities marched in step with a dismal parade including the US government takeover of Fannie Mae and Freddie Mac, the bailout of Bear Stearns, and the entire subprime debacle. (Donaldson, 2012: 5)

The public scandals, regulatory failures and public bailouts of banks have been on a grand scale. For example, the Royal Bank of Scotland in February 2009 reported the biggest annual loss of £24 billion (Werdigier, 2009) in British corporate history, and signed up for Britain's asset protection plan underwritten by the British public (Correy, 2011). Across the Irish Sea the Anglo-Irish Bank received a 4 billion government bailout from the Irish government in 2009 (Correy, 2011). In Iceland, three of the largest banks collapsed when Iceland was found to be $120 billion in debt, which represented the country's entire economy multiplied by a factor of ten (Correy, 2011). In 2008 the giant American insurance company, American International Group Inc. (AIG), was bailed out by the United States government (Correy, 2011) for $182 billion (Grunwald, 2014).

Nankervis et al. (2014: 5) noted 'that the economic interconnectedness of countries (possibly the major hallmark of globalisation), coupled with the unethical behaviour of some senior managers in the finance and other industry sectors, contributed significantly to recent worldwide financial difficulties including the GFC of 2008–9 and subsequent major economic problems in Greece, Spain, Ireland, Cyprus and other European Union (EU) countries' (Nankervis et al., 2014: 5). 'Such events have resulted in the demise of many businesses; more active intervention of governments in company bailouts and the re-regulation of industries; and associated changes in HRM strategies, including mass retrenchments and major revisions to staffing, performance management, executive pay systems, human resource development, rewards and career development programs' (Nankervis et al., 2014: 5).

In the Asian region, there have been several bank runs and bank bailouts as governments have been forced to support banks in order to stabilise the financial system. Banking runs, crises and bailouts were recorded in Malaysia in 1999, Myanmar in 2003 and China in 2014 (Anon., 2014; Fuller, 1999; Tumell, 2003). There are calls for the national banking systems in the region not only to maintain fiduciary and prudential standards, but also to meet community expectations regarding ethical and moral conduct (Chan, 2015). As free trade arrangements are developing across the regions there are calls for improved corporate governance and ethical standards to be implemented across all sectors, not only banking, to support the expansion in trade and investment (Razook, 2015).

The following analysis of two commercially profitable banks operating in Australia is instructive to the banking system within the region. It is also useful in highlighting the importance of an operational and effective HRM system that develops and enforces ethical standards within the organisation.

Australia has a limited number of large banks on a comparative global scale but all are well capitalised and underpinned by a robust retail base, developed capabilities in regard to wealth management and fully serviced activities in trade finance and commercial and corporate advisory infrastructure impacting on the South East Asian Region (Austrade, 2011). However, the reputations of the Australian banks focused on in this chapter are tarnished too as they have harmed many clients who followed what they considered to be professional and ethical advice.

Banks are crucially important institutions within societies as they perform numerous roles that are vital economically (Balluck, 2015). They provide useful information for borrowers and investors to ensure proper use of the funds that they have at their disposal, obtained largely from depositors (Balluck, 2015). Banks also execute key roles in capital markets and theoretically 'contribute to the efficient functioning of financial markets', but as demonstrated in the recent financial crisis, 'banks can create and propagate risks in the financial system given their scale, as well as the interconnected and complex nature of their activities' (Balluck, 2015: 4). When banks lose their ethical compass, from an economic perspective the society is at risk (Bhandari, 2014), as was shown in the financial crisis of 2008/9 (FCIC, 2011).

METHODOLOGY

In this chapter, a qualitative methodological approach involving a review of the relevant literature and an analysis of bank documents was adopted to outline the actual and potential effects of HRM on organisational effectiveness as an analytical framework, reflecting the work of Boyatzis (1998), Braun and Clarke (2006), Thomas (2006) and Hartman and Conklin (2012). The research design uses the key components of HRM as a conceptual framework to illuminate the activities of the banks through the lens of strategic HRM. The ongoing public scrutiny, public criticism and litigation involving major Australian banks reflects poorly on the underlying management and organisational systems of those banks. It is within this context that the chapter examines their HRM systems and their failure to ensure organisational propriety and effectiveness in the light of these ongoing challenges.

LITERATURE REVIEW – HRM AND ETHICS

HRM involves strategically focusing people on the organisation's business goals for mutual satisfaction (Stone, 2013). Nankervis et al. (2014) and Bratton and Gold (2012) considered HRM as a constant factor for organisations to succeed as their staff develop (or redevelop) and improve the services and products, operate and maintain the technology, control and monitor the financial resources, and manage and lead other people in the organisation. Nankervis et al. (2014) considered that human resources are the 'most unpredictable' of all organisational resources when contrasted to financial balance sheets, technical resources and machinery, due to the mixture of emotional (rational and irrational) traits that humans possess. People are frequently the major ongoing cost factor in any organisation, and are likely to be considered an organisation's most valuable asset (Bohlander and Snell, 2010; Bratton and Gold, 2012; Stone, 2013). It is crucial that staff are 'managed effectively, equitably and ethically, and that their personal and work needs are satisfied, if organisational objectives are to be achieved' (Nankervis et al., 2014: 5).

For Bratton and Gold (2012) and Stone (2013), HRM embodies a strategic approach to meet organisational goals, particularly financial goals, through managing employment relations and focusing and leveraging staff capabilities in terms of ongoing commitment to maintaining a position in the marketplace. The key components of HRM include selection, appraisal, human resource development (HRD), rewards (performance management) and ethics (Bratton and Gold, 2012; Nankervis et al., 2014; Stone, 2013) and are the key functions that will be focused on in this chapter.

Drawing from the Harvard model (Beer et al., 1985), other key components of HRM include situational factors, stakeholder interests, HRM policy choices and long-term consequences. These key HRM components are not complicated and are largely self-explanatory, with the possible exception of the link between HRM and ethics which is a key interest of this study. Bratton and Gold (2012) complained that ethics was neglected within the discourse surrounding HRM in the literature despite being a key central issue in the employment relationship. Bratton and Gold (2012) explained that ethics involves a range of issues drawing on moral principles and values and may involve dilemmas where two, or perhaps multiple, values conflict and an ethical position that can be adopted may exceed the concept of a minimum obligation. Under the ethics umbrella Bratton and Gold (2012) incorporated corporate social responsibility (CSR) that brings in the relationship between the organisation and external stakeholders, embracing local communities, the wider society and the planet in relation to sustainability (Bratton and Gold, 2012).

Nankervis et al. (2014: 39) referred to 'a series of spectacular global corporate collapses around the world over the past several years, which reflected dramatically in the 2008–9 GFC and the subsequent disintegration of the economies of several EU countries, thus raising concerns about the role of HRM'. The corporate failures in the US financial sector were characterised by poor investment decisions, poor risk management and inadequate controls over employees. Where staff were rewarded on the basis of sales of mortgages, regardless of the risk profiles of the borrowers and the assets, banks failed in their duty of due diligence and in their responsibilities to uphold ethical behaviour.

This raises the need for HRM ethical systems to be developed. HRM professionals should also be responsible for ethical awareness, training and evaluation. Ethics and values are of crucial importance in all areas of management, but particularly so in the implementation of well-designed HR strategies, processes and plans. 'Equity, fairness, professionalism and respect for employees ensure that employee satisfaction contributes to business success' (Nankervis et al., 2014: 46). This extends to the array of stakeholders that include shareholders, governments, managers, owners, employees, customers and suppliers.

The five professional ethics items governing professional conduct in HRM, according to Nankervis et al. (2014), include *integrity*, meaning the practice of the HRM profession with high levels of integrity, fairness and honesty; *legality*, respecting individual rights and being law-abiding; *proficiency*, working to improve confidence from a professional perspective; *professional loyalty*, supporting the HRM profession and not abusing professional alliances or affiliations for 'personal or business gain'; and finally *confidentiality*, respecting employee confidentiality particularly in relation to privileged information.

Stone (2013) considered ethical issues to be increasingly important to HRM managers, claiming that increased organisational complexity, ambiguity and conflict tested morality and standards of behaviour. He explained that ethics is relatively simple and meant what is good or bad or right or wrong, while conceding that at times there is no clear or discernible distinction between what is unethical and what is ethical. He also referred to the issues of 'whistleblowers' and defined them as persons who expose the inappropriate work of colleagues which they view as unethical, wasteful, harmful and illegal and possibly fraudulent, and underpinned by likely maladministration and corruption (Stone, 2013). The motivation may be to protect the organisation, but often this can impact on the whistleblowers' lives and result in possible subjection to threats, ridicule, abuse or a 'career meltdown' (Stone 2013: 20).

Most HRM authors would agree that HRM has a key responsibility to ensure that systems are compliant and organisational cultures promote ethical behaviour among staff, characterised by trust, open communications and accountability within a culture where it is clear which behaviours and activities are acceptable or unacceptable. They also agree that such ethical cultures contribute to organisational effectiveness and need to be reinforced by clear HRM policies which encourage and support employees to report ethical breaches.

SELECTED AUSTRALIAN BANKS AND THEIR ETHICAL BEHAVIOUR

The Australian retail banking sector is tightly regulated and dominated by four main banks which are provided with 'public lender of last resort' support – they are considered too big to fail. In this oligopolistic market the profit performance had been outstanding, but beneath the large profits are allegations of financial impropriety and corruption towards clients that has seen numerous public inquiries and calls for a Royal

Commission of Inquiry into the sector (Karvelas, 2015). In Australia, the big four banks have been no strangers to accusations of poor ethical behaviour and questionable business practices.

On national television, in Australia four very well-paid executives working within the banking sector were called before an Australian Government Senate Inquiry in 2015 where they were compelled to apologise. According to Alberici (2015), these apologies stemmed from a culture within Australia's largest banks that permitted unprincipled financial advisers to promote investments that were considered risky to clients described as vulnerable.

The operational failures identified in two banks, Bank A and Bank B, are now discussed. These are representative of the failures in due diligence and in governance that have been seen through media and public inquiries to have been systematic and ongoing in the sector. For example, Bank A's chief executive officer (CEO) was recently summoned before a Senate Committee in Canberra and admitted that his organisation had wrongfully ignored an internal whistleblower seven years earlier, when the bank was warned of a rogue financial planner (Iggulden, in Alberici, 2015; Senate Economics References Committee, 2015b). A Bank A staff member had warned his organisation in 2008 'of misconduct in its financial advice area but he was ignored' (Iggulden, in Alberici, 2015: webpage). A key question here is why did it take the bank so long to react (Sales, 2015)? Belatedly Bank A announced a special compensation scheme (Iggulden, in Alberici, 2015), but to date only three customers have received any compensatory money with more than 200 other claimants still awaiting payment. Bank A's profit continuously eclipses its large bank rivals in Australia, and most of the world's banks, consistently recording annual net profits of over A$5 billion (Janda, 2015).

The following is an excerpt from the Senate Economics References Committee Executive Summary (2015c) inquiry conducted in 2015, presenting information at odds with the code of conduct espoused by Bank A, and thus sheds a poor light on Bank A's ethics issues and a range of key HRM practices that are referred to below.

> *Advisers deliberately neglected their duties and placed their personal interests far above the interests of their clients. The assets of clients with conservative risk positions, such as retirees, were allocated into high-risk products without their knowledge to the financial benefit of the adviser, who received significant bonuses and recognition within CFPL as a 'high performer'. There was forgery and dishonest concealment of material facts. Clients lost substantial amounts of their savings when the global financial crisis hit; the crisis was also used to explain away the poor performance of portfolios.*
>
> **(Senate Economics References Committee, 2015c: xviii)**

Bank A was among several other banks in offering customers dubious financial advice (Iggulden, in Alberici, 2015). Bank A clients' money was linked to 'risky investments' they would have objected to but the audit trail was obscured as documents were allegedly forged or shredded to cover up the scandal (Iggulden, in Alberici, 2015: webpage). A former Bank A customer publicly commented that activities involved forgery, fraud and conduct described as deceptive and misleading were seen as reflecting an 'acceptable business model' within the financial planning division of Bank A (Alberici, 2015).

Bank B dismissed 37 senior financial advisers for 'failing to meet standards' including forging documents and clients' signatures, conflicts of interest, inappropriate advice and engaging in inappropriate practices amid a toxic culture (Ferguson, in Karvelas, 2015). The compensation potentially payable to customers is dependent on them raising the issue and it may take years before they can get any resolution of their complaints (Ferguson, in Karvelas, 2015). One politician in the Senate inquiry aid stated that it was like 'déjà vu' to hear of a very similar issue to the Bank A scandal. However, Karvelas (2015) noted differences whereby Bank A had covered up unlawful conduct and gross incompetence among financial planners, and Bank B had sacked its financial planners but only filed five breach reports with the corporate regulator and subsequently did not report them to the regulating authority for further investigation.

An internal Bank B document established that 'rogue advisers' operated within the banks and spoke of additional major occurrences over the last five years where some advisers forged clients' signatures and tampered with documents in attempts to conceal misconduct (Ferguson and Williams, 2015). Ferguson and Williams (2015) described this situation as disturbing, as the document stated that such instances were not revealed through the bank's internal reviews, controls or audits, but resulted from client complaints and queries instigated by the authorities. This observation by Ferguson and Williams (2015) adds weight to the inquiry finding by the Senate Economics References Committee (2015a) which expressed distrust in Bank B's internal checks on its own staff, processes and procedures within its financial planning/advice arm.

The Bank B Wealth boss admitted to the Senate Economics References Committee that the bank had quietly compensated 750 customers who received bad advice with over A$14.5 million paid, most of which was associated with the eight advisers whose conduct was reported to the Australian Securities and Investments Commission in breach reports. Bank B has dismissed 41 advisers and has now provided those names to the Australian Securities Investment Commission (Eyers, 2015b).

Overall, Bank B has paid millions of dollars to compensate hundreds of clients due to inappropriate financial planning advice since 2009 (Ferguson Williams, 2015). The level of malpractice and unethical behaviour among financial planners involving forgery, sackings and millions in compensation places one of Australia's four banks, Bank B, 'under fire inside its financial advice arm' (Ferguson and Williams, 2015: webpage). Added to this, following severe public criticism, Bank B was 'forced to pay hundreds of millions of dollars in compensation to customers in its UK arm for mis-selling of insurance products' (Ferguson and Williams, 2015: webpage).

Bank A and Bank B had persuaded thousands of clients to make very risky investments and thus had exposed them to significant debt as the investments were questionable at best, and for many investors resulted in millions of dollars in terms of financial loss (Sales, 2015). The latest Senate inquiry in 2015 is the 'fifth inquiry into financial advice matters from the major banks and has been occurring over several years with new revelations emerging' (Iggulden, in Alberici, 2015: webpage). Despite a Royal Commission being requested by many observers it has been continually refused by the federal government even though millions of dollars have been lost by innocent victims of the banks (Ferguson, in Karvelas, 2015; Iggulden, in Alberici, 2015).

The above demonstrates a failure of due diligence, governance and ineffective HRM systems. The evidence indicates ongoing problems in meeting the expectations of clients, with identified bank employees able to operate in a manner that adversely impacted on the financial well-being of their clients and at the same time damaging the reputation of the banks in terms of not meeting the stated ethical and professional standards set out in the corporate webpages, as presented below. The banks failed to develop and monitor programmes in their HRM systems that would support ethical and professional standards, and in the process they compromised the proclaimed objectives of the organisations.

ETHICS IN BANKING – RHETORIC AND REALITY

Statements of ethical intent

From their own corporate websites Bank A and Bank B espouse high ethical standards and behaviour among staff that are supposedly supported and developed through the HRM systems. For example:

Statement of professional practice

By accepting employment with the Bank, all staff agree to comply with the Bank's Statement of Professional Practice, ensuring the principles of professionalism, honesty, common sense and fairness.

If they always act honestly, exercise common sense and are never afraid to ask for help if unsure of how to act, staff will not encounter any problems in observing the principles contained in this Statement.

Business of the bank

Staff should know their job and the Bank's instructions applying to it, follow directions, exercise and not exceed the authorities and discretions delegated to them and act in a manner that will enhance the reputation of the Bank. They should comply with the law in all their activities.

(Bank A webpage, 2015)

Our beliefs and behaviours

At our heart is a belief in the potential of our customers and communities, and in each other. It unites and motivates us:

To do the right thing – *Acting in the interests of our customers and communities, taking a long-term view and making decisions and taking actions that support the sustainability of our relationships and brands.*

To realise potential – *This means helping people and . . .*

From these beliefs come our common set of behaviours, that ask us to always:

Be authentic and respectful – *We value the contributions of all our people and treat our employees, our customers and the broader community with dignity and respect.*

Create value through excellence – *Passionate about creating value and exceeding our customers' expectations, we are constantly striving to redefine our standards of excellence.*

Our beliefs and behaviours are the foundation of our culture and our brands. They are the test of every decision and action we take and unite us in a way of thinking, acting and doing business that is unique.

(Bank B webpage, 2015)

HRM, ETHICAL BEHAVIOUR AND ORGANISATIONAL EFFECTIVENESS

The key issues pertaining to the two banks in this study are the links between their HRM practices and ethics. Ethics underpin the majority of the key HRM function, and the following sections of this chapter analyse how closely the rhetoric matches the reality in the chosen banks. Ethics concerns 'the inherent rightness or wrongness of actions' (Nankervis et al., 2014: 41) in all HRM functions, notably recruitment and selection, staff development, enterprise bargaining, performance management, and rewards and remuneration, while 'workplace productivity improvements need an implicit and explicit underpinning of trust and ethics' (Nankervis et al., 2014: 41).

The two banks discussed above seemed to have ignored their ethical responsibilities when it became known that their financial advice section was populated by many staff members of questionable ethics, some potentially bordering on criminality (Ferguson, 2014; Sales, 2015). These organisations also appear to have spurned the business risks associated with unethical behaviours – embodied in the following quotation – as they are too big and powerful perhaps?

> Loss of this trusting culture leads to loss of reputation to attract the best people, markets and shareholder value. The importance of people as a source of competitive advantage becomes more evident as service-oriented and knowledge-based corporations dominate the economy.
>
> **(Nankervis et al., 2014: 41)**

Even so, the message supporting the role of HR as ethical guardian is clear in that the HR function is the driver of ethical compliance (Winstanley and Woodall, 2000). Yet, there are many issues surrounding the ability of the HR department to meet these demands. For example, normative stakeholder theory (see Freeman, 1984), assumes a legitimate claim for employees' interests and well-being to be represented. Yet, to do so may signify a trade-off to other shareholders' economic advantage (Greenwood, 2002). Regardless, HR's responsibility to 'people' business typically embodies the need to observe well founded codes of ethics (Johnson, 2012) and it is within the realm of HR that an ethical culture can be developed (Bratton and Gold, 2012; Stone, 2013; Nankervis et al., 2014).

In the cases above and from the evidence in the public domain there is a failure of HRM systems and practices and inadequate attempts to align HRM strategically to corporate social responsibility and appropriate ethical standards of behaviour by these organisations. The failure is observed at a number of levels, as follows.

Staff recruitment and selection

According to Bratton and Gold (2012) and Stone (2013), the process of staff recruitment and selection involves locating, attracting and hiring the best-qualified candidates from within the organisation or externally for a position that is vacant or newly developed in a cost-effective and timely manner. The recruitment process includes a well-prepared position description through an analysis of the job requirements and attracting employees to apply, followed by careful screening and selection of applicants, appointment and integration of the new employee into the organisation (Nankervis et al., 2014). The evidence from the two chosen banks suggests that there was a failure in recruitment and induction. Key financial advisers were recruited whose behaviour did not meet the ethical and professional standards set by the banks. There are questions around what induction process and training these staff received, in particular around meeting the professional and ethical standards and in supporting the corporate reputation. Such flawed processes predictably resulted in significant harm to the two banks' organisational effectiveness.

Staff appraisal and remuneration

Aligning the measurement of employees' capabilities, skills and competencies with the organisational goals and objectives through development plans that deliver results is the theoretical underpinning of employee performance management (Nankervis et al., 2014). It is clear that some staff in Banks A and B were allowed to act in a way that was unethical and failed to meet the professional standards expected by clients and their organisations. The evidence suggests that staff who did not meet these standards were rewarded, and that complaints regarding their performance were largely ignored. There was a failure in the performance and appraisal systems and a failure in the internal reporting systems. Some sections of the banks were allowed to operate largely without effective oversight.

Rewards and remuneration systems

In general, indirect and non-cash compensation paid to an employee is a common form of reward in addition to wages and salaries (Stone, 2013). Some benefits are compulsory by law (such as social security benefits, unemployment insurance and workers' compensation). Others frequently vary from firm to firm or industry to industry (such as health insurance, life insurance, medical plans, paid vacations, pensions and gratuities). Adequate compensation and other rewards such as recognition, acknowledgement of their input and effective management and leadership may also figure into the equation (Nankervis et al., 2014). Rewards may also depend on achieving an agreed work plan embodying targets or key performance indicators.

The rewards for financial planners in these two banks seem to have been distorted and focused too much on monetary bonuses, fuelling an environment of greed (Morris, 2015; Ferguson, in O'Brien, 2014; Morris, in Senate Economics References Committee, 2014, 2015a, 2015b; Eyers, 2015c).

Morris (Senate Economics References Committee, 2015b) considered that bank executives were earning easily ten times the amount they earned two decades previously, which had corrupted the judgement and the culture in the banks. The all-embracing focus on sales for larger profits was driven by 'remuneration schemes' with tiers of bonuses paid to each level of management. Quite a number of people were getting paid substantial bonuses in these financial institutions based on sales in planning and other areas and the greed was 'out of control' (Morris, in Senate Economics References Committee, 2015b: 5). Financial-planning managers were dependent for their bonuses on the performance of their team of 12–20 staff and adopted the role of a 'jockey with a whip' trying to achieve ever higher sales figures, with a tolerance for planners to overstep ethical boundaries and take risks to write the business (Morris, in Senate Economics References Committee, 2015b: 5).

Reward systems were distorted in these two banks leading to a lack of respect for and effectiveness of HRM policies, functions and monitoring systems.

Human resource development (HRD)

Human resource development (HRD) aims to assist employees to develop their knowledge, skills and abilities for both personal growth and organisational effectiveness. It often incorporates initiating opportunities that may include formal and informal employee training, career development, key employee identification, mentoring, coaching, tuition assistance and organisational development (Stone, 2013).

The whistleblower who furnished Fairfax Media (Ferguson and Williams, 2015) with internal documents spoke of a cultural environment that was 'volatile', 'toxic' and 'Machiavellian' within Bank B Wealth where the financial advisers worked. Witness after witness made the same observation within the Senate hearings (Senate Economics References Committee, 2014, 2015a, 2015b) as did the Bank A whistleblower (Sheedy, in Eyers, 2015d). So the question is what needs to be done by HRM in developing staff to avoid the proliferation of unethical practices. Remedies range from recruitment to performance management and appraisal, but training and development are obviously crucial in terms of reinforcing basic organisational ethics.

Professor Elizabeth Sheedy from Macquarie University says the risk culture in Australian banks is poor (Eyers, 2015c).' Chief executives of Australia's largest banks are ignorant of cultural deficiencies because their staff continue to overlook ethical breaches' (Eyers, 2015c: webpage). The comprehensive study by Macquarie University into bank risk culture has also found that half of the staff in Australian banks believe remuneration plans 'encourage unacceptable risk taking' (Eyers, 2015c: webpage).

It seems therefore that HRD is vital to offset the culture of greed that has been identified as being at the 'the heart' of problems that beset and confront the banks (Eyers, 2015c). Sheedy, who formerly worked as a banker, is currently completing an original research project centred on a survey involving 300 business units within banks and involves 25,000 banker informants (Eyers, 2015c). The study, which has extended over two-and-a-half years is pointing to a finding that the culture in Australia's banks is inferior to Canada's (Eyers, 2015c). Sheedy's research also focuses on the personality issues and traits of bankers that may lead to behaviour that may be described as destructive (Eyers, 2015c). It found staff with 'Machiavellian' personalities (those who manipulate to gain power) could be seen as the most difficult (Eyers, 2015c). Sheedy's research was viewed as timely given the array of 'scandals' within in the wealth divisions of four large Australian banks (Eyers, 2015c).

Internal governance systems and structure of the board of management

Bratton and Gold (2012), Nankervis et al. (2014) and Stone (2013) considered organisational ethics to be (or should be) the domain of the HRM department. Yet, while each of these organisations has an HRM department, unethical behaviour continues. This therefore raises the questions, how strongly represented is HR in the corporate space, and how strongly reinforced are ethical considerations? Scrutiny of each bank's website identifies that from a combined total of 44 governing and executive positions (21 board members and 23 executive members) across the two banks, only one person has any significant HRM experience. For example, the Bank B website identifies a male-dominated board of directors with a particularly strong financial background, however without any history of HRM or people or culture management. Within the male-dominated executive, HRM is again missing from their position titles although one executive previously had a title loosely referencing an HR function.

The Bank A board is also strongly finance- and male-dominated with no direct evidence of HR in the expertise or background of the members. The Bank A executive, however, differs from Bank B with balanced gender representation and an executive HRM position, the current incumbent of which has a strong corporate HRM background.

The contrasts between the constituencies of the executive teams may shed light on our understanding of the differences between the two banks' commitment to upholding their ethical practices, for example the commitment to whistleblowing on other fraud and corruption practices. Bank B's commitment to managing financial crimes such as 'anti-money-laundering and counter-terrorism financing, anti-fraud, anti-bribery and corruption' are clearly referenced on their website, each regarded in terms of the bank's obligation to meet legal and regulatory requirements. The strongly worded commitment to legal and regulatory requirements, however, is softened to words like 'encouragement' and 'guidance' when it comes to ethical matters such as supporting and protecting whistleblowers. For example, where there is a designated HR presence in the executive, ethics and whistleblowing are provided a generous website presence where the stronger focus on commitment and protections are clear. Even so, both banks, irrespective of the emphasis they provide to ethics and HR through people or process, continue to accept behaviour that obviously sits outside ethical enforcement and has been reported by the media and Senate inquiries in the public domain with considerable prominence.

Banks may consider that they are effective as organisations, based on the measures of share prices and profits which remain healthy despite the recent sharp reduction in global stocks, particularly in China. This chapter presents another view through the lens of people management with research indicating that these organisations are not 'too big to fail' in their links between HRM and organisational effectiveness, especially pertaining to financial advisers. Simply stated another dimension of organisational effectiveness has been presented, and there are very serious issues that require further research in academic and judicial contexts, with the Senate Economics References Committee (2015b) clearly calling for intervention by the laws of the land following a royal commission.

CONCLUSION

In terms of the evidence cited from the public domain for Banks A and B focused upon in this chapter, there are ethical failures along the criteria listed by Nankervis et al. (2014). Integrity was compromised, as the evidence suggests that fairness and honesty were not present in the advice offered to clients; legality was compromised to the extent that there have been and there are ongoing court cases involving claims for compensation from clients of the banks; and proficiency was compromised since professional standards were not met in many of the examples cited. In addition, the large banks have had their corporate reputations tarnished, and the trust given them by the public has been damaged.

The banking sector is a key sector in the economy. Across the globe, and especially in Asia with its high growth record and aspirations, the banking system is a crucial support for these aspirations. An efficient and effective banking system facilitates saving, investment, consumer activity and international transactions. In the past decade banking systems globally have failed the public that has been forced to underwrite bad debts, bad loans and bad management. While the banking system is tightly regulated in Australia and the economy avoided the huge bank losses and failures that occurred elsewhere with the GFC, the sector has been under continuing public scrutiny linked to unethical behaviour, predatory business practices and poor systems of corporate governance. The centrality of banking to the sustainability of the economic system requires high levels of public confidence in the banks (they are being effectively underwritten) and due diligence by the banks to reciprocate this public investment.

However, the banking sector internationally has been in the spotlight for breaches of ethical and professional standards that have seen record fines imposed for breaches of national and international law. Allegations against the sector include money laundering, tax evasion, market rigging, breaking international sanctions, investing in armaments and projects damaging the environment, and supporting regimes that breach human rights (Fidelis International Institute, 2010). The Australian examples are relatively minor compared to the scale of unethical practices globally; however, they demonstrate a failure of governance and ethical standards. Across Asia, especially given the impetus for increasing integration within the region, there is an imperative for all banks to support, improve and enforce ethical standards (Chan, 2015).

We have reported on the practices of two banks that are commercially successful and meet regulatory requirements regarding their balance sheets. The evidence reported is in the public domain since we did not have access to internal documents linked to HRM programmes, their implementation and evaluation. While the analysis is incomplete the evidence in the public domain suggests a failure of HRM systems at all levels including recruitment, performance evaluation, pay, training and corporate governance. The banks profess a commitment to high ethical and professional standards on their websites; however, it is clear that HRM has either not been a part of the process of developing or enforcing these standards or it has failed to monitor and enforce the standards. The banks may have codes of ethics but it appears that the HRM function is not effectively addressing ethics in recruitment, performance management and staff appraisal, and HRD. The question, as asked by Wilcox (2012) of other corporate bodies, is whether HRM is complicit in organisations where there has been such ongoing and systemic failure to develop and enforce ethical standards of behaviour.

REFERENCES

Alberici, E., 2015. Big bank bosses grilled at financial advice inquiry. Lateline, Australian Broadcasting Corporation, broadcast by reporter Tom Iggulden. Available at: *http://www.abc.net.au/lateline/content/2015/s4221070.htm* (accessed 10 June 2015).

Anon, 2014. Chinese banks stack money in windows to quell rumours they have run out. Guardian, 26 March.

Austrade (Australian Trade Commission), 2011. Australia's Banking Industry. Australian Government, Canberra. Available at: *http://www.austrade.gov.au/.../2792/Australia's-Banking-Industry.pdf.aspx* (accessed 21 May 2015).

Balluck, K., 2015. Investment banking: linkages to the real economy and the financial system. Bank of England Quarterly Bulletin 55 (1), 4–22.

Bank, A., 2015. Statement of Professional Practice. (accessed 13 August 2015).

Bank, B., 2015. Our Beliefs and Behaviours. (accessed 13 August 2015).

Beer, M., Spector, B., Lawrence, P., Mills, D., Walton, R., 1985. Human resource management: A general manager's perspective, New York, Free Press.

Bhandari, N., 2014. Understanding the differences in codes of ethics of culturally different nations' multinational banks. International Journal of Trade and Global Business Perspectives 3 (1), 853–870.

Bohlander, G., Snell, S., 2010. Managing Human Resources, 15th edn. South-Western Cengage Learning, Mason, OH.

Boyatzis, R., 1998. Transforming Qualitative Information: Thematic Analysis and Code Development. Sage, Thousand Oaks, California.

Bratton, J., Gold, J., 2012. Human Resource Management: Theory and Practice, 5th edn. Palgrave Macmillan, Basingstoke.

Braun, V., Clarke, V., 2006. Using thematic analysis in psychology. Qualitative Research in Psychology 3 (2), 77–101.

Chan, N., 2015. To improve banking standards, bankers themselves must choose ethics over short-term profit. South China Morning Post. Online at: *http://www.scmp.com/comment/insight-opinion/article/1767030/improve-banking-standards-bankers-themselves-must-choose* (accessed 25 August 2015).

Correy, S., 2011. Auditing the auditors. Background Briefing, Radio National Australian Broadcasting Commission 14. Online at: *http://www.abc.net.au/radionational/programs/backgroundbriefing/auditing-the-auditors/2930872#transcript* (accessed 31 August 2015).

Donaldson, T., 2012. Three ethical roots of the economic crisis. Journal of Business Ethics 106, 5–8.

Eyers, J., 2015a. Consumer advocates back expanded powers for ASIC to probe banks. Sydney Morning Herald, 1 June. Online at: http://www.smh.com.au/business/banking-and-finance/consumer-advocates-back-expanded-powers-for-asic-to-probe-banks-20150601-ghclrl (accessed 1 June 2015).

Eyers, J., 2015b. [Bank B] says no to compo review. The Age, p. 4.7.

Eyers, J., 2015c. "Machiavellian" bankers in firing line over scandals. Sydney Morning Herald, 3 June. Online at: *http://www.smh.com.au/business/banking-and-finance/machiavellian-bankers-in-firing-line-over-scandals-20150602-gheree.html* (accessed 14 August 2015).

Eyers, J., 2015d. Greedy bankers in firing line. Business, The Age, 3 June 2015. Fairfax Melbourne.

Ferguson, A., 2014. Banking bad: the emphasis is always on trying to get the maximum share of wallet out of each customer. Four Corners (ABC1). Broadcast, Monday, 5 May. Online at: *http://search.informit.com.au.ezproxy.lib.rmit.edu.au/documentSummary;dn=TSM20140 5050073;res=TVNEWS* (accessed 1 June 2015).

Ferguson, A., Williams, R., 2015. Forgery, sackings and millions in compensation: [Bank B] under fire over financial planners. Sydney Morning Herald. Online at: *http://www.smh.com.au/business/banking-and-finance/forgery-sackings-and-millions-in-compensation,20150220–13kdjk.html* (accessed 6 July 2015).

Fidelis International Institute, 2010. Ethical Issues Facing the Banking System. Online at: *http://www.fidelisinstitute.org/article.php?se=13&ca=22* (accessed 25 August 2015).

Financial Crisis Inquiry Commission (FCIC), 2011. The Financial Crisis Inquiry Report – Final Report of the National Commission on the Causes of the Financial and Economic Crisis in the United States. US Government, Washington, DC.

Freeman, E., 1984. Strategic Management: A Stakeholder Approach. Pitman, Boston.

Fried, J.P., 1998. Swiss Banks reach Holocaust accord. New York Times. Online at: *http://www.nytimes.com/1998/08/13/world/swiss-banks-reach-holocaust-accord.html* (accessed 29 May 2015).

Fuller, T., 1999. Preemptive action puts central bank in control: Malaysia takes over MBf Finance. New York Times, 5th May 1999.

Greenwood, M., 2002. Ethics and HRM: a review and conceptual analysis. Journal of Business Ethics 36 (3), 261–278.

Grunwald, M., 2014. The real truth about the Wall Street bailouts. Time Magazine. Online at: *http://time.com/3450110/aig-lehman/* (accessed 1 August 2015).

Hartman, N., Conklin, T., 2012. A thematic analysis of a leadership speaker series. Journal of Management Development 31 (8), 826–844.

Janda, M., 2015. [Bank A] makes $1m per hour profit but shares slump as earnings stagnate. Australian Broadcasting Commission News ABC1. Online at: *http://www.abc.net.au/news/2015-05-06/commonwealth-bank-makes-1-million-dollars-per-hour/6448130%20 accessed%201%20June%202016* (accessed 1 June 2015).

Johnson, C., 2012. Organizational Ethics: A Practical Approach, 2nd edn. Sage, Thousand Oaks, CA.

Karvelas, P., 2015. Business and economics: [Bank B] leaks. Radio National, Australian Broadcasting Commission, 25 February. Online at: *http://www.abc.net.au/radionational/programs/drive/business-and-economics3a-nab-leaks/6262284* (accessed 26 February 2015).

Makin, J., 2015. Barclays handed biggest bank fine in UK history over "brazen" currency rigging. Research Gate. Online at: *http://www.researchgate.net/publication/277005145_ Barclays_handed_biggest_bank_fine_in_UK_history_over_%27brazen%27_currency_rigging* (accessed 7 June 2015).

Morris, J., 2015. [Bank B] and its dead-parrots society. Sydney Morning Herald, 13 March. Online at: *http://www.smh.com.au/business/comment-and-analysis/its-deadparrots-society-20150312–142cja.html* (accessed 15 March 2015).

Nankervis, A., Baird, M., Coffey, J., Shields, J., 2014. Human Resource Management: Strategy and Practice, 8th edn. Cengage Learning, Melbourne.

O'Brien, K., 2014. Banking bad: the emphasis is always on trying to get the maximum share of wallet out of each customer. Online at: *http://search.informit.com.au.ezproxy.lib.rmit.edu.au/documentSummary;dn=TSM201405050073;res=TVNEWS* (accessed 2 August 2015).

Razook, C., 2015. Corporate governance challenges facing Southeast Asia. Ethical Boardroom. Online at: *http://ethicalboardroom.com/global-news/corporate-governance-challenges-facing-southeast-asia/* (accessed 25 August 2015).

Ritchie, A., 2011. Irish ruling party thrashed and trashed by the voters. Sydney Morning Herald, 27 February. Online at: *http://www.smh.com.au/world/irish-ruling-party-thrashed-and-trashed-by-the-voters-20110226-1b9am.html* (accessed 21 May 2015)].

Sales, L., 2015. Financial scandal apology fails to hold off call for stronger inquiry into banks: some of Australia's most powerful chief executives have been humbled today before a Senate inquiry. 7.30 Report, Australian Broadcasting Commission, ABC1, 21 April. Online at: *http://search.informit.com.au.ezproxy.lib.rmit.edu.au/documentSummary;dn=TS M201504210173;res=TVNEWS* (accessed 1 June 2015).

Senate Economics References Committee, 2014. Performance of the Australian Securities and Investments Commission. Australian Government, Canberra. 26 June. Online at: *http://www.aph.gov.au/senate_economics* (accessed 12 June 2015).

Senate Economics References Committee, 2015a. Scrutiny of financial advice (public). Australian Government, Canberra. 6 March. Online at: *https://www.mlc.com.au/content/dam/mlc/documents/pdf/investments/senate_economics_references_committee_hansard.pdf*.

Senate Economics References Committee, 2015b. 'Scrutiny of financial advice (public)', Canberra, by authority of the Senate [proof copy]. Commonwealth of Australia. 21 April. Online at: *http://www.aph.gov.au/Parliamentary_Business/Committees/Senate/Upcoming_Public_Hearings* (accessed 10 June 2015).

Senate Economics References Committee, 2015c. Executive summary. Commonwealth of Australia. Online at: *http://www.aph.gov.au/Parliamentary_Business/Committees/Senate/Economics/ASIC/Final_Report/b02* (accessed 31 August 2015).

Stone, R., 2013. Managing Human Resources, 4th edn. Wiley & Sons, Brisbane, Queensland.

Thomas, D., 2006. A general inductive approach for analyzing qualitative evaluation data. American Journal of Evaluation 27 (2), 237–246.

Tumell, S., 2003. Myanmar's banking crises. ASEAN Economic Bulletin 20 (3), 272–282.

Verick, S., Islam, I., 2010. The Great Recession of 2008–2009: Causes, Consequences and Policy Responses, Discussion Paper No. 4934. Forschungsinstitut zur Zukunft der Arbeit (Institute for the Study of Labor), Bonn. Online at: *http://ftp.iza.org/dp4934.pdf* (accessed 1 March 2015).

Werdigier, J., 2009. Record loss at Royal Bank of Scotland. New York Times. Online at: http://www.nytimes.com/2009/02/27/business/worldbusiness/27rbos.html?_r=0 (accessed 2 March 2015).

Wilcox, T., 2012. Human resource management in a compartmentalized world: whither moral agency? Journal of Business Ethics 111, 85–96.

Winstanley, D., Woodall, J., 2000. The ethical dimension of human resource management. Human Resource Management Journal 10 (2), 5–20.

CHAPTER 5

HRM as a strategic business partner: the contributions of strategic agility, knowledge management and management development in multinational enterprises – empirical insights from India

S. Ananthram

INTRODUCTION

Demographic challenges, the effects of globalisation and the emergence of new technologies, workplace changes and dynamic labour markets have all had significant impacts on human resource management (HRM) theory and practice. These contextual factors have strengthened the imperative for HRM to develop as a strategic business partner (Ulrich, 2008) contributing to organisational productivity, effectiveness and competitiveness (Bach and Bordogna, 2011; Tissen et al., 2010). This chapter reconsiders HRM theory and its progress from its administrative and functional origins towards strategic human resource management (SHRM) and human capital management perspectives. This progression in HRM theory has been impelled by growing demands on HRM practitioners to demonstrate their business contributions through effective evaluation systems (measurement, accountability, reporting) (Ananthram and Nankervis, 2014; Roca-Puig, 2012). The chapter explores these new responsibilities of HRM professionals, in particular the key role of a strategic business partner, in a sample of Indian and foreign multinational enterprise (MNEs) firms operating in India, with a particular focus on three key components, namely strategic agility, knowledge management and management development.

Asia Pacific Human Resource Management
and Organisational Effectiveness
ISBN 978-0-08-100643-6

As a global economy, with a transitional industrial structure comprised of an amalgam of government authorities, local private companies and MNEs, India was selected as the study context (non–Western) in order to assess the capabilities of their HRM professionals as strategic business partners in addressing its significant development challenges. The field of HRM has undergone significant changes in the last two decades in India (Budhwar and Sparrow, 1997) with the HR function evolving from providing basic support to playing more of a strategic role (Saini and Budhwar, 2004). Cappelli et al. (2010) provided some evidence on the proactive nature of HRM in large Indian and foreign MNEs in India in which HRM was involved in more strategic roles that led to the growth of the respective businesses. This study deliberately explored these characteristics from the perspectives of HRM and non–HR managers in established Indian and overseas MNEs operating in India, in order to reduce the possible bias associated with self-reporting by HRM professionals. The three components chosen for the study were derived from the literature on strategic HRM and international management and are explained in the next section.

LITERATURE REVIEW

HRM theory may be summarised as comprising three core components – human beings as employees, employees as critical human resources and the design of efficient and effective management techniques and strategies for the maximisation of tangible and intangible benefits for the firm (Ananthram and Nankervis, 2013a; Lepak et al., 2006; Soderquist et al., 2010; Storey and Sisson, 1990). HRM research has increasingly been concerned with obtaining evidence of the links between HRM strategies and processes and organisational performance (Prowse and Prowse, 2010).

The resource–based view (RBV) (Wright et al., 1994; Ray et al., 2004) underpinned early HRM models and was characterised by its emphases on 'resources' and 'capabilities', scarcity of resources and competitiveness, with the key objective of HRM being the maximisation of the value of human resources towards organisational goals (Becker and Huselid, 1998; Kogut and Kulatilaka, 2001; Ulrich and Lake, 1990). Barney and Wright (1998: 32) posited that the RBV is 'an economic foundation for examining the role of human resources in firm competitive advantage'. Several researchers sought empirical evidence to support such concepts, based upon literature from disciplines such as economics and accounting (Boudreau, 1990; Guest and

Hoque, 1994; Huselid, 1995; Snell and Youndt, 1995). Most of these studies focused on cost–benefit based measures of HRM practices. Stavron and Brewster (2005), for example, contended that possible outcomes of HRM programmes might include greater productivity, customer service and efficiency.

Subsequently, HRM theory was revised to encapsulate the concept of workers as human capital. Thereafter, empirical research focused on establishing links between effective human capital management and organisational performance. Human capital is considered to include the combined knowledge, attitudes, experience and skills of the entire workforce (Snell and Dean, 1992). Several authors have noted that human capital is most critical as it has the potential to convert the other resources at the disposal of the firm into wealth for the firm (Nankervis et al., 2011; Mahalingam, 2001).

Empirical studies have generally concentrated either on the influence of distinct HRM functions (Delery and Doty, 1996; Lim et al., 2010; Nankervis and Stanton, 2010) or on the contributions of broad HRM strategies to business objectives (Akhtar, Ding and Ye, 2008; Andersen et al., 2007; Chow et al., 2008). These studies have suggested that 'a coherent system' (Barney and Wright, 1998) of HR strategies and processes is the most effective approach in order to align with business strategies. As noted by Becker and Huselid (2006) and Ananthram et al. (2013: 284), 'this approach accords with overall strategic HRM theory, as it reflects a focus on organisational (rather than individual) performance, emphasises the role of HRM systems as solutions to business problems, and therefore contributes to building sustainable competitive advantage.'

Researchers have argued that human assets (employees) are a critical source of competitive advantage to their respective firms and hence need strategic direction in order to invest in them (Wright et al., 1994; Snell et al., 1996; Becker and Huselid, 1998). These authors also noted that a lack of strategic direction in human asset investment has potential for adverse organisational performance. As Bhattacharya and Wright (2004) suggested, human resource/human asset management concepts recast HRM professionals as 'firm asset managers' with their key responsibility being to invest successfully in the firms' human assets. These new HRM concepts and models assume knowledge and expertise in risk management to determine the potential worth and value of every single human resource, the scale, scope, amount and direction of organisations' local and global operations, labour market and currency fluctuations as well as other associated external factors that impact on them, and the ongoing costs of these investments

(Ananthram et al., 2013; Bhattacharya and Wright, 2004; Hamel and Prahalad, 1994). Other relevant variables include opportunity costs, employee wastage, products and services, or structural changes, opportunities and dynamic labour markets (Ananthram and Nankervis, 2013a; Bhatnagar et al., 2010; De Vos and Meganck, 2008). Bhattacharya and Wright (2004: 17) succinctly summarise that the available opportunities for HR specialists in managing their strategic human resource assets include 'four domains addressing the identified risks and uncertainties – namely, growth and learning options (training, recruitment, skill-based pay), turnover and productivity management options (competitive pay, employee stock options, employee voice), options to alter scale (contingent, contractual and/or part time employment), and options to alter costs (variable pay, performance-based incentive plans)'.

Strategic human resource/capital/asset management encompasses three broad areas – strategic agility, knowledge management and management development. Strategic agility is the capacity of HR professionals to adapt their systems and processes to dynamic global, national and industry contexts (Doz and Kosonen, 2008). Broad perspectives of knowledge management incorporate organisational knowledge, human capital skills and abilities, along with a systematic knowledge collection, analysis, dissemination and storage system of a strategic nature (Ananthram et al., 2013; Lim et al., 2010). Finally, management development encompasses all HRM activities designed to revitalise organisational systems and employee relations processes. The next section of the chapter provides a deeper discussion of these components of SHRM – strategic agility, knowledge management and management development.

Strategic agility

Strategic agility may be defined as the proactive development and implementation of strategies in response to the inherent dynamism in the organisation's external environments (Ananthram and Nankervis, 2013a; Doz and Kosonen, 2008) with a particular focus on human resources/assets. Doz and Kosonen (2010) suggest that strategic agility is comprised of three key components: namely 'strategic sensitivity' (current HR knowledge of and expertise in responding to internal and external labour markets), HR professionals' capacities for dynamic decision-making and 'resource fluidity' (adaptable and flexible HR systems). Strategic agility is also categorised as 'organisational resilience' (Hamel, 2003); and 'dynamic capabilities'(Eisenhardt and Martin, 2000). A central focus of these conceptualisations of strategic agility includes 'the centrality of human resource management capacities in creating dynamic, flexible and agile environments that promote and enable organisations to achieve competitive business advantage' (Ananthram et al., 2013: 286).

Strategic agility thus demands that HR professionals adopt 'strategic business partner' and 'strategic architect' roles (Lepak and Snell, 1999; Ulrich, 2008, 2009), incorporating flexible HRM systems and processes (Ananthram and Nankervis, 2013a).

Knowledge management

The process of knowledge management (KM) is considered a critical source of competitive advantage for organisations (Ananthram et al., 2013; Chen and Chen, 2005; Liebowitz, 2002; Smale, 2008). Successful firms have clearly defined knowledge management strategies, systems and processes (Nonaka and Takeuchi, 1995). Hellström and Jacob (2003) suggested that KM applications are complex and often include process and product elements. There are varied definitions of 'knowledge' including treating knowledge as an object or as a cognitive state (Chen and Chen, 2005) to more applied explanations involving abilities and expertise (Davenport and Prusak, 1998), but most studies emphasise that its effective management is crucial to the firm's competitive advantage (Ananthram and Nankervis, 2013a; Ananthram et al., 2013).

Chen and Chen (2005: 381) defined KM as the 'creation, conversion, circulation, and completion of knowledge'. Swan et al. (1999: 669) argued that KM encompasses '… any process or practice of creating, acquiring, capturing, sharing and using knowledge, wherever it resides, to enhance learning and performance in organizations'. Several researchers concur that knowledge is a critical strategic asset and contend that the development and utilisation of appropriate KM systems is imperative. Brinkerhoff (2006: 305) recommended '… an evaluation strategy with the overall purpose of building organization capability to increase the performance and business value of the training investment … essentially an organizational learning approach that is well-aligned with the overall (HRM) mission'.

Management development

Bhatnagar (2006) asserted that 'the competitive edge will come from an organization's ability to innovate, create and use the entrepreneurial energies of its people' (p. 417). The author went further to make a link between knowledge management and learning capabilities – 'formal and informal processes and structures in place for the acquisition, sharing and utilizing of knowledge and skills' (p. 420). Such capabilities include learning theories, strategies, structures, resources and core values (Ananthram and Nankervis, 2013b; Ananthram et al., 2013), and their linkages with HRM strategies have been explained thus: 'In terms of transformational change, the HR role is found to be important especially when devising innovative HR practices which are designed to support business strategy, influence the attitudes and mindsets of employees, and align business strategies to HR strategies' (Bhatnagar et al., 2010: 494). Key concomitants of these strategies are HRD processes such as the enhancement of employees' technical or functional, managerial and human capabilities.

With particular respect to management development, many authors agree that it is generally a long-term and ongoing process designed to provide current and potential managers with the capabilities and competencies required to fulfil new responsibilities and challenges. Among the specific competencies that managers need to develop in dynamic global business environments are a global mindset, cross-cultural sensitivity, adaptability and open-mindedness, cross-cultural communication and knowledge of markets (Ananthram and Nankervis, 2013b). Borwankar and Velamuri (2009) suggested that these competencies together 'help managers to recognize their capabilities (self-confidence); understand their own preferences better; prioritization of tasks; uncertainty management; [and] interpersonal communication skills' (p. 339). These competencies can consequently be inculcated through systematic management development programmes.

The above discussions provide underpinning for the following conceptual model (Figure 5.1) which constitutes the framework for this chapter. The next section discusses the methodology utilised to empirically assess this framework.

METHODS

Data collection

The study employed a qualitative research methodology using an interview questionnaire. The interview schedule included a series of questions which were developed from a comprehensive review of the relevant literature related to the historical and current status of HR in the Indian context, the importance of strategic agility, knowledge management and management development for MNEs, and the role and influence of HR in the same.

Figure 5.1 Strategic business partner conceptual model

The interview schedule was fine-tuned by the researchers after several rounds of discussions. Subsequently, the final draft version was tested with two academic scholars who formed the committee of experts (Kvale, 2007) who suggested minor changes mainly in vocabulary to suit the Indian organisational context. These changes were subsequently emailed to six senior executives in India who were purposely selected to provide feedback on the questions. The feedback from the executives was positive and they noted that the questions were appropriate and relevant for the purpose of the study in an Indian business environment. The final questionnaire is included in Appendix 5.1.

In the absence of a publicly available list of Indian MNEs and foreign MNEs operating in India published by national and/or state government bodies or industry associations, the researchers developed their own list (Poulis et al., 2013). Initially, the HR departments in 12 MNEs in the private sector based in a major metropolitan city, Mumbai, were contacted via telephone using the researcher's personal networks. An information sheet providing brief details of the study was forwarded to the firms via email and they were asked to identify a potential interviewee who was currently a member of the top management team (TMT) directly involved in organisational-level strategic decision-making (Carpenter et al., 2004; Nielsen and Nielsen, 2011). Eight MNEs consented to participate in the study and identified a TMT member. A snowballing technique was employed and the consenting MNEs were requested to identify other such firms that might consider participating in the study. A total of 47 other MNEs in the private sector in Mumbai were identified using this process and their HR departments contacted via telephone. Brief details of the study were then forwarded to these firms. Eighteen of the firms consented to participate in the study and identified a TMT member, making the total number of firms providing consent to 26. All MNEs were well-established. The demographic details of the respondents are presented in Table 5.1. Twelve senior managers were employed in Indian MNEs and 14 by foreign MNEs operating in India. The respondents represented a range of industry sectors. Eleven respondents had direct HR responsibilities. Five participants were female.

The interviews were conducted in English by an interviewer who had significant experience in conducting interviews in an Indian business environment and was well-versed with Indian national and business culture. Twelve of the interviews were conducted over the phone while the others were conducted face-to-face at the respective MNE's office premises. The interviewer applied the interview techniques and strategies recommended by Kvale (1996) for successful interviewing – being knowledgeable about interview themes, relevant structure, etiquettes, cultural sensitivity, being open-minded, being flexible and open to new directions and allowing the interviewee to raise any concerns before/during/after the interview. The interview format was semi-structured which allowed the researcher to ask follow-up questions seeking clarification or further explanation. The interviewees were encouraged to provide examples using anecdotal and/or experiential evidence. This resulted in unexpected and emergent themes (Welch et al., 2008).

The interviews lasted 40 minutes on average. The interviews were recorded with the consent of the participants and transcribed verbatim by the interviewer. The transcripts were subsequently checked for accuracy by randomly selecting sections from six different transcripts and comparing them with the recordings by an independent experienced professional and there were no discrepancies.

Social desirability bias

Qualitative studies using interview techniques are subject to social desirability bias. In addition, social desirability bias becomes more prevalent in collectivist societies (Robertson and Fadil, 2009) like India. Six strategies were adopted to reduce social desirability bias. Firstly, MNEs and interviewees volunteered to participate in the interview and their names were

Table 5.1 Summary of participants' details

	Face-to-face/ telephone	Position	Role (HR, non-HR)	Industry	Local/ foreign MNE	Gender
E1	Face-to-face	Vice President	Non-HR	Consumer products	Foreign	Male
E2	Telephone	Chief Executive Officer	Non-HR	Information technology and communications	Local	Male
E3	Telephone	Associate Director	Non-HR	Telecommunications	Foreign	Male
E4	Telephone	Chief Executive Officer	HR	Consulting	Local	Female
E5	Telephone	Senior Manager	Non-HR	Chemical industry	Foreign	Male
E6	Face-to-face	Divisional Head	Non-HR	Automobile industry	Foreign	Male
E7	Face-to-face	Assistant Vice President	Non-HR	Banking	Local	Male
E8	Face-to-face	Vice President	Non-HR	Banking	Local	Male
E9	Face-to-face	Divisional Head	HR	Airlines	Local	Male
E10	Face-to-face	Chief Executive Officer	Non-HR	Information technology and communications	Local	Male
E11	Face-to-face	Divisional Head	HR	Information technology and communications	Local	Male
E12	Face-to-face	Vice President	Non-HR	Banking	Foreign	Male
E13	Telephone	Senior Manager	HR	Consultancy	Foreign	Male
E14	Face-to-face	Vice President	Non-HR	Banking	Foreign	Male
E15	Face-to-face	Senior Manager	Non-HR	Consumer products	Local	Female
E16	Face-to-face	Senior Manager	HR	Banking	Foreign	Male
E17	Face-to-face	Senior Manager	Non-HR	Shipping services	Foreign	Male
E18	Face-to-face	Senior Manager	HR	Telecommunications	Local	Male
E19	Telephone	Vice President	Non-HR	Banking	Local	Male
E20	Face-to-face	Divisional Head	HR	Chemical industry	Foreign	Female
E21	Telephone	Senior Manager	HR	Airlines	Local	Male
E22	Telephone	Divisional Head	HR	Consumer products	Local	Male
E23	Telephone	Senior Partner	Non-HR	Consultancy	Foreign	Male
E24	Telephone	General Manager	HR	Consumer products	Local	Male
E25	Telephone	Senior Manager	Non-HR	Banking	Foreign	Female
E26	Telephone	Divisional Head	HR	Telecommunications	Local	Male

kept anonymous so as not to place undue pressure to respond in a socially acceptable way. Secondly, interviewees were only provided a brief overview of the study at the outset. Steenkamp et al. (2010: 1–2) noted that this strategy helped 'avoid priming respondents to answer in particular socially acceptable ways but creates scope to explore their values and priorities unfettered, before homing in on the main topic of interest'. A third strategy included employing a 'committee of experts' (Kvale, 2007) that provided advice on the relevance and sensitivity of the interview questions which were incorporated in the final interview schedule. Fourthly, the interviews were conducted by an experienced interviewer using Kvale's (1996) strategies of a successful interviewer. In addition, it was ensured that there was no power relationship between the interviewer and the interviewees (Nederhof, 1985). A fifth strategy was in line with Brunk (2010: 257), who suggested that one-on-one interviews should be conducted, wherever possible, in 'the familiar and comfortable surroundings of their home', thus this study conducted one-on-one interviews with the TMT members at a time and place convenient to them. Finally, interviewees were briefed that there were no right or wrong answers and encouraged them to use anecdotes and experiential evidence to support their views. These strategies combined provided confidence that social desirability bias could be reduced.

Data analysis and interpretation

The interview transcripts were analysed using Nvivo (v.10) software for systematic content analysis of qualitative data (Richards, 1999). This helped provide a more rigorous analysis of the data (Lindsay, 2004; Sinkovics et al., 2008) leading to the discovery of new conceptual insights and themes (Welch et al., 2008; Buckley and Chapman, 1997). A variable-oriented strategy was employed to find themes that cut across cases (Miles and Huberman, 1994). An initial set of codes was developed from the relevant literature. Two researchers coded the data in Nvivo independently (Bogdan and Biklen, 1992; Spradley, 1979). Miles and Huberman (1994) acknowledged that coding by multiple independent coders has the potential to reduce coder bias as compared to employing one coder. After the initial round of coding, the researchers applied the interactive and comparative approach to coding which included discussing the codes and the grouping and development of concepts and categories to maximise inter-rater reliability (Keaveney, 1995). After ongoing discussions between the coders and five iterations, linkages between the codes were identified and grouped into four main components. The inter-rater reliability of the coding process was 90 per cent (Miles and Huberman, 1994). The four main components were:

- descriptions of strategic agility and links with SHRM;
- knowledge management imperatives and links with SHRM;
- management development initiatives within the context of SHRM; and
- the role of HR as a proactive strategic business partner.

The empirical findings along these four main components are presented next. It must be noted that there was an extensive volume of quotations obtained from the interviewees; however, the chapter presents a summary of the four components in the following section via a liberal use of quotations which are representative of the views expressed by the interviewees (Thein et al., 2010).

RESEARCH FINDINGS

Descriptions of strategic agility and links with SHRM

All executives (both HRM and non-HR) unanimously agreed that firms engaged in global business are required to be proactive and strategically agile. Several interpretations of strategic agility were put forth by the executives such as adaptability, dynamic capabilities and strategic flexibility (Doz and Kosonen, 2010). All these interpretations provided by executives from Indian MNEs as well as overseas MNEs operating in India, however, provided underpinning to the relative importance of their firm's ability to remain strategically agile. The following quotation sums up the executives' views:

> Let me give you an example of our firm's agility from a strategic point of view. Our industry is challenged with cut-throat competition wherever we operate as there are many of us in the industry. Every environment is a challenge for us, some more difficult than others. If our firm does not have the capability to understand our strengths and weaknesses in light of the challenges the internal and external environment presents and more importantly act on it by taking advantage of opportunities and negotiating our threats, we will be finished. We constantly scope out our resources and reconfigure them. We had to bite the bullet and curtail operations in two countries as it was not viable. We moved resources rapidly to other places to consolidate operations there.
>
> **(E11 – Non-HR executive)**

Several authors have established the link between strategic agility and SHRM (Ulrich et al., 2012; Wright and Snell, 1998). Twenty executives agreed that HR can provide vital input towards the firm's strategic agility and consequently its strategic ambitions. The six executives who had a negative view of HR in this regard were all non-HR professionals. The executives provided examples to explain this critical link along the lines of the relocation of resources and redesigning of structures. It was noted that both Indian and overseas MNEs held similar views regarding this linkage. Two relevant comments included:

> To me it is a no-brainer. Firms cannot be agile without involving HR. I mean top management takes decisions which involve all types of resources including other people. How can you then not involve HR when you have to move human resources around? HR strategy needs to play a central or even foremost role here.
>
> **(E20 – HR executive)**

> Obviously structure follows strategy. For a multinational company like ours, the HR department is consulted while designing or redesigning structures for whatever reason it was not working at some location. I know of firms who don't value HR much, let alone use their expertise and knowledge in designing relevant structures. But we take this seriously and our HR department is pretty much equipped to provide advice on such matters. Even our legal experts are called upon as our industry is heavily regulated. Thankfully, we have got that bit right.
>
> **(E25 – Non-HR executive)**

In summary, the executives' comments echo firstly the critical requirement for firms engaged in cross-border business to be strategically agile, and secondly the role that SHRM plays in ensuring the proactive approach to developing and maintaining strategic agility in the firm's worldwide operations.

Knowledge management imperatives and links with SHRM

A majority of the respondents agreed that knowledge is a critical asset for the firm and a vital source of competitive advantage (Chen and Chen, 2005; Nonaka and Takeuchi, 1995). While knowledge included business data, innovative ideas, human capital, talent and innovation capability, knowledge management was referred to as a conscientious process of systematically utilising knowledge for tangible and intangible benefits. Some of the knowledge management systems that were developed and utilised by the respondent firms included low-key intranet systems, sophisticated data management systems, enterprise resource planning systems and corporate universities. The following comments provide underpinning towards these issues:

> Our organization values knowledge. It is at the heart of everything we do. That includes knowledge creation, distribution and storage. We have our own in-house training center – it acts like a corporate university though we do not call it that.
>
> **(E2 – Non-HR executive)**

Of course we have to value our staff – they bring the knowledge to the table, they are the talent. If we do not harness that, then why spend so much time and money in bringing the right candidates from around the globe into our various locations. The way in which we harness that is by tapping into our knowledge base, our knowledge capital. The top management understands this – we even have a Chief Knowledge Officer whose role is to look into these aspects of knowledge management and sharing.

(E12 – Non-HR executive)

Regarding the link between knowledge management and SHRM, the respondents firstly explained that HRM is in a prime position to manage knowledge as demonstrated by the following quote:

We understand that knowledge is everything. Really, in our industry, if we do not innovate, we will be finished by the end of the year. Who has this knowledge – people of course? And who knows who has this knowledge? The HR people.

(E26 – HR executive)

The respondents also explained how HRM can be involved in the knowledge management process. The following comments provide examples of such initiatives which incorporated HRM planning including job design, attraction and retention processes, project management, performance management and HRM databases. These comments thereby provide evidence of the link between knowledge management and SHRM.

HR has to be involved in the knowledge management process. While it is not involved in the design phase in our company, it is involved in the implementation phase. Let me give you an example. Our knowledge management system which is totally online – HR has solid input into the same . . . by that I mean that HR ensures that details of every project are stored which can be retrieved later on by anyone in any location. A new person does not have to reinvent the wheel you see. We use our knowledge management system for training purposes and HR is directly involved with that.

(E23 – Non-HR executive)

HR has to be involved in the knowledge management system implementation. They don't have the technical knowledge to design it, but in our firm they help with the implementation. One element of the system is its offering of flexibility. This is important in the automobile industry, especially the knowledge part.

(E6 – Non-HR executive)

Management development initiatives within the context of SHRM

The respondents agreed that the traditional role of HRM in developing managers and executives' knowledge base and skill-sets and competencies is critical. Firstly, the interviewed executives recognised that continuous management development was critical.

> Investment in people is the most important. Most importantly, we need the right-minded individuals to head our organizations, our divisions, our departments, our branches. If they are not a good fit with the organization, then we will be doomed.
>
> **(E7 – Non-HR executive)**

> I cannot think how a company can achieve competitive advantage without the best managers who have the appropriate skills and decision-making abilities. Not just skills, necessary values and attitude are also crucial for these fellows.
>
> **(E9 – HR executive)**

Second, the executives explained the role of specific management development programmes that HR in their firms are engaged in which allow for the development and upgrading of the relevant managerial knowledge base, skill-sets and competencies for success in a dynamic and complex global business environment. Specifically, they provided examples of management development programmes such as cross-cultural simulations and cultural sensitivity training which are facilitated through boundary-spanning activities, overseas postings and cross-national teams with the assistance of HRM (Bhatnagar, 2006; Lovvorn and Chen, 2011). The respondents also reflected on the knowledge management initiatives such as in-house training, learning centres and corporate universities that were established with the assistance of HRM in management development initiatives.

> It is my responsibility to make sure that our management across all levels is continuously developed. It is unwise to assume that they all have the required abilities – maybe they did when they were brought into our firm. Times are changing, technology is changing, cultures are coming closer. This is global – it's all global now. Management needs to constantly update their skills – if not they will be left behind and will not be able to function in such a dynamic global world. In our firm, development of managers is looked after by HR – in fact it is one of their most important functions. And they are well known for that.
>
> **(E24 – HR executive)**

The managers also noted that it was better to keep the training in-house and that the management development programmes were required to be associated with other HRM activities such as capacity building, performance management, talent management and career development strategies (Nankervis et al., 2011).

> Yes, of course management development is critical. Think about it this way. If you have been a senior manager for 20 years and your thoughts and ideas and skills are from that era – how will you fit in with the changing times? Our HR department

spends a lot of energy upskilling/training/developing our management. We find it is better if our local HR does it though sometimes we bring people who are experts from outside. Internal is better as they understand the culture.

(E9 – HR executive)

The role of HRM as a proactive strategic business partner

The previous three sections have identified the links between strategic agility, knowledge management, management development and SHRM. The respondents were asked to link these three roles within the context of SHRM and explain the key role HRM plays/could play in their respective firms. A majority of the executives explained that in order for HRM to lend its weight and become involved in providing strategic direction along the three areas, it needs to function as a strategic business partner (Francis and Keegan, 2006; Ulrich, 2009; Ulrich et al., 2012). The following three comments summarise these convictions:

HR is an equal partner in our firm. They are involved in high level strategies.

(E4 – HR executive)

HR strategy has to be at the centre. I don't see how organisations cannot agree to that. HR has to be treated as a strategic partner.

(E14 – Non-HR executive)

More importantly, HR has to be proactive. If HR acts like a fire department and only aids in putting out fires, then they would not be of much use. HR needs to take initiative and they need that support from the top. Our HR boss was headhunted for that very purpose. She had brought about such change in another MNC before she was poached from there and brought here. She has made it clear at the outset that there needs to be a culture change, a sort of mindset change towards HR and only then can this happen.

(E10 – Non-HR executive)

The executives explained that not all firms appreciate such a proactive role for HRM. When asked how HR can be made into a strategic business partner, they explained that there needed to be a culture change with regard to how firms viewed HRM and that senior leadership needs to bring about this change (Doz and Kosonen, 2008). The executives also explained that HRM needed to better understand the business and also have clear key performance indicators:

Our CEO and top management values HR. We have set KPIs for our HR along with other functional areas. As I have mentioned earlier, if top leaders do not appreciate HR, then they will not add much value to the firm. So it has to come from the top.

(E20 – HR executive)

In my previous firm, the CEO and CFO only worried about the bottom line. They felt HR are useless and provided no real value in money terms, so the culture in the firm was such that HR had no real role – only conducted exit interviews, basic payroll and other simple functions. They might as well have outsourced the HR. It is the complete opposite of what happens in my current firm. Here HR is respected and their contributions valued.

(E21 – HR executive)

We talked about dynamic capabilities, knowledge management, talent management, global mindset training and a whole heap of other issues earlier. I mean that's where HR can contribute and provide real strategic input. It is not easy but there is potential there. In our firm, HR is tending towards that way of functioning. It's happening because we have new leadership including myself who have said at our top-level meetings that we want this to happen. And it has taken 2–3 years to happen.

(E2 – Non-HR executive)

In summary, the findings provide support to the key role of HRM as a strategic business partner, equipped with a profound understanding of business goals and strategies and the capacity to align overall HR strategies and systems with them. Continuous changes in business environments and technology and ever-increasing competition demand strategic agility and flexibility for the firm and HR specialists are required to be proactive in that regard. These capabilities include ongoing human resource planning and re-allocation, the effective management of knowledge (in all its forms), and perceptions of management development programmes as a significant investment in the firm's human resources.

LIMITATIONS AND SUGGESTIONS FOR FUTURE RESEARCH

This study acknowledges several limitations and offers suggestions for future research. First, our findings are based on interviews with 26 TMT members from 26 Indian and foreign MNEs operating in India and it would be impossible to ascertain whether the findings mirror those of all such MNEs. We encourage future qualitative and quantitative studies to conduct research with larger sample sizes to add to the generalisability of the study findings. We also encourage future studies to incorporate small and medium sized firms in their sample and compare and contrast the findings with those of well-established MNEs in order to extrapolate any similarities and differences across the strategic business partner roles. A second limitation of the study includes a focus on only three components of the strategic business partner role. This was attributed to the sample size and the nature and size of the MNEs. It is suggested that future studies include larger sample sizes from a cross-section of industry sectors in order to validate and extend the theoretical contentions along different strategic business partner roles. Thirdly, despite our efforts to reduce social desirability bias using a combination of six strategies, due caution needs to be exercised in interpreting the study findings. Future studies are encouraged to identify, test and report additional strategies to reduce social desirability bias to build confidence in qualitative studies utilising interview techniques.

CONCLUSION

This study focused on the perceptions of HRM roles from a sample of senior managers in large Indian MNE firms. In particular, the study analysed the nature of the strategic business partner role highlighted in contemporary SHRM literature. In order to gain a deeper understanding of the strategic business partner role and its contributions to firms, three key pillars extracted from the literature were developed into a framework – namely strategic agility, knowledge management and management development (see Figure 5.1). While the focus was on three components and as such may be considered a limitation, the study's main contributions are the development of an innovative lens for exploring the strategic business partner role in more depth, the application of the framework in a non-Western business context, and the perspectives of senior (primarily non-HR) managers about HR roles. It was especially interesting to note that executives in non-HR roles were strongly committed to the key role of HRM as a strategic business partner in line with the changing nature of HRM in India (Capelli et al., 2010).

The findings are generally supportive of the existence of a strategic business partner role, at least in large local and global corporations operating in India. These positive perceptions are reflective of their exposure to global HRM practices.

With respect to the three designated components of the strategic business partner role – strategic agility, knowledge management and management development – most Indian respondents expressed perceptions consistent with the literature on the applications of Western strategic HRM theory (Bhatnagar et al., 2010; Doz and Kosonen, 2008, 2010; Nonaka and Takeuchi, 1995). *Strategic agility* was considered an essential capability of HRM professionals, incorporating human resource planning, talent management, workplace redesign and structural reform, in response to both internal and external business developments – 'a central or foremost role'. Components such as 'strategic sensitivity', strategic decision-making and 'resource fluidity' (Doz and Kosonen, 2010; Trigeorgis, 1996) were displayed in several respondents' comments. The 'creation, distribution and storage' of employee and organisational *knowledge* was also considered a crucial component of the HRM strategic business partner role, including harnessing talent, stimulating innovation, creating organisational flexibility in response to external business demands and managing 'knowledge capital' – consistent with the 'organisational learning' perspective described by Brinkerhoff (2006). In this case, apart from HRM contributions to the design of knowledge management systems, several respondents suggested that their key responsibility is to ensure the effective implementation of such programmes.

Using the parlance of SHRM theory, most respondents reported that their firms perceived *management development* as an opportunity to invest in their human capital in order to contribute to their competitiveness and profitability. Given their global exposure, this is hardly surprising. The human 'investments' reported include acquiring and retaining 'right-minded individuals', ensuring 'organisational fit' and, in particular, developing 'managers with the appropriate skills and decision-making abilities … necessary values and attitudes'. Again, this reflects earlier Western theory (Bhatnagar et al., 2010). In summary, the study suggests that large Indian firms have begun to adopt Western-style approaches to SHRM, in particular the strategic business partner role, as a consequence of their exposure to global influences. These findings support the observations made by Cappelli et al. (2010) and Prayag (2010) who reported the changing nature of the HRM function in an Indian context to include more strategic roles. However, it is likely that these roles are modified according to local demands and circumstances and there could potentially be variations across industry sectors as well as between small, medium and well established organisations.

APPENDIX 1: FINAL INTERVIEW QUESTIONNAIRE

1. What are the major challenges faced by global/international organisations such as yours in this complex and uncertain business environment?
2. Describe some of the day-to-day challenges faced by global managers.
3. What are the main roles of HR in your organisation? How are the key HR functions represented in your organisation?

4. We define *dynamic capabilities* as 'the firm's ability to integrate, build, and reconfigure internal and external resources to address rapidly changing environments'. How important is it for your organisation to possess such capabilities?

5. Does your organisation possess such dynamic capabilities? If so, how is your organisation currently developing these capabilities, especially with respect to HR strategies and operations?

6. What is your organisation's strategic and operational approach to development, maintenance and protection of core knowledge, information and skills?

7. How does your organisation transfer knowledge, information and skills among divisions and/or employees?

8. What can organisations do to develop appropriate management competencies and skills to operate effectively and efficiently in the current global business environment?

9. How effective is your HR area in developing competencies and skills for global/international managers?

REFERENCES

Akhtar, S., Ding, D., Ge, G.L., 2008. Strategic HRM practices and their impact on company performance in Chinese enterprises. Human Resource Management 47 (1), 15–32.

Ananthram, S., Nankervis, A., 2013a. Strategic agility and the role of HR as a strategic business partner: an Indian perspective. Asia-Pacific Journal of Human Resources 51 (4), 454–470.

Ananthram, S., Nankervis, A., 2013b. Global managerial skill-sets, management development, and the role of HR: an exploratory qualitative study of North American and Indian managers. Contemporary Management Research: An International Journal 9 (3), 299–322.

Ananthram, S., Nankervis, A., 2014. Outcomes and benefits of a managerial global mindset: an exploratory study with senior executives in North America and India. Thunderbird International Business Review 56 (2), 193–209.

Ananthram, S., Nankervis, A., Chan, C., 2013. Strategic human asset management: evidence from North America. Personnel Review 42 (3), 281–299.

Andersen, K.K., Cooper, B.K., Zhu, J.Z., 2007. The effect of SHRM practice on perceived financial performance: some initial evidence from Australia. Asia Pacific Journal of Human Resources 45 (4), 176–192.

Bach, S., Bordogna, L., 2011. Varieties of new public management or alternative models? The reform of public service employment relations in industrialized democracies. International Journal of Human Resource Management 22 (11), 2281–2294.

Barney, J., Wright, P.M., 1998. On becoming a strategic partner: the role of human resources in gaining competitive advantage. Human Resource Management 37 (1), 31–46.

Becker, B., Huselid, M., 1998. High performance work systems and firm performance: a synthesis of research and managerial implications. Research in Personnel and Human Resource Management 16 (1), 53–101.

Becker, B.E., Huselid, M.A., 2006. Strategic human resource management: where do we go from here? Journal of Management 32 (6), 898–925.

Bhatnagar, J., 2006. Measuring organizational learning capability in Indian managers and establishing firm performance linkage: An empirical analysis. The Learning Organization 13 (5), 416–433.

Bhatnagar, J., Budhwar, P., Srivastava, P., Saini, D.S., 2010. Organizational change and development in India: a case of strategic organizational change and transformation. Journal of Organizational Change Management 23 (5), 485–499.

Bhattacharya, M., Wright, P.M., 2004. Managing Human Assets in an Uncertain World: Applying Real Options Theory to Human Resource Management. Cornell University, Center for Advanced Studies, New York.

Bogdan, R., Biklen, S.K., 1992. Qualitative Research for Education. Allyn & Bacon, Boston.

Borwankar, A., Velamuri, R., 2009. The potential for management development in NGO-private partnerships. Journal of Management Development 28 (4), 326–343.

Boudreau, J., 1990. Measurement as a Strategic Human Resource Management Decision Tool. Paper presented at the IPMA/IPMNZ Conference, Auckland, New Zealand.

Brinkerhoff, R., 2006. Increasing the impact of training investments: an evaluation strategy for building organizational learning capabilities. Industrial and Commercial Training 38 (6), 302–307.

Brunk, K.H., 2010. Exploring origins of ethical company/brand perceptions – a consumer perspective of corporate ethics. Journal of Business Ethics 63 (3), 255–262.

Buckley, P.J., Chapman, M., 1997. A longitudinal study of the internationalisation process in a small sample of pharmaceutical and scientific instrument companies. Journal of Marketing Management 13, 43–55.

Budhwar, P., Sparrow, P., 1997. Evaluating levels of strategic integration and development of human resource management in India. International Journal of Human Resource Management 8, 476–494.

Cappelli, P., Singh, H., Singh, J., Useem, M., 2010. The India Way: How India's Top Business Leaders are Revolutionizing Management. Harvard Business School Press, Boston.

Carpenter, M.A., Geletkanycz, M.A., Sanders, W.G., 2004. Upper echelons research revisited: antecedents, elements, and consequences of top management team composition. Journal of Management 30 (6), 749–778.

Chen, M., Chen, A., 2005. Integrative options model and knowledge management performance measures: an empirical study. Journal of Information Science 31 (5), 381–393.

Chow, I.H., Huang, J.C., Liu, S., 2008. Strategic HRM in China: configurations and competitive advantage. Human Resource Management 47 (4), 687–706.

Davenport, T.H., Prusak, L., 1998. Working Knowledge: How Organizations Manage What They Know. Harvard Business School Press, Boston.

De Vos, A., Meganck, A., 2008. What HR managers do versus what employees value: exploring both parties' views on retention management from a psychological contract perspective. Personnel Review 38 (1), 45–60.

Delery, J.E., Doty, D.H., 1996. Modes of theorizing in strategic human resource management: tests of universalistic, contingency and configurational performance predictions. Academy of Management Journal 39 (4), 802–835.

Doz, Y., Kosonen, M., 2008. The dynamics of strategic agility: Nokia's rollercoaster experience. California Management Review 50 (3), 95–118.

Doz, Y., Kosonen, M., 2010. Embedding strategic agility: a leadership agenda for accelerating business model. Long Range Planning 43 (2), 370–382.

Eisenhardt, K.M., Martin, J.A., 2000. Dynamic capabilities: what are they? Strategic Management Journal 21 (11), 1105–1121.

Francis, H., Keegan, A., 2006. The changing face of HRM: in search of balance'. Human Resource Management Journal 16 (3), 231–249.

Guest, D.E., Hoque, K., 1994. The good, the bad and the ugly: employment relations in the new non-union workplaces. Human Resource Management Journal 5 (1), 1–14.

Hamel, G., 2003. The quest for resilience. Harvard Business Review 81 (9), 52–63.

Hamel, G., Prahalad, C., 1994. Competing for the Future. Harvard Business School Press, Boston.

Hellström, T., Jacob, M., 2003. Knowledge without goals? Evaluation of knowledge management programs. Evaluation 9 (1), 55–72.

Huselid, M.A., 1995. The impact of human resource management practices on turnover, productivity, and corporate financial performance. Academy of Management Journal 38 (3), 635–672.

Keaveney, S., 1995. Customer switching behavior in service industries: an exploratory study. Journal of Marketing 59, 71–82.

Kogut, B., Kulatilaka, N., 2001. Capabilities as real options. Organization Science 12 (6), 744–758.

Kvale, S., 2007. Doing Interviews. Sage, Thousand Oaks, CA.

Lepak, D.P., Snell, S.A., 1999. The human resource architecture: toward a theory of human capital allocation and development. Academy of Management Review 24 (1), 31–48.

Lepak, D.P., Liao, H., Chung, Y., Harden, E.E., 2006. A conceptual review of human resource management systems in strategic human resource management research. Research in Personnel and Human Resource Management 25, 217–271.

Liebowotz, J., 2002. The role of the Chief Knowledge Officer in organisations. Research and Practice in Human Resource Management 10 (2), 2–15.

Lim, L.L.K., Chan, C.C.A., Dallimore, P., 2010. Perceptions of human capital measures: from corporate executives and investors. Journal of Business and Psychology 25 (4), 673–688.

Lindsay, V., 2004. Computer-assisted qualitative data analysis: application in an export study. In: Marschan-Piekkari, R., Welch, C. (Eds.), Handbook of Qualitative Research Methods for International Business. Edward Elgar, Cheltenham, pp. 486–506.

Lovvorn, A.S., Chen, J.S., 2011. Developing a global mindset: the relationship between an international assignment and cultural intelligence. International Journal of Business and Social Science 2 (9), 275–283.

Mahalingam, S., 2001. Of human capital. Praxis 3 (2), 18–21.

Miles, M.B., Huberman, A.M., 1994. Qualitative Data Analysis: An Expanded Sourcebook, 2nd edn. Sage, Thousand Oaks, CA.

Nankervis, A., Stanton, P., 2010. Managing employee performance in small organisations: challenges and opportunities. International Journal of Human Resources Development and Management 10 (2), 136–151.

Nankervis, A.R., Compton, R., Baird, M., Coffey, J., 2011. Human Resource Management: Strategy and Practice, 7th edn. Cengage, South Melbourne.

Nederhof, A.J., 1985. Methods of coping with social desirability bias: a review. European Journal of Social Psychology 15, 263–280.

Nielsen, B., Nielsen, S., 2011. The role of top management team international orientation in international strategic decision-making: the choice of foreign entry mode. Journal of World Business 46 (2), 185–193.

Nonaka, I., Takeuchi, H., 1995. The Knowledge-Creating Company. Oxford University Press, Oxford.

Poulis, K., Poulis, E., Plakoyannaki, E., 2013. The role of context in case study selection: an international business perspective. International Business Review 22 (1), 304–314.

Prayag, A., 2010. HR shifts gear to talent management. BusinessLine, 9 December.

Prowse, P., Prowse, J., 2010. Whatever happened to human resource management performance? International Journal of Productivity and Performance Management 59 (2), 145–162.

Ray, G., Barney, J.B., Muhanna, W.A., 2004. Capabilities, business processes, and competitive advantage: choosing the dependent variable in empirical tests of the resource based view. Strategic Management Journal 25 (1), 23–37.

Richards, L., 1999. Using NVivo in Qualitative Research. Sage, London.

Robertson, C., Fadil, P.A., 2009. Ethical deicion making in multinational organizations: A culture-based model. 19 (4), 385–392.

Roca-Puig, V., Beltrán-Martin, I., Cipres, M.S., 2012. Combined effect of human capital, temporary employment and organizational size on firm performance. Personnel Review 41 (1), 4–22.

Saini, D., Budhwar, P., 2004. Human resource management in India. In: Budhwar, P. (Ed.), Managing Human Resources in Asia-Pacific. Routledge, London, pp. 113–139.

Sinkovics, R.R., Elfriede, P., Ghauri, P.N., 2008. Enhancing the trustworthiness of qualitative research in international business. Management International Review 48 (6), 689–714.

Smale, A., 2008. Global HRM integration: a knowledge transfer perspective. Personnel Review 37 (2), 145–164.

Snell, S.A., Dean, J.W., 1992. Integrated manufacturing and human resource management: a human capital perspective. Academy of Management Journal 35 (1), 467–504.

Snell, S.A., Youndt, M.A., 1995. Human resource management and firm performance: testing a contingency model of executive controls. Journal of Management 21 (4), 711–737.

Snell, S.A., Youndt, M., Wright, P., 1996. Establishing a framework for research in strategic human resource management: merging resource theory and organisational learning. Research in Personnel and Human Resource Management 14, 61–90.

Soderquist, K.E., Papalexandris, A., Ioannou, G., Prastacos, G., 2010. From task-based to competency-based: a typology and process supporting a critical HRM transition. Personnel Review 39 (3), 325–346.

Spradley, J.P., 1979. The Ethnographic Interview. Rinehart & Winston, New York.

Stavron, E., Brewster, C., 2005. Configurational approach to linking SHRM bundles with business performance: myth or reality? Management Revue 16 (2), 186–203.

Steenkamp, J.B.E.M., Jong, M.G. de., Baumgartner, H., 2010. Socially Desirable Response Tendencies in Survey Research. Journal of Marketing Research, 47 (2), 199–214.

Storey, J., Sisson, K., 1990. Limits to transformation: HRM in the British context. Industrial Relations Journal 21 (1), 61–72.

Swan, J., Scarbrough, H., Preston, J., 1999. Knowledge management – the next fad to forget people. In proceedings of European Conference on Information Systems, Copenhagen, Denmark, June 23-25, 668–678.

Thein, H.H., Austen, S., Currie, J., Lewin, E., 2010. The impact of cultural context on the perception of work/family balance by professional women in Singapore and Hong Kong. International Journal of Cross-Cultural Management 10 (3), 303–320.

Tissen, R.J., Deprez, F.R.E., Burgers, R.G.B.M., van Montfort, K., 2010. Change or hold: re-examining HRM to meet new challenges and demands: the future of people at work: a reflection on diverging human resource management policies and practices in Dutch organizations. International Journal of Human Resource Management 21 (5), 637–652.

Trigeorgis, L., 1996. Real Options: Managerial Flexibility and Strategy in Resource Allocation. MIT Press, Cambridge, MA.

Ulrich, D., 2008. A new mandate for human resources. Harvard Business Review 76 (1), 124–134.

Ulrich, D., 2009. The role of strategy architect in the strategic HR organization. People and Strategy 32 (1), 24–31.

Ulrich, D., Lake, D., 1990. Organizational Capability: Competing from the Inside/Out. Wiley, New York.

Ulrich, D., Younger, J., Brockbank, W., Ulrich, M., 2012. HR from the Outside. In: Six Competencies for the Future of Human Resources. McGraw-Hill, New York.

Welch, C.L., Welch, D.E., Tahvanainen, M., 2008. Managing the HR dimension of international project operations. International Journal of Human Resource Management 19 (2), 205–222.

Wright, P.M., Snell, S.A., 1998. Toward a unifying framework for exploring fit and flexibility in strategic human resource management. Academy of Management Review 23 (4), 756–772.

Wright, P.M., McMahan, G.C., McWilliams, A., 1994. Human resources and sustained competitive advantage: a resource-based perspective. International Journal of Human Resource Management 5 (2), 301–326.

CHAPTER 6

An exploratory study of HRM roles and competencies in Vietnam, India and Malaysia

V. Prikshat, N.M. Salleh, A. Nankervis

INTRODUCTION

Much current human resource management (HRM) research has been focused on establishing clear linkages between HRM strategies and organisational effectiveness, a key driver of the notion of 'competitive advantage'. It has generally been accepted that competitive advantage is derived from the optimal utilisation of organisational resources, notably human resources or human capital, ensured through the internal alignment of HRM strategies and processes with key business strategies, and their external alignment with industry and national socioeconomic contexts (Ulrich et al., 2012). This has been the key assumption underlying contemporary taxonomies of HRM roles and competencies, which together facilitate such successful alignments. However, it has been acknowledged that diverse HRM approaches and competencies may be required for different countries, industries and organisations (Nankervis et al., 2012). It is also suggested that not all HRM professionals will possess or require all of the designated competencies, and that distinct industry sectors and diverse stages of business development will demand different sets of HRM skills and competencies.

The contributions of this chapter include an addition to our knowledge of the applicability of global frameworks of HRM roles and competencies in these three Asian countries within the broad spectrum of organisation effectiveness for a better understanding of diverse HRM approaches in different Asian contexts; and the consideration of some practical implications of these roles and competencies for HR professionals. The key research foci were: to explore the nature of HRM in organisations in Vietnam, India and Malaysia; to determine the extent to which HRM professionals in these countries adopt a strategic orientation; to assess the predominant HRM

Asia Pacific Human Resource Management
and Organisational Effectiveness
ISBN 978-0-08-100643-6

roles, competencies and functions in organisations in these countries; and thus to explore if (and how) these HRM roles, competencies and functions might be linked to organisational effectiveness.

International HRM theory (Nankervis et al., 2012) emphasises the challenges associated with the transference of Western management strategies and systems to non-Western and emerging country contexts, and it is this focus which is addressed in this chapter. In particular, we explore the applicability of both Western and indigenous frameworks of HR roles and competencies to three emerging Asian countries, namely Vietnam, India and Malaysia, with the intention of discerning similarities and differences between them.

The chapter begins with a discussion of the dynamic economic contexts of these three South Asian countries, followed by an analysis of the literature concerning HRM roles, competencies and functions in terms of a more strategic orientation. The following sections cover the methodology used; empirical research findings associated with the demographic profiles (organisation size and type, education status and job titles of respondents); and the key identified HRM roles, competencies and functions in the respective countries. The final section discusses the orientation of HR departments in these countries towards strategic HRM and discusses its possible contributions to organisational effectiveness.

DYNAMIC ECONOMIC CONTEXTS

In the wake of the sustained economic growth buoyed by more strategic business imperatives, Vietnamese, Indian and Malaysian industries seem to be experiencing a gradual if patchy shift towards 'strategic' human resource management (SHRM) as opposed to more traditional functional approaches. Vietnam has developed into one of the fastest growing economies in the Asian region as a result of economic 'renovation' (*doi moi* – 1986). Its recent initiative of a Socio-Economic Development Strategy (SEDS) 2011–20 and emphasis on structural reforms, environmental sustainability, social equity and emerging issues of macroeconomic stability have strengthened the need for robust human resource management (HRM) systems promoting human resources/skills development and thus laying the foundations for a modern industrialised Vietnam (Nankervis et al., 2015; World Economic Forum, 2014). Similarly, the Indian economy, in its transformation from a regulated to a free-market environment, has demanded that its managerial cadre bring about large-scale professional changes in their organisations in order to build capabilities, resources, competencies and strategies, and macro as well as micro HRM activities which translate into strategic HR roles and enhanced organisational learning capabilities (Pareek and Rao, 2007; Som, 2002). Malaysia, like India, has the legacy of Western and indigenous HR traditions and practices, characterised by the transference of earlier HRM practices by nineteenth-century British professionals (Hamid, 2014). The inauguration of 'Vision 2020', the New Economic Model (NEM-2010), and multilateral agreements such as the ASEAN Free Trade Agreement (AFTA) have brought about systematic and radical organisational changes in human resource and general management in Malaysia (Islam, 2010; MITI, 2013; Tataw, 2012). There is a growing need to determine the competence and capabilities of the HR professionals to play more strategic roles, especially in the context of these emerging economies (Bhatnagar and Sharma, 2005; Chen et al., 2003; Khatri and Budhwar, 2002; Selmer and Chiu, 2004).

The following section examines the broad generic and more localised literature from these three Asian economies concerning the available HRM frameworks and their applications with respect to the evolution and development of their HR roles and competencies.

LITERATURE REVIEW

One of the persistent issues in contemporary management research has been analysis and discussion of the significance of 'competencies' in job design, learning and development, and rewards systems among leaders and their subordinates (Nankervis et al., 2015). Competencies have been considered to be valid and reliable descriptors of the practical and theoretical job knowledge, cognitive skills, behaviors and values of employees and their managers (Robinson et al., 2007; Raven and Stephenson, 2001), HRM theorists have focused in particular on the identification of the key professional competencies which define their strategy, policy and operational functions (Boudreau and Ramstad, 2003; Brockbank et al., 1997: Wright et al., 2001). They represent a search for professional legitimacy on the one hand – 'the HR profession can evolve into a true decision science . . . and aspire to the level of influence of disciplines such as finance and marketing' (Boudreau and Ramstad, 2003: 86), and prescriptive frameworks for professional practice on the other – 'a competency model can serve as an integrative framework for an organisation's entire human resources system' (Ramlall, 2006: 29). The latter author, for example cited several recent research studies which 'show a strong correlation between HR technical competence and strategic contribution' (p. 37), undoubtedly the key plank of SHRM theory and the (missing) link between strategic HRM and organisational effectiveness. HRM roles and competencies provide practitioners with the perspectives to make sense of their complex workplace and external environments, to design business-focused human capital strategies, and to engage multiple stakeholders in pursuit of those objectives (Nankervis et al., 2015).

These earlier frameworks reflect two key notions of SHRM theory, namely 'internal-external fit' (Wright and Snell, 1998) and 'horizontal-vertical integration' (Becker et al., 2001; Huselid and Becker, 1999). They assert, on the one hand, that HRM strategies and processes should represent an amalgam of responses to the challenges of the external business environment and internal company imperatives, and that all HRM functions should be integrated with each other (horizontal) and with HRM strategies (vertical), on the other (Nankervis et al., 2013; Nankervis et al., 2015). As Crouse et al. (2011) explained, 'the former functional HRM role has been supplanted by a more strategic role which requires new competencies' (p. 379). The common features of such frameworks include business knowledge (marketing and financial acumen), change-management, data collection and analysis, consulting skills, HRM functional competence, program evaluation and accountability (Nankervis et al., 2015).

Subsequent models of HRM roles, capabilities and competencies contain similar features and have been validated empirically. As examples, Ulrich's (1997) research at the University of Michigan distilled four interrelated broad competencies – strategic partner, change agent, employee champion and administrative expert (Barney and Wright, 1998; Boselie and Paauwe, 2005). Subsequent University of Michigan studies (2002, 2007, 2012) have attracted large global research samples, leading to successive revisions of these competencies. The most recent study (2012) which attracted 20,000 respondents (HR and non-HR managers) in ten countries resulted in an HR competency model including 'strategic positioner', 'capability builder', 'change champion', 'technology proponent', 'HR innovator and integrator' and 'credible activist' (Ulrich et al., 2012: 24).

At the professional level, HR associations in the United States, United Kingdom and Australia (among others) have attempted to translate these broad theoretical competencies into more specific and measurable capabilities. Thus, after extensive research, the US Society of HRM has defined nine competencies (technical expertise, relationship management, consultation, organisational leadership, communication, diversity and inclusion, ethical practice, critical evaluation and business acumen), together with one technical competency and eight behavioural competencies/professional standards (Dolan, 2013; Nankervis et al., 2015).

The UK Chartered Institute of Personnel Development (CIPD, 2010) has designed an 'HR Profession Map' (HRPM) which incorporates ten professional areas, eight professional behaviours and four 'bands' (levels) of competency (CIPD, 2010: 7–8). In Australia, the federal Public Service Commission has formulated six 'capabilities' for its HR professionals – namely, knowledge, credibility, alignment, innovation, relationships and 'performance achieving high quality business results', while the Western Australian Public Service Commission has designed a 'capability framework' which includes strategic alignment, workforce capability, results-driven, relationship management, credible influence, professional expertise, culture and change management competencies (Dolan, 2013; Nankervis et al., 2015).

Finally, the Australian Human Resources Institute (AHRI) has for several years used a 'Model of Excellence', developed in conjunction with the University of Michigan, as a framework for both the recognition of its members' proficiency and the formal accreditation of all Australian vocational and higher education HRM qualifications (see Figure 6.1).

In this model, human resource management is comprised of seven interrelated HR roles that combine to drive organisational capability and business performance, which then drive ten associated HR competencies. To achieve and maintain a sustainable competitive advantage, the HR practitioners need to better design and implement a robust system comprising HR competencies that enhance organisational effectiveness (Ngo et al., 2014). Two types of fit (internal and external) have been viewed as critical elements in generating competitive advantage and enhancing organisational effectiveness and performance. Internal fit refers to the extent to which HR practices are orchestrated in a coherent and consistent way while external fit aligns HR policies and practices with the business strategy (Baird and Meshoulam, 1988; Boxall, 1992; Delery and Doty, 1996; Wood, 1999; Wright et al., 1998). The latest research in this direction (Huselid et al., 1997; Ulrich and Brockbank, 2005) indicates that competencies related to external fit (strategic HR competencies) have a strong impact on financial competitiveness, which is almost double that of other competencies identified in their study (i.e. business knowledge, personal credibility, HR delivery, HR technology) which are more or less related to internal fit. This reinforces the logic that HR practices must integrate key HR competencies to create and sustain organisational capabilities in order to significantly impact business

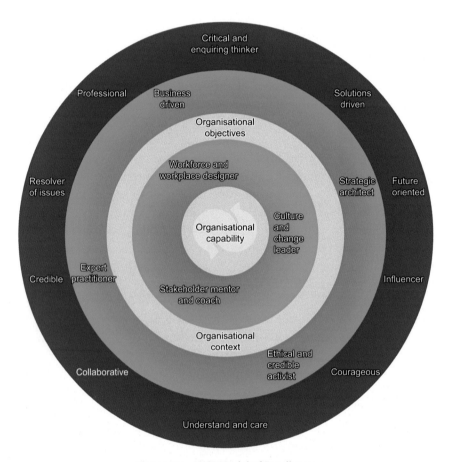

Figure 6.1 AHRI Model of Excellence

performance and organisational effectiveness. Greater emphasis should be placed on HR competencies that add the greatest value to the business, such as connecting people though technology, aligning strategy, culture, practices and behaviour and sustaining change (Ulrich et al., 2012).

The HR departments of organisations are charged with the responsibility of developing organisational effectiveness based on key HR competencies and therefore play key roles in building resources and capabilities. However, serious gaps in existing literature still remain with respect to the causal HR competencies involved in the HRM–organisational effectiveness relationship (Purcell et al., 2003; Wright et al., 2005). Specifically, in analysing the impact of HRM on organisational effectiveness, each of the HRM – performance/effectiveness linkage models developed complements the others by adding constructs, variables, competencies or relationships

(Alcazar et al., 2005). Although there have been attempts to create a common list of generic HRM competencies, to date there is no clear unison due to the different contexts and concepts of HRM employed by the authors of the studies (Katou, 2008).To summarise, it may be argued that while there is a growing body of theory and empirical research demonstrating relationships between HRM policies, collective employee attributes and firm outcomes – namely, performance and effectiveness, additional studies in this area are needed (Harter et al., 2002; Purcell and Kinnie, 2007).The following sections of the chapter explore HRM roles and competencies through the prism of the above models and discussion in Vietnam, India and Malaysia.

HR roles and competencies in Vietnam

HRM in Vietnam can be termed as 'embryonic'.There has been a significant paradigm shift for Vietnam from a centrally planned economic system to a market-oriented approach with a multi-sectoral economic structure and a multi-ownership system. It has resulted in the transformation of traditional (socialist) personnel management and HRM models to a new model of HRM (Zhu et al., 2008). Importantly, in response to Vietnam's dynamic economy and labour market, there is growing support for HR planning and policy development functions in all organisation types (Collins et al., 2013; Montague, 2013; Nguyen et al., 2013; TCLMS, 2008). HR roles and practices are, however, not convergent at the same level of adoption across different ownerships (Thang and Quang, 2005; Zhu et al., 2008), and ownership form is the critical variable that influences the adoption of different HR practices (Zhu et al., 2007). State-owned enterprises (SOEs) and privately-owned enterprises (POEs) generally demonstrate egalitarianism, while foreign-invested enterprises (FIEs) emphasise individualism and democracy in managing people (Zhu, 2005). Moreover, the Vietnamese economy is characterised by numerous coexisting hybrid examples of traditional models, personnel management (PM) and HRM (Collins, 2009; Edwards and Phan, 2013; Zhu, 2011). It can be argued that a majority of SOEs have simply changed their personnel function to 'HR' without any change in its administrative focus or the adoption of a strategic role (Cox, 2013; Quang and Thang, 2004; Quang et al., 2008; Warner, 2013). Although the private sector is relatively new in Vietnam and POEs are generally faster in adopting new management systems (Quang, 2006), the roles of HR departments in POEs are often less developed as they have not reached the potential of the models promoted by Western HRM theorists. HR departments in POEs are still often considered to be internal consultants (Caldwell, 2003; Nguyen et al., 2013; Schuler, 1990; Tsui, 1987).

HR roles and competencies in India

Since the 1980s, the Indian industrial relations culture has been significantly impacted by the intensification of globalised markets. During this time and beyond, there has been a clear departure from traditional personnel management (Chatterjee, 2007). The overall role of HR in India has been elevated from clerical to administrative, administrative to managerial, managerial to executive and, in some cases, from executive to strategic partner (Bhatnagar, 2007; Bhatnagar and Sharma, 2005; Budhwar, 2009; Venkata Ratnam and Srivastava, 1991). The Indian economy has also witnessed a change from a regulated traditional welfare-focused approach to a market-driven strategic environment, and HR professionals are becoming increasingly sensitive to the need to align HRM with business needs and strategies to build capabilities, resources, competencies, strategies, and macro as well as micro HRM activities, which translate into strategic HR roles (Bhatnagar and Sharma, 2005; Cooke and Saini, 2010; Rao et al., 2001; Som, 2002). HR professionals are now increasingly being viewed as partners in Indian organisations' growth strategies rather than being merely administrators (Ernst & Young, 2012). This phenomenon of transformation from the legal compliance approach to that of culture building, communication, change-management, performance management and measuring the effectiveness of HR systems and interventions can be attributed partly to the progressive policies brought and pursued by foreign MNCs (Japanese and many American firms), and the professionally managed Indian organisations including some public sector enterprises (Budhwar and Bjorkman, 2003).

However, there are only a few empirical studies concerning the prevalent HR competencies in the Indian context, despite many theoretical frameworks outlining the needs of robust HR competency models. Recent studies designed to understand the trend in competency-based HRM in Indian organisations have observed that that there are considerable variations in the approaches implemented (Premarajan and Goyal, 2010). These accord with variations in competencies observed according to national situation, labour markets, particular organisations and time (Brewster and Mayhofer, 2013).

The Confederation of Indian Industry (CII), together with the National Human Resource Development Network (NHRDN) and XLRI (Jamshedpur), developed the 'HR Compass Model' to transform, set standards and benchmark the quality of HR professionals in India (NHRD, 2010). This model is a result of five years of in-depth research with comprehensive tests and detailed reports, and the involvement of practitioners, academia and other stakeholders. It specified 17 roles for HR professionals across four competencies (Functional/Behavioural HR, Generic Behavioural HR Competencies, Generic Technical Competencies, Functional Technical Competencies). The roles outlined in the HR compass model again reflect a combination of various sub-factors illustrating six HR competency domains (Ulrich et al., 2012). Similarly the TVRLS (TV Rao Learning Systems) Competency Model (Rao, 2008), based on existing studies by Ulrich and a host of India-based research, evaluated the HRD 'maturity' level of any organisation and identified ten competencies critical to HR professionals (Business Knowledge, Functional Excellence, Leadership and Change Management, Strategic Thinking, Personal Credibility, Technology 'Savvy', Administration Skills, Vision, Learning Attitude and Execution Skills) resembling again the six HR competency domains (Rao, 2008). Both the HR compass model and the TVRLS competency model are compared with Ulrich's et al. (2012) model in Figure 6.2.

It can be observed that Indian HR departments reflect traditional roots (respect for seniority, status and group affiliation), but global competition has driven them to follow more strategic technological, innovator and integrator competency approaches. This is predominantly reflected in the traditional Indian value model blended with new organisational imperatives such as work quality, customer service and innovation (Chattterjee, 2007).

HR roles and competencies in Malaysia

Contemporary Malaysian HRM practices are driven by both the British traditions and ethnic-oriented values (e.g. Chinese, Malay and Indian) (Chew, 2005). These practices are in a stage of transition impelled by the government in the wake of strategies to accelerate the transformation of Malaysia ('Vision 2020') towards a knowledge-based society (Huui and Siddiq, 2012; Liu et al., 2014; Man, 2012; Samaratunge et al., 2008). The role of innovation has been highlighted as the key factor affecting the performance of Malaysian small and medium enterprises (SMEs), with the launch of the SME Masterplan 2012–2020, particularly to drive productivity (NSDC, 2012). Its key purpose is to stimulate SMEs to adapt global HRM practices in order to retain and motivate employees towards the enhancement of their innovative behavior (Ar and Baki, 2011; Tan and Nasurdin, 2010; Zakaria et al., 2014).

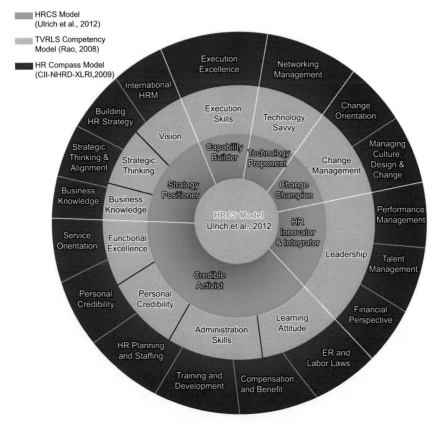

Figure 6.2 Indian HR Compass Model/TVRLS Competency Model – a comparison with Ulrich's et al. (2012) Model

There is a paucity of research on HR competencies in Malaysia, but recently a few research studies have appeared in the Malaysian literature (Hamid et al., 2011; Long and Khairuzzaman, 2008, 2010). Some studies have observed that Malaysian human resource practices focus on performance, evaluation, training and recruitment and are influenced by Islamic principles (honesty, trustworthiness and continuous determination to work for the best) (Hashim, 2009; Osman et al., 2011). Malaysian HR management can be described as more 'personnel' in approach and the acceptance of the term HRM by Malaysians is slow and cautious (Rowley and Abdul Rahman, 2007). Business and human resource competencies, change-management capacities, organisational culture capabilities, personal communication, legal compliance, effective relationships, performance management and personal credibility are the HR competencies assessed by researchers as urgently needed by human resource managers from the top management perspective in Malaysia (Hamid, 2004; Junaidah, 2007; Long and Khairuzzaman, 2008).

The above sections highlight the findings from the literature on the gradual development of HRM roles and competencies in Vietnamese, Indian and Malaysian economies over recent decades. It must be noted that all three countries' HR professionals mirror their Western counterparts in their selection of HRM practices that promote innovation in organisations. All three countries are on the road to economic growth, and sustained efforts are being made by researchers to confirm the developing roles and competencies of HR professionals in these countries. Although considerable research has been conducted recently in these developing economies exploring the strategic role of HRM, it appears that all three economies are far from adopting robust strategic HRM roles and the associated competencies.

In both Vietnam and Malaysia, research studies have suggested that change is occurring towards the conscious adoption of strategic HRM roles and competencies by different sectors; on the other hand, in India more varied findings are reported. There is research evidence underlying the importance of a strategic business partner role, but there are only a few organisations (software services, pharmaceuticals and biotechnology) in which the greater significance of HRM is emphasised (Chatterjee, 2007). Similarly in Malaysia, due to its deep-seated cultural values and the mix of Western and indigenous influences, these outcomes are as yet uncertain.

RESEARCH METHODOLOGY

This section takes into consideration existing empirical research and takes a step further by analysing research data collected to understand HRM roles and competencies in Vietnam, India and Malaysia. These roles and competencies were assessed using the 'AHRI – Model of Excellence' with its three key HRM roles – namely strategic business partner, functional HRM specialist and administrative expert – and the associated seven designated competencies comprising business-driven, strategic architect, stakeholder manager, workforce designer, credible activist, expert practitioner and culture and change agent. The data were collected from surveys of managers working in different types of organisations ranging from government, private and international/multinational organisations in the three countries.

A questionnaire incorporating all these items was administered to the executives of the organisations which have a separate HR/personnel department manned with at least one HR professional. It was ensured that the respondent executives had a minimum of two years of work experience so that they have had sufficient exposure to the HR department and its HR professionals. The initial completed questionnaires received from the executives in Vietnam, India and Malaysia were analysed and the findings are presented through simple statistical representations. The sample sizes were quite disparate with 73 (Vietnam), 55 (India) and 214 (Malaysia). Given these different and relatively modest sizes, it is not possible to make broad generalisations about the findings. Hence it is an exploratory comparative study.

The three specific research questions were:

1. What are the key characteristics of HRM departments in a variety of organisational types in Vietnam, India and Malaysia?
2. Which are the predominant HRM roles, competencies and functions adopted in these organisations?
3. How are these HRM roles and competencies similar and different in the three countries?

Associated implications of these findings, including potential links between HRM and organisational effectiveness, are discussed later in the chapter.

RESEARCH FINDINGS

Demographic profile

The following sections explore the demographic profile in terms of organisation size, type, educational status, job title and industry type of the respondents from Vietnam, India and Malaysia (see Table 6.1).

Vietnam

The data from Vietnam represented the views of respondents largely from small (64 per cent) and medium–large (16 per cent) organisations and fewer from large organisations (20 per cent), working in government departments or agencies (43 per cent), local private organisations (35 per cent), and a smaller number of respondents from multinational enterprises (MNCs) (12 per cent). These proportions generally reflect the sectoral size distributions in the overall economy. Their employers were based in either Ho Chi Minh City (46 per cent) or Can Tho province (50 per cent), which reflected the

Table 6.1 Demographic profile of respondents

Size	Vietnam	India	Malaysia
Small–medium	64%	30%	21%
Medium–large	16%	21%	61%
Large	20%	49%	18%
Education			
Graduates	64%	27%	42%
Postgraduates	27%	57%	5%

Nature of organisation	Vietnam	India	Malaysia
Government	43%	30%	61%
Private	35%	21%	35%
Multinational	12%	49%	4%
Positions			
HR managers	16%	67%	43%
Middle and senior managers	68%	23%	26%
Team Leaders	16%	8%	9%

networks of the survey partners, with only a small proportion from Hanoi (4.2 per cent). Most (64 per cent) of the Vietnam respondents had a graduate degree and 27 per cent were postgraduates. Most (72 per cent) of the Vietnamese respondents did not have HRM-related qualifications. Of those who had them, 47 per cent had an HRM degree, while 53 per cent held general business degrees with HRM subjects. The respondents covered a broad range of managerial positions, including directors, deputy managers, general managers, office managers, project managers, marketing executives, compliance team leaders, a quality manager and HRM staff. Most of these (68 per cent) were in the category of middle or senior managers. The majority of Vietnamese respondents were employed in education and training (20 per cent), administrative and support (19 per cent) or manufacturing (16 per cent) sectors (together amounting to 55 per cent of responses), but there was a wide spread of other sectors represented as well.

India

Indian data included more participation by large organisations (49 per cent) followed by small–medium (30 per cent) and medium–large (21 per cent) organisations. The majority of the representation was from multinationals (49 per cent) and government departments (30 per cent) with only 21 per cent from private organisations. The Indian respondents with Masters' qualifications (57 per cent) were proportionately greater, and 27 per cent had undergraduate degrees. The number of these respondents (both graduates and postgraduates) having HRM-related qualifications was also high at 63 per cent. Most (42 per cent) of the Indian respondents did not have HRM-related qualifications, and of those who had them, 11 per cent had an HRM degree, while 7 per cent had general business degrees with HRM subjects. A majority of respondents (67 per cent) were working as HR managers with 23 per cent in senior roles. The Indian respondents included in the study were 25 per cent from manufacturing organisations, followed by education and training, and information media and telecommunications (18 per cent each), construction firms (14 per cent) and health and social assistance (7 per cent) organisations.

Malaysia

A large majority of the respondents from Malaysia represented medium–large business (61 per cent), small (20 per cent) organisations and fewer in large organisations (18 per cent), and most were Malaysian-owned. The respondents were mainly from government departments (61 per cent) and private organisations (35 per cent); the multinational representation was only 4 per cent. Malaysian respondents at the rank of middle to senior managers had either a Bachelor's (42 per cent) or a Master's (5 per cent) qualification. The majority of respondents (43 per cent) were HR managers, with 26 per cent in middle and senior level roles. These were from education and training (16 per cent), financial and insurance (13 per cent), administrative and support (12 per cent) and agriculture, forestry and fishing (9 per cent). There was a spread of other sectors represented as well.

Key HRM roles, competencies and functions
Key HRM roles
With respect to the three key HRM roles discussed earlier in the paper, Figure 6.3 illustrates their representation in HR departments in Vietnam, India and Malaysia.

The majority of Vietnamese respondents in this study considered that their HRM professionals adopt a 'functional HRM specialist' (73 per cent) rather than either 'strategic business partner' (18 per cent) or 'administrative expert' (9 per cent) roles. Similarly, Indian respondents of the sample organisations for the study also indicated that they were mainly performing their roles as functional HRM specialists (52 per cent), followed by 28 per cent claiming to practise a strategic business partner role. The administrative expert role was demonstrated by 20 per cent of the sample organisations. The Malaysian respondents considered that their HRM professionals should adopt an 'administrative expert' (42 per cent) rather than either 'strategic business partner' (25 per cent) or 'functional HRM specialist' (33 per cent) role.

Table 6.2 shows the key roles of HR departments in these three countries according to organisational type and size.

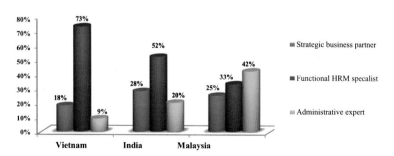

Figure 6.3 Key roles of HR departments

Table 6.2 Key roles of HR departments as per type and size

| Type | Strategic business Partner | | | | | | Functional HRM specialist | | | | | | Administrative expert | | | | | |
	Vietnam		India		Malaysia		Vietnam		India		Malaysia		Vietnam		India		Malaysia	
(a) Government	3	(10%)	0	–	33	(25%)	22	(71%)	17	(80%)	47	(36%)	3	(19%)	4	(20%)	51	(39%)
(b) Private	7	(27%)	7	(28%)	21	(28%)	19	(73%)	12	(52%)	20	(26%)	0		6	(20%)	35	(46%)
(c) International	1	(11%)	8	(89%)	1	(14%)	7	(78%)	0		3	(0%)	1	(11%)	1	(11%)	3	(43%)
Total	**11**		**15**		**55**		**48**		**29**		**70**		**4**		**11**		**89**	
Size																		
(a) <20	0		–		8	(18%)	4	(100%)	–		21	(47%)	0		–		16	(35%)
(b) >20, <199	6	(14%)	2	(13%)	23	(23%)	33	(79%)	11	(37%)	34	(34%)	3	(7%)	3	(18%)	45	(44%)
(c) >200, <499	3	(25%)	4	(27%)	9	(9%)	6	(50%)	6	(21%)	7	(24%)	3	(25%)	2	(18%)	13	(45%)
(d) >500	4	(27%)	9	(60%)	15	(38%)	10	(67%)	12	(42%)	9	(22%)	1	(6%)	6	(55%)	16	(45%)
Total	**13**		**15**		**55**		**53**		**29**		**71**		**7**		**11**		**90**	

In the case of Vietnam, the functional HRM specialist role was most evident in government departments and agencies followed by local private businesses, while the strategic business partner role was more prominent in private businesses than in government agencies. All of the respondents (100 per cent) from small organisations (<20 employees) rated the functional HRM specialist as the key role of their HR department. Although respondents from organisations with employee numbers of 200–499 gave the lowest rank to the functional HRM specialist role relative to those from other organisation sizes, the majority of them (50 per cent) still considered it the key role of their HR department.

Similarly, Indian HR professionals reported the functional HRM specialist role in the majority (80 per cent) of government organisations, followed by 52 per cent of privately owned organisations. No government respondents reported a strategic role for the HR department. The strategic business partner role was predominantly seen in international organisations (89 per cent) and to a lesser extent in private organisations (28 per cent). There was a healthy trend towards the strategic business partner role, demonstrated by 28 per cent of the organisations, mainly private or multinational organisations.

Table 6.2 further shows that the 'Administrative Expert' role was most evident in Malaysia's government departments and agencies (39 per cent), followed by 'functional HRM specialist' (36 per cent) and then 'strategic business partner' (25 per cent) roles. In private business, the administrative expert role was also the most evident, but strategic business partner (28 per cent) and functional HRM specialist roles (26 per cent) were considered of similar levels of importance as the difference between the roles was only 2 per cent. There was a tendency for the roles to change according to the ownership types of the organisation. In smaller organisations, more HR professionals were involved in 'functional HRM specialist' roles (47 per cent). In medium-sized organisations, the role of HR professionals as an administrative expert was perceived to be more evident (44 per cent).

HRM competencies

Across the broad spectrum of HRM competencies which form the 'AHRI Model of Excellence' – given that the mean scores of all the competency variables are greater than the theoretical mean (3.0) – it may be concluded that most of the respondents from the three countries believed that their levels of expertise were relatively high on all the measured competencies

Table 6.3 HRM competencies

Competencies	Vietnam			India			Malaysia		
	N	Mean	SD	N	Mean	SD	N	Mean	SD
Business-driven	73	3.42	0.90	55	4.14	0.848	214	3.51	0.917
Credible activist	73	3.56	0.93	55	4.30	0.539	215	3.41	0.832
Expert practitioner	73	3.60	0.92	55	4.10	0.761	216	3.39	0.867
Culture and change agent	73	3.67	0.90	55	3.98	0.827	215	3.38	0.810
Strategic architect	73	3.45	1.11	55	3.87	0.883	215	3.35	0.940
Workforce designer	72	3.46	1.06	55	4.14	0.755	215	3.24	0.801
Stakeholder manager	72	3.47	0.90	55	4.10	0.916	215	3.19	0.956

(see Table 6.3). The table shows the current HR managers' perceived competencies in three countries. Incidentally, all countries' respondents displayed support for different competencies in order of preference. While in Vietnam the greatest support was given to 'culture and change agent' (mean = 3.67) followed by 'expert practitioner' (3.60) and 'credible activist' (3.56), in India the 'credible activist' (4.30) competency was given most support, followed by 'business-driven' (4.14) and 'workforce designer' (4.14) competencies. Malaysian respondents gave most support to the 'business-driven' (3.51) competency followed by 'credible activist' (3.41) and 'expert practitioner' (3.39) competencies.

There was no evidence of significant differences between the measured competencies. All these competencies reinforced earlier findings that the functional HRM specialist role is key in all three countries, especially one performed within a transitional industry context. The strategic architect and culture and change agent competencies received the lowest ranking in terms of perceived expertise in all three countries.

Cross-correlation analyses were also undertaken with respect to the associations between organisation type/company size and the specific HRM competencies. Table 6.4 reports the level of expertise that the HR professionals perceived against the seven HR competencies and skills across the three types of organisation in all three countries.

Table 6.4 Organisational types and HR competencies and skills

Competencies	Government			Private			International		
	Vietnam	India	Malaysia	Vietnam	India	Malaysia	Vietnam	India	Malaysia
Business-driven	Medium	High–very-high	High	High	High–very-high	High	Medium	High–very-high	High
Strategic architect	High	Medium-high	Medium-high	High–very-high	Medium-high	High	High	High–very-high	High
Stakeholder manager	High	Medium-high	Medium-high	High	High–very-high	Medium	Medium	Medium-high	Medium-high
Workforce designer	High	Medium-high	Medium-high	High	High–very-high	Medium	High	Medium-high	High–very-high
Credible activist	Medium	High–very-high	Medium-high	Very high	High–very-high	Medium	Medium	High–very-high	High–very-high
Expert practitioner	High	High–very-high	Medium-high	High	High–very-high	High	Medium	High–very-high	High
Culture and change agent	Medium-high	Medium-high	Medium	Medium-high	High–very-high	Medium-high	High	High–very-high	Medium
Business-Driven	Medium	High–very-high	High	High	High–very-high	High	Medium	High–very-high	High
Strategic Architect	High	Medium-high	Medium-high	High–very-high	Medium-high	High	High	High–very-high	High
Stakeholder Manager	High	Medium-high	Medium	High	High–very-high	Medium	Medium	Medium-high	Medium-high
Workforce Designer	High	Medium-high	Medium	High	High–very-high	Medium	High	Medium-high	High–very-high
Credible Activist	Medium	High–very-high	Medium–high	Very high	High–very-high	Medium	Medium	High–very-high	High–very-high
Expert Practitioner	High	High–very-high	Medium–high	High	High–very-high	High	Medium	High–very-high	High
Culture and Change Agent	Medium-high	Medium-high	Medium	Medium-high	High–very-high	Medium-high	High	High–very-high	Medium

Competencies by organisation type
Government

Vietnamese HR professionals who worked for government agencies considered themselves as having a high level of expertise on four key competencies (strategic architect, stakeholder manager, workforce designer and expert practitioner). Some of these competencies suggest that they recognised the importance of a strategic business partner role but are yet unable to fully adopt it, due either to their own lack of confidence or experience, or absence of support from senior management. Indian government HR professionals' perceived competence appears to be as credible activist, expert practitioner and business–driven, with medium to high expertise in stakeholder management and stakeholder manager competencies. The competencies of strategic architect and culture and change agent received the lowest ranking in terms of perceived expertise. Whereas Malaysian HR professionals who worked for government agencies perceived themselves as having a high level of expertise on five key competencies (business-driven, strategic architect, stakeholder manager, credible activist and expert practitioner).

Private

The HR professionals in local Vietnamese private businesses assessed themselves as experts on five of the seven competencies and skills, setting aside credible activist and culture and change agent competencies. Indian private organisations' HR departments reported high levels of expertise for credible activist, expert practitioner and business–driven competencies, but at the same time these organisations also demonstrated some movement towards the strategic architect and culture and change agent competencies. The HR professionals in local Malaysian private businesses assessed themselves as experts on four out of the seven competencies and skills (business driven, strategic architect, expert practitioner and culture and change agent).

Multinational

HR professionals working for Vietnamese MNCs perceived their key competencies as reflecting a mere three of the seven HR competencies, namely strategic architect, culture and change agent and workforce designer, reinforcing their greater confidence in a strategic business partner role. In the case of India, competencies such as strategic architect, workforce designer and culture and change agent were ranked more highly in terms of expertise by MNCs. Malaysian HR professionals working for international companies perceived their key competencies as workforce designer, credible activist, business-driven, strategic architect and expert practitioner.

HRM by organisation size

The findings demonstrate that HR professionals in smaller Vietnamese organisations consider that they have less expertise on the seven competencies and skills than HR professionals in larger organisations. For example, the HR professionals in organisations with less than 20 employees perceived themselves as having a high level of expertise in one competency (strategic architect), while their counterparts who were working for companies with more than 500 employees perceived themselves as possessing a high level of expertise on five out of seven competencies and skills (stakeholder manager, workforce designer, credible activist, expert practitioner and culture and change agent). There was a mixed finding for HR professionals who worked for medium size companies (20 to less than 199).

In the case of India the research findings further reflect high to very high expertise levels for the competencies by HR professionals in large organisations (more than 200 employees). In contrast, the organisations with a smaller number of employees (less than 200 employees) demonstrated variable expertise levels ranging from medium to very high. For Malaysia, the findings showed that HR professionals in smaller organisations consider that they have expertise in seven competencies and perceive their highest level of skill to be an expert practitioner and their lowest level as strategic architect. HR professionals in larger organisations favoured the credible activist competency, with little support for workforce designer, stakeholder manager and expert practitioner skills. However, the medium size organisations' respondents perceived themselves to possess high skills on the business-driven competency, as well as in all seven competencies. HR professionals in organisations with more than 200 and less than 499 employees perceived that business-driven skills were more evident in their operations.

Top five HRM functions

Respondents were asked to rank the top five functions of their HR department among the 16 given HR functions (see Table 6.5).

Vietnam

The frequency analysis demonstrated that 'HR policy development' was perceived as the most highly ranked HR function, with 34.2 per cent of the respondents ranking it as the most important function of their HR

Table 6.5 HR functions

HR function	Vietnam Rank						India Rank						Malaysia Rank					
	1	2	3	4	5	Total	1	2	3	4	5	Total	1	2	3	4	5	Total
HR policy development	34.2	6.3	1.3	0.0	5.1	46.9	3.6	10.9	9.0	3.6	7.2	34.3	69	50	8	4	17	148
HR planning	25.3	21.5	7.6	3.8	2.5	60.7	10.9	10.9	0.0	3.6	9.0	34.4	65	46	19	7	19	156
HR information system design/management	7.6	13.9	7.6	6.3	3.8	39.2	5.4	0.0	3.6	3.6	7.2	19.8	15	34	31	8	11	99
Knowledge management	6.3	5.1	11.4	7.6	2.5	32.9	5.4	0.0	0.0	1.8	3.6	10.8	22	21	21	11	24	99
Ethics, governance and/or corporate social responsibility (CSR)	11.4	7.6	12.7	6.3	3.8	41.8	12.7	9.0	3.6	3.6	1.8	30.7	23	18	9	9	22	81
Work/job design/analysis/evaluation	22.8	8.9	13.9	5.1	3.8	54.5	3.6	5.4	20.0	18.1	5.4	52.5	31	28	24	14	18	115
Recruitment and selection	16.5	20.3	16.5	10.1	6.3	69.7	12.7	21.8	7.2	16.3	10.9	68.9	20	40	19	7	16	102
Talent management	13.9	5.1	8.9	5.1	1.3	34.3	10.9	3.6	7.2	9.0	7.2	37.7	18	16	19	12	9	74
Career management	8.9	5.1	7.6	5.1	0.0	26.7	7.2	7.2	9.0	9.0	5.4	37.8	26	23	19	13	7	88
Employee training and development	13.9	11.4	15.2	25.3	0.1	75.9	1.8	0.0	12.7	3.6	9.0	27.1	28	35	34	25	27	149

Employee counselling and/ or discipline	2.5	7.6	7.6	5.1	0.0	26.7	5.4	0.0	12.7	12.7	7.2	38.0	14	22	16	10	10	72
Performance management	11.4	7.6	2.5	11.4	3.9	46.8	10.9	10.9	9.0	1.8	10.9	43.5	24	15	18	8	14	79
Employee rewards and benefits	6.3	2.7	3.8	3.8	1.4	38.0	1.8	10.9	1.8	12.7	7.2	34.4	19	23	22	29	28	121
Industrial relations	12.7	6.3	8.9	3.8	5.1	36.8	3.6	1.8	3.6	0.0	7.2	16.2	20	14	15	5	5	59
Occupational health and safety	10.1	8.9	6.3	2.5	6.3	34.1	5.4	3.6	0.0	0.0	0.0	9.0	18	9	24	12	12	75
HR evaluation and accountability	10.1	7.6	3.8	1.3	7.6	30.4	3.6	0.0	0.0	0.0	0.0	3.6	20	33	9	9	9	80

department. More than a quarter of the respondents considered that 'HR planning' is the most important HR function, with less support given to 'work and job design/analysis/evaluation' (22.8 per cent), 'recruitment and selection' (16.5 per cent) and 'employee training and development' (13.9 per cent). Although 'employee training and development' was only ranked in fifth place as the most important HR function (see Figure 6.4), it got the highest percentage (75.9 per cent) when the top five HR functions were considered at the same time. Similarly, 'recruitment and selection' was only ranked in fourth place as the most important HR function, but it got the second highest rank (69.7 per cent) when multiple (5) functions were considered. These findings were generally consistent with functional HRM specialist roles and expert practitioner, credible activist, workforce designer, stakeholder manager and culture and change agent professional competencies, while not surprisingly HR policy and planning capabilities and skills were consistent with the management of staff within a dynamic economic context. There was considerably less support for HR information management, knowledge management, career development, employee rewards and benefits systems or talent management competencies, which might be more reflective of strategic business partner roles.

Cross-correlations between organisation type/size and HR functions were also undertaken. The results showed that the HR professionals who worked for government organisations perceived that seven activities were the

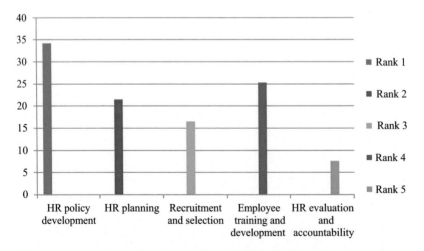

Figure 6.4 Top five HR functions – Vietnam

most important of the 16 HR functions (ranked first: HR policy development, HR planning, ethics, governance and/or corporate social responsibility, work/job design/analysis/evaluation, industrial relations, occupational health and safety and HR evaluation and accountability). The HR professionals in local private organisations seemed to agree with their counterparts as they rated HR policy development, HR planning, work/job design/analysis/evaluation, industrial relations and HR evaluation and accountability as the most important HR functions (ranked first). Cross-correlational analyses between organisation size and HR functions indicated that the larger organisations tend to see most of the HR functions as top priorities as compared with smaller organisations (ranked first). More specifically, the HR professionals in companies with less than 20 employees ranked four HR functions as top out of 16 functions (HR policy development, HR planning, career management and industrial relations) while the HR professionals who work for large organisations (>500) identified eleven functions as the most important (ranked first).

India

The frequency analysis showed that 'recruitment and selection' was perceived as the most highly ranked HR function, with 12.7 per cent of the respondents ranking it as the most important function of their HR department. It was followed equally by HR planning, talent management and performance management (10.9 per cent), perceived as the most highly ranked HR functions. Recruitment and selection also got the highest percentage (68.9 per cent) when the top five Indian HR functions were considered (see Figure 6.5) at the same time. HR policy development, HR planning and employee rewards and benefits (10.9 per cent) were second ranked HR functions in Indian context. The work/job design/analysis/valuation function clearly took third place with 20 per cent of respondents. It also took second place in terms of perceived importance when multiple (5) functions were considered. The ranking of these HR functions again demonstrate the functional and administrative expert orientation of most of the surveyed Indian organisations. Some of the organisations (local private business and MNCs) ranked HR information system design/management and knowledge management but were few in number, which demonstrates that the Indian HR context is as yet undeveloped with respect to the technology proponent and change management competency domains. The major concern was about the 'training and development' function, which was poorly ranked by all the respondents.

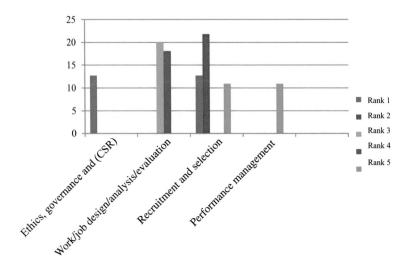

Figure 6.5 Top five HR functions – India

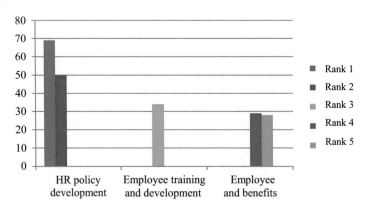

Figure 6.6 Top five HR functions – Malaysia

Malaysia

The frequency analysis for Malaysian respondents showed that 'HR policy and development' was perceived as the first and the second most important functions followed by employee training and development (see Figure 6.6). Employee rewards and benefits were ranked fourth and fifth respectively. The results showed less support being given to industrial relations and ethic and social responsibility (CSR).

Cross-tabulation analyses between organisational size and HR functions indicated that the larger organisations tend to see most of the work/job design analysis and evaluations as top priorities as compared with smaller organisations that ranked HR planning as the most important. More specifically, the HR professionals in a company with less than 20 employees ranked four HR functions as of top importance out of 16 functions (HR planning, HR policy development and employee training and development).

DISCUSSION

The statistical analysis of the respondent data suggests that HR roles and practices in all three countries are still 'developing and emerging' and at the same time are showing a tendency to follow the Western path and to adopt many of the 'best practice' models across different ownership styles (Connor and McCartney, 2011; Zhu et al., 2007). The Vietnamese respondents surveyed demonstrate a transitional phase in the development of various HR roles and competencies, and these results are in conformity with similar earlier studies (Benuyenah and Phoon, 2014; Boselie and Paauwe 2005; Boudreau and Ramstad, 2003; Nankervis et al., 2015; Warner, 2013). The Indian respondents portrayed trends of 'crossvergence', or the blending of Western and Indian HR practices, as an outcome of the exigencies of globalisation, and many organisations have adopted strategic HR practices in their operations with minor modifications (Budhwar and Bjorkman, 2003; Saini and Budhwar, 2004). The HRM roles in Malaysian organisations showed that organisations are still grappling with the 'administrative expert' and 'functional HRM specialist' roles (Long and Khairuzzaman, 2008; Ulrich, 2008), and that the concept of strategic business partner is not aggressively pursued by most HR practitioners.

It is interesting to note that in all the three economies, organisation size plays a part in terms of the strategic business partner role. The data in this study reveal an ascending order in terms of this role, i.e. the larger the organisation size, the greater importance given to the strategic business partner role of their HR department. This finding echoes the mainstream studies conducted in Western economies (Armstrong, 2012; Kearns, 2010; Truss et al., 2012). The analysis of the data suggests that the majority of Vietnamese and Indian respondents consider that their HRM departments have adopted a functional HRM specialist role, whereas a majority of the Malaysian respondents believe that their HRM department's role is that of an administrative expert. It was also noted across all three countries that the adoption of HRM practices is not convergent at the same level across different types of ownership of organisations, reconfirming previous studies in the literature (Brewster and Mayhofer, 2013; Nguyen et al., 2013; Premarajan and Goyal, 2010; Thang and Quang, 2005; Zhu et al., 2008). The functional HRM specialist role was dominant in government organisations in both Vietnam and India. Correspondingly, the government organisations in Malaysia display an administrative expert role, in contrast to those in either Vietnam or India. Indian organisations' respondents demonstrate more evidence of moving towards a strategic business partner role, followed by Vietnam and Malaysia. The strategic business partner role was more evident in Vietnam and Indian private/MNCs as compared to Malaysia, where the private organisations demonstrated more reliance on the administrative expert role, followed by almost equal weighting for the strategic business partner and functional specialist roles. Interestingly enough, the Vietnamese and Indian respondents exhibited less emphasis on the administrative expert role, suggesting that their HRM departments are on the path of functional and strategic evolution, whereas Malaysian HRM departments are struggling to catch up with Vietnamese and Indian counterparts (Benschop, 2001).

In terms of competencies, the key finding of this study is that most of the respondents from the three countries believed that their levels of expertise were relatively high on all the measured competencies. Vietnamese respondents considered themselves to have a high level of expertise in four key competencies – namely strategic architect, stakeholder manager, workforce designer and expert practitioner. Indian respondents' perceived competencies appear to be credible activist, expert practitioner and business-driven, with medium to high expertise in stakeholder management and stakeholder manager competencies; meanwhile, Malaysian respondents perceived themselves as high in the competencies of business-driven, strategic architect, stakeholder manager, credible activist and expert practitioner. Another common feature observed across the three countries was that the respondents from smaller organisations demonstrated less expertise on the seven listed competencies.

The results of this study in terms of the top five HRM functions in HRM departments of these countries suggested a reliance on HRM functions in alignment with the perceived role (administrative, functional and strategic) of their departments. In order to reduce skill shortages (Montague, 2013) and improve talent development (Chatterjee et al., 2013), much of the emphasis the HR functions was on the creation of talent pipelines and talent management to reduce skill gaps and improve the quality of human capital (Connell and Stanton, 2014).Vietnamese respondents rated HR policy development, work and job design/analysis/evaluation and recruitment and selection as the most important HR functions. Indian respondents ranked recruitment and selection, HR planning, talent management and performance management as the most important HR functions, whereas Malaysian respondents gave most importance to the function of industrial relations, followed by HR evaluation and accountability, employee counselling and/or discipline. The main point of concern evident from this study was the ranking of the employee training and development function across the three economies. Though, it got highest percentage when the top five HR functions were considered at the same time across the three economies it did not rate among the top five HR functions. Given the impending skill shortages in these economies due to increasingly significant mismatches between worker skills and job requirements (Dobbs and Madgavkar, 2014), training and development can be seen as an issue that warrants further investigation (Nguyen et al., 2013).

CONCLUSION

Effective implementation of HRM functions, roles and competencies is a measure of the effectiveness of the HR department of an organisation (Ahmad et al., 2015) and this effectiveness is seen as HRM's contribution to a firm's performance (Long and Ismail, 2011; Ruel et al., 2007). The study contributes to the literature of HRM on the various functions, roles and competencies utilised in Vietnam, India and Malaysia, and also emphasises their importance in ensuring organisational effectiveness. The chapter has explored the key characteristics (HRM roles and competencies) that HR professionals must demonstrate to be personally effective and to affect business performance (Brockbank et al., 2012) in a variety of organisational types in the three countries (Vietnam, India and Malaysia). The alignment of HR systems with business strategy is expected to enhance organisational effectiveness and competitiveness (Delery and Doty, 1996; Schuler and Jackson, 1987). The results of this study indicate that all three economies are far from adopting robust strategic HRM roles and the associated competencies. The Vietnamese and Indian HRM functions demonstrate more reliance on the functional specialist role with moves towards a strategic business partner role in some sectors, whereas Malaysian HRM seems to be still in a nascent stage, with a predominance of the administrative expert role, at least partly due to its diverse cultural context.While HR practice in Vietnam and

India shows a gradual development towards a strategic partner role driven by their rapidly changing economies and industrial environments, Malaysian HRM has adopted a slow and cautious approach towards the strategic partner role. In order to enhance HR's organisational contribution to the economies of these three countries, HR managers will not only need to transform their HRM functions, roles and competencies, but also to adopt a more strategic orientation, in order to have a significant impact on organisational performance and effectiveness.

It is important to reiterate that the present study is mainly concerned with HRM roles and HR competencies in three economies and does not attempt to empirically establish the relationship between the various HR competencies and organisational effectiveness or performance. Moreover, the sample sizes were both modest and diverse, thus it is not possible to make broad generalisations about the findings. For more comprehensive and statistically reliable evidence of these relationships in these economies, it would be necessary to extend the research through thorough analysis of the HR orientation of their HR departments, to determine whether they follow a more strategic, administrative or functional approach and what the impact is of that stance on organisational effectiveness and performance.

REFERENCES

Ahmad, A., Kausar, A.R., Azhar, S.M., 2015. HR professionals' effectiveness and competencies: a perceptual study in the banking sector of Pakistan. International Journal of Business and Society 16 (2), 201–220.

Alcazar, F.M., Fernandez, P.M.R., Gardey, G.S., 2005. Researching on SHRM: an analysis of the debate over the role played by human resources in firm success. Management Revue 16, 213–241.

Ar, I.M., Baki, B., 2011. Antecedents and performance impacts of product versus process innovation: empirical evidence from SMEs located in Turkish science and technology parks. European Journal of Innovation Management 14 (2), 172–206.

Armstrong, M., 2012. Armstrong's Handbook of Human Resource Management Practice, 12th edn. Kogan Page, London.

Baird, L., Meshoulan, I., 1998. Managing two fits of strategic human resource management. Academy of Management Review 13, 116–128.

Becker, B.E., Huselid, M.A., Ulrich, D., 2001. The HR Score Card: Linking People, Strategy, and Performance. Harvard Business School Press, Boston.

Benschop, Y., 2001. Pride, prejudice and performance: relations between HRM, diversity and performance. International Journal of Human Resource Management 12, 1166–1181.

Benuyenah, V., Phoon, M., 2014. Population, property and productivity: a theoretical prediction of economic growth in Vietnam. Journal of Global Business and Economics 8 (1), 1–13.

Bhatnagar, J., 2007. Predictors of organizational commitment in India: strategic HR roles, psychological empowerment and organizational learning capability. International Journal of Human Resource Management 18 (10), 1782–1811.

Bhatnagar, J., Sharma, A., 2005. The Indian perspective of strategic HR roles and organizational learning capability. International Journal of Human Resource Management 16 (8), 1711–1739.

Boselie, J.P., Paauwe, J., 2005. Human Resource Functional Competencies in European Companies. Visiting Fellow Working Papers, No. 11. School of Industrial and Labor Relations, Cornell University.

Boudreau, J., Ramstad, P., 2003. From Professional Business Partner to Strategic Talent Leader: What's Next For Human Resource Management. Cornell Centre for Advanced Human Resource Studies, Ithaca, NY.

Boxall, P., 1992. Strategic human resource management: beginnings of a new theoretical sophistication? Human Resource Management Journal 2, 60–79.

Brewster, C.J., Mayhofer, W., 2013. Handbook of Research in Comparative Human Resource Management. Edward Elgar, London.

Brockbank, W., Ulrich, D., James, C., 1997. Trends in HR competencies. University of Michigan School of Business, Ann Arbor, MI.

Brockbank, W., Ulrich, D., Younger, J., Ulrich, M., 2012. Recent Study shows impact of HR Competencies on business performance. Employment Relations Today. http://dx.doi.org/10.1002/ert. http://onlinelibrary.wiley.com/doi/10.1002/ert.21348/pdf.

Budhwar, P.S., 2009. Human resource management in the Indian context. In: Budhwar, P.S., Bhatnagar, J. (Eds.), The Changing Face of People Management in India. Routledge, London.

Budhwar, P., Bjorkman, I., 2003. A Corporate Perspective on the Management of Human Resources in Foreign Firms Operating in India. In: Proceedings of International HRM Conference, pp. 4–6 June, Limerick, Ireland.

Caldwell, R., 2003. The changing roles of personnel managers: old ambiguities, new uncertainties. Journal of Management Studies 40, 983–1004.

Chatterjee, S.R., 2007. Human resource management in India: "where from" and "where to?". Research and Practice in Human Resource Management 15 (2), 92–103.

Chatterjee, S.R., Nankervis, A.R., Connell, J., 2013. Talent shortages in China and India: nature, antecedents and challenges. In: Srivastava, B., Mohapatra, M. (Eds.), Capability Building for Cutting Edge Organizations. Excel Books, New Delhi, pp. 40–49.

Chen, L.H., Liaw, S.Y., Lee, T.Z., 2003. Using an HRM pattern approach to examine the productivity of manufacturing firms: an empirical study. International Journal of Manpower 24 (3), 299.

Chew, Y.T., 2005. Achieving organisational prosperity through employee motivation and retention: a comparative study of strategic HRM practices in Malaysian institutions. Research and Practice in Human Resource Management 13 (2), 87–104.

CIPD, 2010. UK Chartered Institute of Personnel Development – see. http://www.cipd.co.uk/cipd-hr-profession/profession-map.

Collins, N., 2009. Economic Reform and Employment Relations in Vietnam. Routledge, London and New York.

Collins, N., Sitalaksmi, S., Lansbury, R., 2013. Transforming employment relations in Vietnam and Indonesia: case studies of state-owned enterprises. Asia Pacific Journal of Human Resources, Special Issue: HRM in Vietnam 51 (2), 131–151.

Connell, J., Stanton, P., 2014. Skills and the role of HRM: towards a research agenda for the Asia Pacific region. Asia Pacific Journal of Human Resources 52, 4–22.

Connor, J., McCartney, C., 2011. Next Generation HR: The Growth Option: Turbo Charging HR's Impact in Asia. CIPD, London.

Cooke, F.L., Saini, D.S., 2010. (How) does the HR strategy support an innovation oriented business strategy? An investigation of institutional context and organizational practices in Indian firms. Human Resource Management 49 (3), 377–400.

Cox, A., 2013. Human resource management in Vietnam. In: Varma, A., Budhwar, P. (Eds.), Managing Human Resources in Asia-Pacific, 2nd edn. Routledge, London and New York.

Crouse, P., Doyle, W., Young, J.D., 2011. Trends, roles, competencies in human resource management practice: a perspective from practitioners in Halifax, Canada. In: Proceedings of the ASBBS Annual Conference, Las Vegas, NV, pp. 377–390.

Delery, J., Doty, D.H., 1996. Modes of theorizing in strategic human resource management: test of universalistic, contingency and configurational performance predictions. Academy of Management Journal 39, 802–835.

Dolan, A.-M., 2013. AHRI Model of Excellence Redevelopment Project: Literature Review, August. AHRI, Melbourne.

Dobbs, R., Madgavkar, A., 2014. The world at work: matching skills and jobs in Asia. Prospects 44 (2), 197–210.

Edwards, V., Phan, A., 2013. Managers and Management in Vietnam: 25 Years of Economic Renovation (Doimoi). Routledge, London and New York.

Ernst, Young, 2012. Human Resources Solutions Industry: Stepping into the Next Decade of Growth. Ernst & Young 2012, Ernst & Young Pvt. Ltd. Published in India.

Hamid, A., 2004. Competencies Mapping and Certification Program for Human Resource Practitioners. Paper presented at 3rd STCEX Conference, Riyadh, KSA.

Hamid, A., 2014. Development of an HR practitioner competency model and determining the important business competencies: an empirical study in Malaysia. International Journal of Management Excellence 3 (2), 446–461.

Hamid, A., Fauzi, R.M.R.A., Juhary, A., 2011. The development of the human resource practitioner competency model perceived by Malaysian human resource practitioners and consultants: a structural equation modeling (SEM) approach. International Journal of Business Management 6 (11), 240–255.

Harter, J.K., Schmidt, F.L., Hayes, T.L., 2002. Business-unit-level relationship between employee satisfaction, employee engagement, and business outcomes: a meta-analysis. Journal of Applied Psychology 87, 268–279.

Hashim, J., 2009. Islamic revival in human resource management practices among selected Islamic organizations in Malaysia. International Journal of Islamic and Middle Eastern Finance and Management 2, 251–267.

Huselid, M.A., Becker, B.E., 1999. An interview with Mike Losey, Tony Rucci, and Dave Ulrich: three experts respond to HRMJ's special issue on HR strategy in five leading firms. Human Resource Management 38 (4), 353–365.

Huselid, M.A., Jackson, S.E., Schuler, R.S., 1997. Technical and strategic human resource management effectiveness as determinants of firm performance. Academy of Management Journal 40, 171–188.

Huui, L.M., Siddiq, M.S.B., 2012. Human resource disclosure: the current practice and its association with corporate characteristics in Malaysia. Interdisciplinary Journal of Contemporary Research in Business 4 (6), 68–93.

Islam, R., 2010. Critical success factors of the nine challenges in Malaysia's Vision 2020. Socio-Economic Planning Sciences 44 (4), 199–211.

Junaidah, K., 2007. Examining human resource managers' competencies. Journal of Malaysian Institute of Management 42 (1), 123–141.

Katou, A.A., 2008. Measuring the impact of HRM on organisational performance. Journal of Industrial Engineering and Management 1 (2), 119–142.

Kearns, P., 2010. HR Strategy: Creating Business Strategy with Human Capital, second ed. Elsevier Press, London.

Khatri, N., Budhwar, P.S., 2002. A study of strategic HR issues in an Asian context. Personnel Review 31 (1/2), 166.

Liu, Y., Pearson, C.A., Chatterjee, S.R., 2014. Selection practices and customer relationship activities mediated by cultural ideologies: an empirical study with Malaysian organisations. Asian Journal of Business Management 6 (1), 34–46.

Long, C.S., Ismail, W.K., 2011. An analysis of the relationship between HR professionals' competencies and firms' performance in Malaysia. International Journal of Human Resource Management 22 (5), 1054–1068.

Long, C.S., Khairuzzaman, W., 2008. Understanding the relationship of HR competencies and roles of Malaysian human resource professionals. European Journal of Social Science 7 (1), 88–103.

Long, C.S., Khairuzzaman, W., 2010. Readiness of Malaysian human resource professionals to be a strategic partner. Intangible Capital 6 (1), 26–50.

Man, M.M.K., 2012. Malaysian human resource development needs: challenges and suggestions. International Journal of Management Innovation 4 (2), 41–53.

MITI, 2013. Free Trade Agreement: Malaysia's FTA Involvement. Retrieved from: http://www.miti.gov.my/cms/content.jsp?id=com.tms.cms.section.Section_8ab55693-7f000010-72f772f7-46d4f042 (accessed 10 April 2013).

Montague, A., 2013. Vocational and skill shortages in Vietnamese manufacturing and service sectors, and some plausible solutions. Asia Pacific Journal of Human Resources, Special Issue: HRM in Vietnam 51 (2), 208–227.

Nankervis, A., Baird, M., Coffey, J., Shields, J., 2013. Strategic Human Resource Management: Strategy and Practice, eight ed. Cengage Learning Australia, Melbourne.

Nankervis, A., Montague, A., Prikshat, V., 2015. Scarcity in Plenty': Skills Shortages and HRM Practices in Vietnam: Building Workforce Capacities in the Asia Pacific. Routledge (forthcoming), London.

Nankervis, A., Stanton, A.R.P., Foley, P., 2012. Exploring the rhetoric and reality of performance management systems and organisational effectiveness – evidence from Australia. Research and Practice in Human Resource Management 20 (1), 40–56.

NEM, 2010. New Economic Model for Malaysia. National Economic Advisory Council. Putrajaya Malaysia.

Ngo, H.N., Jiang, C.Y., Loi, R., 2014. Linking HRM competency to firm performance: an empirical investigation of Chinese firms. Personnel Review 43 (6), 898–914.

Nguyen, D., Teo, S., Mylett, T., 2013. An exploration of the roles of HR departments in Vietnam. Journal of General Management 39 (2), 83–113.

NHRD, 2010. NHRD Network Journal. 3(4): October.

NSDC, 2012. SME Annual Report 2011/12: Redefining the Future. Retrieved from: http://www.smecorp.gov.my/images/Publication/Annual-report/BI/Annual-report-2011.pdf (accessed 30 January 2013).

Osman, I., Ho, T., Galang, M.C., 2011. Are human resource departments really important? An empirical study on Malaysian small and medium enterprises (SMEs) in the service sector. International Journal of Business and Management 6 (2), 147–153.

Pareek, U., Rao, T.V., 2007. From a sapling to a forest: the saga of the development of HRM in India. NHRD Journal 1 (Special Issue), 100–106.

Premarajan, P., Goyal, S., 2010. Competency based HRM in Indian organizations: interim results of an ongoing survey. NHRD Network Journal, October.

Purcell, J., Kinnie, N., 2007. Human resource management and business performance. In: Boxall, P., Purcell, J., Wright, P. (Eds.), The Oxford Handbook of Human Resource Management. Oxford University Press, Oxford.

Purcell, J., Kinnie, N., Hutchinson, S., Rayton, B., Swart, J., 2003. Understanding the People and Performance Link: Unlocking the Black Box. Chartered Institute of Personnel and Development, London.

Quang, T., 2006. Human resource management in Vietnam. In: Nankervis, A., Chatterjee, S., Coffey, J. (Eds.), Perspectives of Human Resource Management in the Asia Pacific. Pearson Education, . Australia, pp. 213–252.

Quang, T., Thang, L.C., 2004. HRM in Vietnam. In: Budhwar, P.P. (Ed.), Managing Human Resources in Asia Pacific. Routledge, London and New York.

Quang, T., Thang, L.C., Rowley, C., 2008. The changing face of human resource in Vietnam. In: Rowley, C., Abdul- Rahman, S. (Eds.), The Changing Face of Management in Southeast Asia. Routledge, London and New York.

Ramlall, S.J., 2006. Identifying and understanding HR competencies and their relationship to organizational practices. Applied HRM Research 11 (1), 27–38.

Rao, T.V., 2008. HRD Score Card 2500: Based on HRD Audit. SAGE Publications, India.

Rao, T.V., Rao, R., Yadav, T., 2001. A study of HRD concepts, structure of HRD departments, and HRD practices in India. Vikalpa 26 (1), 49–63.

Raven, J., Stephenson, J., 2001. Competency in the Learning Society. Peter Lang, New York.

Robinson, M.A., Sparrow, P.R., Clegg, C., Birdi, K., 2007. Forecasting future competency requirements: A three-phase methodology. Personnel Review 36 (1), 65–90.

Rowley, C., Abdul-Rahman, S., 2007. The management of human resources in Malaysia: locally-owned organisations and multinational organisations. Management Review 18 (4), 427–453.

Ruel, H.J.M., Bondarouk, T.V., Velde, M.V., 2007. The contribution of e-HRM to HRM effectiveness: results from a quantitative study in a Dutch ministry. Employee Relations 29 (3), 280–291.

Human resource management in India. In: Saini, D.S., Budhwar, P.S. (Eds.), 2004. Managing Human Resources in Asia. Routledge, New York.

Samaratunge, R., Alam, Q., Teicher, J., 2008. The new public management reforms in Asia: A comparison of South and Southeast Asian countries. International Review of Administrative Sciences 74 (1), 25–46.

Schuler, R.S., 1990. Repositioning the human resource function: transformation or demise? Academy of Management Executive 4, 49–60.

Schuler, R.S., Jackson, S.E., 1987. Linking competitive strategies with human resources management practices. Academy of Management Executive 1 (3), 207–219.

Selmer, J., Chiu, R., 2004. Required human resources competencies in the future : a framework for developing HR executives in Hong Kong. Journal of World Business 39, 324–336.

Som, A., 2002. Role of Human Resource Management in Organizational Design'. Unpublished doctoral dissertation. Indian Institute of Management, Ahmedabad.

Tan, C.L., Nasurdin, A.M., 2010. Human resource management practices and organizational innovation: an empirical study in Malaysia. Journal of Applied Business Research 26 (4), 105–115.

Tataw, D., 2012. Toward human resource management in inter-professional health practice: linking organizational culture, group identity and individual autonomy. International Journal of Health Planning and Management 27 (2), 130–149.

TCLMS, 2008. Youth Employment in Vietnam: Report of Survey Findings for VCCI, ILO. University of Leicester, TCLMS, Leicester.

Thang, L.C., Quang, T., 2005. Human resource management practices in a transitional economy: a comparative study of enterprise ownership forms in Vietnam. Asia Pacific Business Review 11, 25–47.

Truss, C., Mankin, D., Kelliher, C., 2012. Strategic Human Resource Management. Oxford University Press, Oxford.

Tsui, A.S., 1987. Defining the activities and effectiveness of the human resource department: a multiple constituency approach. Human Resource Management 26, 35–69.

Ulrich, D., 1997. Human Resource Champions. The next agenda for adding value and delivering results. Harvard Business School Press. Harvard Business School Press, Boston, Massachusetts, USA.

Ulrich, D., Brockbank, W., 2005. The HR Value Proposition. Harvard Business School Press, Boston.

Ulrich, D., 2008. The journey of HR. HR competencies : mastery at the intersection of people and business (pp. xi, 271 p.). Society for Human Resource Management, Alexandria, VA.

Ulrich, D., Brockbank, W., Ulrich, M., Younger, J., 2012. Global HR Competencies: Mastering Competitive Value from the Outside In. McGraw-Hill, USA.

Venkata Ratnam, C.S., Srivastava, B.K., 1991. Personnel Management and Human Resources. Tata McGraw-Hill, Delhi.

Warner, M., 2013. Comparing HRM in China and Vietnam: an overview. Human Systems Management 32, 217–229.

Wood, S., 1999. Human resource management and performance. International Journal of Management Reviews 1 (4), 367–413.

World Economic Forum, 2014. Vietnam World Economic Forum. Retrieved from: http://reports.weforum.org/global-competitiveness-*report-2012-2013*.

Wright, P.M., Snell, S.A., 1998. Toward a unifying framework for exploring fit and flexibility in strategic human resource management. Academy of Management Review 23 (4), 756–772.

Wright, P.M., Dunford, B., Snell, S., 2001. Human resources and the resource based view of the firm. Journal of Management 27, 701–721.

Wright, P.M., Gardner, T., Moyniham, L.M., Allen, M., 2005. The HR performance relationship: examining causal direction. Personnel Psychology 58, 409–446.

Wright, P.M., McMahan, G.C., McCormick, B., Sherman, S.C.W., 1998. Strategy, core competence, and human resource involvement as determinants of HR effectiveness and refinery performance. Human Resource Management 36, 17–29.

Zakaria, N., Abdullah, N.A.C., Yusoff, R.Z., 2014. The role of human resource management (HRM) practices in promoting organizational innovation in Malaysian SMEs: some preliminary findings. Journal of Global Management 8 (1).

Zhu, Y., 2005. The Asian crisis and the implications for human resource management in Vietnam. International Journal of Human Resource Management 16, 1261–1276.

Zhu, Y., 2011. Labour markets in Vietnam. In: Benson, J., Zhu, Y. (Eds.), The Dynamics of Asian Labour Markets. Routledge, London and New York, pp. 148–164.

Zhu, Y., Warner, M., Rowley, C., 2007. Human resource management with "Asian" characteristics: a hybrid people management system in East Asia. International Journal of Human Resource Management 18, 745–768.

Zhu, Y., Collins, N., Webber, M., Benson, J., 2008. New forms of ownership and human resource practices in Vietnam. Human Resource Management 47, 157–175.

CHAPTER 7

HRM roles in paradise: strategic or administrative? A study of tourist resorts in the Maldives

A. Najeeb

INTRODUCTION

Much of the growing body of research on human resource management (HRM) has promoted an increasingly strategic role of HRM (Ananthram and Nankervis, 2013; Kramar, 2014; Ulrich et al., 2013) and its contribution to organisational effectiveness (Guest, 2011; Nankervis et al., 2012; Rowley and Warner, 2013). However, research has thus far inconsistently conceptualised strategic human resource management (SHRM), casting doubt on the extent to which SHRM is actually practised in organisations (Tompkins, 2002). Moreover, there has often been more speculation than empirical examination of what it takes for HR to become strategic. Similarly, although there has been a great deal of normative writing about the role HR should play, there has been little empirical investigation of whether it is actually playing this role (Al-Taee and Alwaely, 2012; Lawler and Mohrman, 2003). Similarly, although research has identified HR competencies that go along with HRM roles, a question still remains as to the applications of these competencies (Darvish et al., 2012).

Existing SHRM research has paid less attention to (among other matters) the scope of HRM and issues associated with the effectiveness of the execution and implementation of HRM (Guest, 2011; Lengnick-Hall et al., 2009). SHRM literature also fails to adequately address the influence of different stakeholder perceptions and national and industry contexts (Stanton et al., 2010). Investigation of these issues in the hospitality industry is particularly limited (Najeeb, 2013). Much of the earlier literature also considers HRM in organisations in the hospitality industry as largely disconnected from organisational strategy (Alleyne et al., 2008) since HRM practices in organisations in the industry are administrative and operational, as opposed to strategic (Baum, 2012).

Asia Pacific Human Resource Management
and Organisational Effectiveness
ISBN 978-0-08-100643-6

Hospitality is a labour-intensive industry that depends heavily on the knowledge, skills, attitudes and commitment of the employees working in the industry (Naidu and Chand, 2014). Therefore people are the primary resources for competitiveness and success in this industry. The focus of this chapter is on 'hospitality' rather than broad 'tourism'. As the recognition of the need to include the context of hospitality in theory development has increased due to the importance of employees in hospitality firms and as HRM practices begin to become key factors in their growth and development, more literature has begun to appear on SHRM in the hospitality industry (Najeeb, 2011). However, the extant research on SHRM has largely treated all sectors in the industry as a generic unit, viewing them in a relatively homogeneous manner (Knox, 2002). Consequently, HRM in the industry has been generally characterised as 'adversarial and ad hoc' (Knox, 2002: 60). However, there are significant differences in terms of the nature, operation and management of firms within the industry. For instance, the way that restaurants are managed is very different from the way luxury hotels are managed. As a result, HRM practice also differs from sector to sector (Najeeb, 2011). The ways in which hospitality organisations manage their employees has implications for the quality of service they provide and for organisational effectiveness as a result. Given the differences that exist within the sectors of the hospitality industry, there is a need to study SHRM in relation to specific industries in order to appreciate the differences (Najeeb, 2013).

Managing employees in the hospitality industry continues to be challenging in the small developing island economies (Baum, 2012). Due to contextual factors such as institutional and cultural dissimilarities, HRM in the hospitality industry is very different in these countries from that in developed countries (Baum, 2012). A contextual approach to SHRM assumes that as with industry-specific factors influencing HRM in a particular industry, country-specific factors also influence SHRM practices in a particular country (Brewster and Mayrhofer, 2012). As HRM and its roles are affected by contextual factors, there have been increasing calls for an exploration of HRM within their contexts, especially in the case of emerging economies, with a view to expanding the applications of SHRM (Brewster and Mayrhofer, 2012; Lengnick-Hall et al., 2009; Schuler et al., 2002).

In order to address the SHRM issues outlined above, this chapter aims: (1) to explore the HRM roles and competencies of HR professionals in tourist resorts in the Maldives; (2) to examine whether HRM roles and practices in tourist resorts bear the characteristics of SHRM; (3) to investigate the factors that shape the nature and roles of HRM in these resorts; and (4) to investigate whether HRM roles and practices in local resorts are similar to or different from those of international hotel chains operating in the Maldives. The Maldives was chosen as the locus of this chapter in order to understand the SHRM concepts in a relatively unexplored new context.

The contributions of the study are threefold. First, as the majority of SHRM research has been conducted in developed countries, this chapter contributes to the literature by drawing data from resorts in the Maldives, thereby shedding light on a new context. Second, the empirical data generated by this research and the findings help distinguish SHRM in high-end tourist resorts from other sectors within the hospitality industry. Third, this study highlights the importance of a broader stakeholder perspective in SHRM research.

The remainder of the chapter is organised as follows. The next section presents an overview of the literature on SHRM and HRM roles and competencies that frame the analysis of the nature and roles of HRM in resorts in the Maldives. This is followed by a discussion of the research methods. The findings are presented in the third section, followed by discussion and implications of the findings. The chapter concludes by summarising the findings and outlining the directions for future research.

LITERATURE REVIEW

SHRM, defined as 'the patterns of planned HR developments and activities intended to enable an organisation to achieve its goals (Wright and McMahan, 1992: 298), emerged in the early 1980s as a strategic perspective of managing people in an increasingly turbulent and rapidly changing environment (Kramar, 2014). Since then SHRM has largely been grounded in the literature on competitive advantage, organisational effectiveness and the resource-based view. This literature argues that as employees' core competences and capabilities are key resources that need to be leveraged strategically to gain competitive advantage (Altarawneh and Aldehayyat, 2011), HRM practices need to be aligned not only with each other but also with the strategic orientation of the organisation (Nankervis et al., 2012; Ulrich et al., 2012). In summary, this literature reflects four key components that demonstrate SHRM in practice (Alleyne et al., 2008; Storey, 1992): (1) HRM strategy is determined by the organisational business strategy, integrating HRM fully with strategic planning; (2) HRM strategy is consistent with other functional strategies; (3) HRM strategy considers all levels of staff; and (5) the HRM function seeks to ensure that organisational culture, structure and employees' quality, motivation and commitment contribute to the achievement of organisational goals. Other SHRM characteristics include: HR managers' participation in business strategy formulation and the sharing of HR activities between HR professionals and line managers (Ulrich et al., 2013).

Best practice and best fit approaches

SHRM literature identifies two main schools of thought for SHRM: 'best practices' and 'best fit' approaches. The best practice approach is closely associated with the organisational effectiveness perspective and argues that any organisation can adopt a set of best practices in the management of people to improve performance (Boxall and Purcell, 2011; Kramar, 2014). It promotes the universalism of HRM with an assumption that all organisations that adopt a range of agreed HRM practices tend to create a high performance workplace as organisations compete on the basis of high quality and productivity.

The best fit school argues for an approach to HRM which is fully integrated with the specific organisational and environmental contexts in which they operate. In other terms, it argues for external and internal fits. External fit requires HRM activities to fully integrate with the demands of the external environment. Internal fit refers to HRM strategies reinforcing each other (Jackson and Seo, 2010). Best fit can be achieved when HR strategies are aligned with an organisation's preferred business strategy ,such as cost leadership, differentiation (innovation and quality enhancement) or focused strategies (Schuler and Jackson, 1987), through which organisational effectiveness is achieved.

HRM roles and competencies

In the context of HRM in Europe, Kohont and Brewster (2014) suggested that there are three main players in the HRM field: line managers, HRM specialists and employee representatives. From the perspective of hospitality resorts in the Maldives, Najeeb (2013) identified three major HR participants: senior managers (mainly general managers), HR and line managers. This categorisation is consistent with the importance of senior, middle and line managers in promoting the implementation of HRM policy through organisational hierarchies (Stanton et al., 2010). Therefore, the chapter focuses on the HRM roles of these participants. These roles are shaped by multiple contextual factors, including institutional context, company environment, the social dimension of culture and organisational contingencies (Lengnick-Hall et al., 2009; Steers et al., 2013).

There are various typologies of HR roles (Ulrich et al., 2012; Kohont and Brewster, 2014). Ulrich (1997) suggested that HR professionals must play four key roles in order to add value to the organisation. These roles are both strategic and operational in nature, and have both long-term and short-term perspectives. These roles involve activities ranging from managing processes to managing people. They are: (1) the strategic partner role; (2) the administrative expert role; (3) the employee advocacy or champion role; and (4) the change agent role. Some researchers have divided HR professionals into specialists and strategists (Ulrich et al., 2012), while others categorise them as generalists and functional specialists (Antoine, 2015). These researchers also identified HR competencies or behaviours that encompass knowledge, skills and attributes required for successful HR performance (Darvish et al., 2012) that flow from each of these role categories. For example, competencies associated with the HR generalists' role include organisational design, development and effectiveness, relationship management and project and product management. Competencies such as business acumen, strategic influence and change management are associated with the HR strategist's role.

Antoine (2015) argued that to be strategic partners, HR managers need to have credibility with line managers, possess line experience and be able to offer solutions to business problems. Similarly, senior and line managers need to heed and value HR partners who can counsel and provide advice. All members of this partnership also need to be change agents. To be more specific, HR professionals need to be operational executors, credible activists, change stewards, talent managers, organisational designers, strategy architects and business allies. Although strategic and operational roles are conflicting in many respects and performing both roles in an integrated fashion will remain an ongoing challenge (Tompkins, 2002), this has to be accepted as part of an HR professional's job.

Drawing on Brewster et al. (2004), Kohont and Brewster (2014) divided HR competencies into four groups: (1) competencies that form the individual style of operations; (2) enterprise competencies; (3) competencies needed for leadership, guidance and mentoring such as vision and alignment, strategic thinking, networking, resource management and team work; and (4) competencies that are necessary for the operational activities of HR managers. These competencies are also shaped by contextual, national and organisational factors, and the time frames within which they operate. These HR competencies are crucial in increasing organisational effectiveness for two reasons (Ramlall, 2006): first, to get assurance from HR managers that the organisation has the human resource capabilities to implement its strategies; second, to ensure that effective HR practices are in place for the effective implementation of organisational strategies. Although the greatest opportunity for HRM to contribute to organisational effectiveness may be to play a role in the development and implementation of the corporate strategy, the absence of HR competencies to carry out strategic HR roles has been identified as a possible reason for the lack of HR involvement in strategy development (Tompkins, 2002).

Managing HR through partnerships

There is a plethora of literature concerning how HRM is managed by HR professionals and line managers. Line managers are renowned for criticising the contribution that HR specialists make to organisational performance. This broadly takes one or more of four forms. First, HR practitioners are regarded as out of touch with commercial realities and not really being aware of how the business operates or its customer needs, and instead promote principles – such as welfare or employee rights – that may run counter to business goals. Second, HR is often seen to constrain the autonomy of line managers to make decisions which they feel are in the best interests of business. Third, HR managers are unresponsive and slow to act, always wanting to check options thoroughly rather than taking action immediately. Finally, HR practitioners are criticised for promoting policies that may be fine in theory but hard to put into effect. Although there have been suggestions that HR should be disbanded altogether, a more realistic option is for line managers and HR professionals to work together as partners (Marchington and Wilkinson, 2012; Ulrich, 1998). Such partnerships require increasing the trust in line managers and transferring HR accountability to them in many areas where previously HR has exercised control. Managing human resources through such partnerships reflects SHRM theory in effective practice (Guest, 2011; Rupidara and McGraw, 2011).

SHRM in the hospitality industry

There have been mixed views on the nature of HRM in the hospitality industry. Earlier research in developing and developed countries provided a very bleak picture of HRM in the industry (Baum, 2007), labelling it essentially administrative in nature (Taylor and Finley, 2008). This is particularly true for the catering sector and small organisations in the hospitality industry. However, since the early 2000s, empirical studies have been increasingly suggesting that organisations in the hospitality industry are beginning to adopt SHRM practices (Taylor and Finley, 2008). This appears particularly true for luxury hotels. Findings from hospitality HRM research in small island states are also consistent with this claim (Alleyne et al., 2008; Baptiste and Bailey, 2003).

RESEARCH METHODS
The context of the study

The research was conducted in seven resorts in the Maldives. The Republic of Maldives is located in the Indian subcontinent, consisting of 1,190 small coral islands, 200 of which are inhabited (Department of National Planning (DNP), 2014). The hospitality industry in the Maldives is considered synonymous with resorts (Najeeb, 2013) because resorts provide 79.9 per cent of the beds in the tourism industry in the Maldives (Ministry of Tourism, Arts and Culture (MTAC), 2014). This industry is the lifeline of the Maldivian economy. In 2013, the industry contributed 27 per cent to GDP, 17.3 per cent to government revenue and approximately 70 per cent of the country's foreign currency earnings (MTAC, 2014). The industry has also been the largest private sector employer, supporting 87,000 jobs or providing employment for an estimated 63 per cent of the country's labour market during 2011 (World Travel and Tourism Council, 2011). As illustrated in Table 7.1, resorts primarily serve the high-end tourist market. By the end of December 2014, the Maldives received more than 1.2 million tourists – four times the population of the country (Hamid, 2015).

Resorts selected for this research are self-contained in nature. They were developed under the country's 'one island, one resort policy', based on the 'enclave tourism' philosophy (Najeeb, 2014). These resort islands are 'off limits to the [indigenous] people' unless they are employed at the resort (Najeeb, 2013). Thus only employees and guests are found in these resorts. In 2013, of the 109 resorts registered, 41 per cent were operated by local companies, 16 per cent by foreign companies and 42 per cent by joint venture (local and foreign) companies (DNP, 2014). As most of the resorts belong either to a local hotel group or to an international hotel chain, they operate as independent strategic business units, employing a largely independent management team.

Table 7.1 Structural profile of the resorts

Characteristics	Resorts						
	A	B	C	D	E	F	G
Size							
Number of employees	380	560	985	318	302	285	216
Number of rooms	65	225	426	125	148	75	44
Age	16	39	13	17	30	38	32
Ownership							
Local resorts		√	√	√		√	
International hotel chain	√				√		√
Target market/level of service							
High-end	√			√		√	√
High-end and middle-level		√	√		√		
Middle level							
Perceived star ranking★	5	4	4	5	4	5	5

★There is no official star ranking for resorts

Research design, data collection and analysis

Data for this study were gathered as part of a four-year doctoral research project investigating the shaping of HRM practices in resorts in the Maldives. Ethical approval for this research was granted by the University of Wollongong. Based on the nature of the research problem and the context, a qualitative approach was adopted. Qualitative methods are more appropriate to 'explore exotic cultures, understudied phenomena, or very complex social phenomena (Miles and Huberman, 1994: 94). Based on a multiple case study approach (Yin, 1994), seven resorts were selected: four locally owned and managed resorts and three that belong to international hotel chains. As access to these cases was granted on the condition of anonymity, pseudonyms are used to describe the resorts and participants. The background and contextual information on the seven resorts are presented below in tabular form. Resorts have different profiles in terms of size (number of employees and rooms) and level of service, as presented in Table 7.1.

Consistent with the multiple case study approach, empirical material was collected through a range of methods: semi-structured interviews, field observation and contextual documents comprising company web pages, reports and strategy and policy documents, employee handbooks, best practice manuals, and relevant posts in newspapers and online blogs. A total of

Table 7.2 Number of interviews with participants

Participants	Pseudonyms	Number
Senior managers	SNM	7
Line managers	LNM	7
HR managers	HRM	7
Non-managerial employees	NME	28
Government officials	GOO	2
Industry experts	INE	2
Tourism Employee Association (TEAM) executives	EAM	2
Total		55

55 semi-structured interviews were held across all seven case studies. Details of the respondents considered for the interviews are presented in Table 7.2.

The interviews were exploratory and aimed at eliciting views and opinions from multiple perspectives. The data for this study were gathered from the background and career-related questions asked of the interviewees. Respondents were asked questions such as: 'Can you please tell me about your career in general?', 'What's your position in your organisation?' and 'What's the nature of the work you are involved in?' In most cases, interviewees started to talk freely about their role in the organisation in general, and about HRM or relationships they have with each other in particular. Most interviews lasted between 30 and 75 minutes. Respondents were offered the option to conduct interviews in either English or Dhivehi (local language of the Maldivian people), and the interviewer adopted the language they preferred. Interviews conducted in Dhivehi were translated into English before analysis. All interviews were digitally recorded and transcribed verbatim. Interview transcripts were read several times and corroborated with the documentary evidence and field notes that helped develop each case as a stand-alone entity and perform a within-case analysis (Miles and Huberman, 1994). Data from each case were coded and patterns emerging out of each case were identified before they were generalised across the seven cases (Eisenhardt, 1989). Patterns that emerged from the cross-case analysis (comparison) were categorised according to the research aims and concepts identified from the literature.

RESEARCH FINDINGS

The findings are organised based on the themes that emerged from the analysis, including the definition of HRM, the status and position of the HR department, the devolution of HRM to line managers, and the integration of HR functions with each other and with the strategic orientation of the firm.

Contextual and perceptual definition of HRM – rhetoric or reality?

In order to heed the calls for defining and understanding HRM in context (Brewster and Mayrhofer, 2012; Lengnick-Hall et al., 2009) and to gain insight into the extent to which resort stakeholder views reflect the characteristics of SHRM, the study analysed interviewees' definitions of HRM. Most managers defined HR as the most important resource and HRM as a means to achieve competitive advantage. The following quotes from managers typify this view:

Human resource in modern hospitality is absolutely paramount to the success of a resort. The new strategic leadership of tomorrow comes from guidance with human resources. HR plays absolutely a key role in maintaining balance of leading, guiding and supporting the workforce within the resort. I think human resources are very much about training, which is the most challenging aspect of HRM in resorts.

(SNM20, Resort F)

HR is the most important resource in this resort. The only way we can see a smiling face of a guest is to make employees happy, the intangible element. The care and kindness of our staff, friendliness of our staff, accepting customers as they are, providing services that the customers want, attending customer requests promptly. Creating an environment where employees and guests are happy is what I see HRM. How do we create such an environment? There are things that need to happen at the back stage – motivating employees, bringing their professional levels up, working for their well-being, and making them happy. Employees are in a trapped environment here so make the environment vivid and complete for them.

(SNM30, Resort C)

HRM is all about interactions and relationships.

(SNM32, Resort G)

These definitions reflect the broader role of HRM in resorts. These definitions also reflect important HRM roles and leadership and management competencies (Kohont and Brewster, 2014), such as leading, guiding, networking, team work and maintaining fairness and equality in managing employees.

HRM is also largely viewed as an organisational function whose support and integration is key to the effectiveness of all other business functions. As the following response suggests:

If you look after your employees that deliver great services, the guests come back and the profit and the finance start to look after themselves. So get it right with your employees.

(HRM39, Resort A)

The definition also emphasises HRM's contribution to service quality, profitability or to the bottom-line of the organisation, which is indicative of SHRM (Kramar, 2014). It also to some extent reflects the market-driven approach to HRM, as employees are treated well because these resorts serve high-end markets and guests demand high-quality personalised services, which can only be delivered through well-managed human resources.

While managerial definitions of HRM largely reflect strategic aspects of HRM, employees' and their representatives' views of HRM focus on employees as end-users. They view HRM and its functions as looking after their welfare, developing, empowering and supporting them achieve their goals:

HRM is about managers dealing with us professionally by building and maintaining a good relationship, supporting us and meeting our needs, looking after us well and helping us reach our goals by developing us.

(NME49, Resort B)

HRM is about employees running their affairs.

(TEAM15)

Although managers and employees viewed HRM from different angles, as the interview responses indicate, they agreed on a similar set of competencies required to perform HRM roles such as networking, interpersonal relationships or team skills.

In summary, although all interviewees invariably acknowledged the importance of HRM in resorts, consistent with Janssens and Steayaert's (2009) findings, the perceptions of HRM vary among stakeholders as their interests and roles within the organisations are different. The perceptions of HRM reflect and/or are shaped by the context (e.g. the unique context of resorts), as are the strategic challenges posed to the managers, such as the importance of human capital development in the provision of high-quality services due to skill shortages. With regard to the managerial view of HRM, although their views reflect SHRM, further analysis would determine whether it is a reflection of their aspirations rather than the reality.

The status and role of HR managers – strategic partners or administrative subordinates?

Chow (2004) argued that the development of HR in an industry can be inferred from such indicators as having a separate HR department to carry out HR functions, having specialised HR professionals employed, and the extent of using state-of-the-art HRM techniques. Although the number of HR experts and other staff working in HR vary from resort to

Table 7.3 HR profile of resorts

Characteristics	A	B	C	D	E	F	G
Resorts							
The department in charge of HR functions							
HR department	✓	✓	✓	✓	✓	✓	✓
The person in charge of HR functions							
Human Resource Director	✓	✓					✓
Human Resource Manager			✓			✓	
Assistant Human Resource Manager				✓			
Others					✓		
No. of staff responsible for HR functions	6	5	10	2	2	4	3
No. of staff from professional HR background	4	3	1	1	0★	3	3

★HR functions are centralised at Malé office

resort, all resorts in this study have separate HR departments. As Table 7.3 shows, most resorts employed an HR professional to lead the department.

As Table 7.3 indicates, the number of employees in the HR department varies between one and four, including the HR director or manager. A wide range of titles are applied to HRM jobs. Most resorts have a senior manager in charge of the HR function. However, in some resorts HR functions are entrusted to other senior roles. In general, employees reach a senior level in HR through internal promotions within the department, resort or organisation. It is also common for people from other professional backgrounds such as ticketing and reservations to be employed for senior HR roles. This appears to have assisted HR practitioners to develop competencies such as business acumen to be a more effective strategic partner, and has also prepared HR to partner with line managers to implement HRM in resorts effectively (Antoine, 2015).

Having qualified HR professionals in resorts is an incentive for the senior managers to take HR on board and to involve them in decision-making. With the exception of resort E, HR managers in all resorts are given a central role, and their views are considered in almost all decision-making at the resort level. In resort E, only an administrative assistant of HR is based in the resort; hence HR does not have much say in decision-making. The parent company of resort E is managing HR using the 'hub' concept. HR functions are coordinated by a manager located in the Malé (Maldives capital) office who is also responsible for looking after the HR functions of all the resorts that belong to the parent company operating in the Maldives, leaving a greater HR role for line managers in the resort. These findings show that, consistent with international hotel chains operating in other parts of the world, hotel chains in the Maldives have also started adopting the 'hub' concept in managing hotels (Davidson et al., 2011). Although HR managers both in local and international hotel chains are involved in strategic decision-making, most HR decisions which involve finance in local resorts are made by the headquarters in Malé. Therefore, some of the HR roles in these resorts are administrative and operational in nature.

HRM roles to a certain degree are also shaped by the perceptions and expectations of various stakeholders. For example, the general expectation of the general manager of the HR department is to play a role in bridging the gap between employees and management, advising management on HR issues, and guiding, supporting and modelling employees. These roles reflect Ulrich's (1997) typology of HRM roles, namely strategic, administrative, operational and employee advocacy roles. From HR managers' point of view, senior managers not only influence HRM roles in resorts, their support is also critical for HR managers to perform HRM roles effectively:

> ... On a day-to-day basis, what's crucial is how your general manager feels about HR, because if they are not supportive of and do not believe in HR, then you have to struggle. Here the GM is extremely supportive of HR, very host-orientated, which again makes life much easier.
>
> **(HRM12, Resort D)**

Although general managers often associate HRM with Ulrich's (1997) role categories, line managers and employees often perceive HR as a place to lodge complaints and prioritise its role in resolving employment issues. As a consequence of the latter, the operational role of the HR department increases, limiting HR managers' opportunities to engage in strategic roles. There are also other contextual and institutional factors that drive HRM roles. Among them, the operational arrangements and the unique context of resorts is particularly noticeable:

> We are responsible for hosts always as they stay here 24/7 resorts are island based. So the breadth of the role is bigger. We have a more welfare kind of a role.
>
> **(HRM45, Resort B)**

The HR department's welfare role is consistent with employees' view of HRM. As the HR department has to play this welfare role due to the unique context of the resorts, in this context, some managers see the role of looking after employees in these resorts as 'strategic', as the delivery of a high-quality service depends on employee satisfaction which in turn makes positive contributions to organisational effectiveness.

Besides the nature of HRM roles, the utilisation of a wide range of HR techniques is also an indicator of strategic HRM (Storey, 1992). Resorts implement a wide range of HRM practices. For example, Resort A implements (in its managers' responses) 94 HR best practices which include some very sophisticated HRM practices such as two-way recruitment and 360 degree employment selection processes whereby employees are chosen through an evaluation and judgement of a range of stakeholders with whom the employee has either already been engaged in a previous job or would potentially be engaged.

In summary, consistent with Altarawneh and Aldehayyat (2011) who studied SHRM practices in hotels in Jordan, and Alleyne et al.'s (2008) study of hotels in Barbados, HR functions in many resorts in the Maldives go beyond delivering services and maintaining records, and demonstrate strategic elements to some extent by being members of the management team, contributing to strategic decision-making and having a more profound role in organisational decisions and overall effectiveness. HR managers are generally highly regarded (credible activists) and play a central role in the implementation of HRM practices. HR managers in high-end international hotel chains tend to have a more proactive role and appear to implement SHRM practices more often than their competitors.

Devolving HR responsibilities to line managers – through change management

A high level of line manager involvement in HRM, or at least the devolution of HRM roles to line managers, is considered as SHRM in the hospitality industry (Maxwell and Watson, 2006). Resorts in the Maldives are increasingly devolving HR responsibilities to line managers through change management programmes. However, HR managers find it challenging to empower line managers to play a crucial role in managing people. Interviews conducted with HR and line managers reveal that there are three reasons why line managers are reluctant to take up HR roles or in some cases are not able to perform HR functions when they are allocated them roles through these programmes. First, line managers lack people management skills and leadership competencies. Second, they are overloaded with operational tasks. Third is the taken-for-granted view that HR is not part of their responsibility, and the way they practice HRM in resorts is the 'right way of doing it'. An example is the recruitment practice in some resorts whereby potential employees are selected as the position becomes vacant without any screening or due process. Although expatriate HR managers who often act as change agents in international hotel chains see recruiting employees this way as not best practice, local managers often view the practice as the right way of recruiting people. As the following respondent comment shows:

> *Some managers queue up to recruit new employees. When employees come into the interview and assign them yes or no or give them the job isn't the right way to go. We ask managers to give us a couple of days, we will give you 4 or 5 CVs, and then you pick up the best ones not the first one that turned up. But they see this process as slow.*
>
> **(HRM39, Resort A)**

As the above comment indicates, a high level of expectations and demands from employees and management on HR departments to do things 'as usual' limit their ability to improve the existing HR system or to introduce SHRM practices. The resistance shows how challenging it is to change practices that are deeply embedded in the organisational culture and which have been institutionalised for a long period. As HR managers play the change agent's role, due to the pressure from line managers, HR managers sometimes give into line managers' demands and deviate from the proposed HR systems. A case in point is the abandonment of an induction programme by the HR department in Resort B when line managers refused to involve their employees in welcoming and hosting new employees recruited for their departments because they viewed it as an HR responsibility.

As the preceding example shows, tensions often exist between HR and line managers as the former to a certain extent are forced to undertake some roles that are supposed to be performed by line managers. This increases the workload of HR managers, limiting their ability to engage in strategic planning. One reason for this tension is that HR and line managers' roles are not very distinctive in the implementation of HRM practices during this change process (Gilbert et al., 2011). However, these tensions in resorts (such as resort A) are overcome by the presence of a strong corporate culture of sharing and collaboration. Sometimes, a strong consultative process is initiated between the managers and employee committees with the aim of avoiding conflicts.

In summary, HR professionals in resorts play a leadership role in implementing SHRM practices through change management processes. HR managers try to manage people through partnerships (Marchington and Wilkinson, 2012). However, despite the best efforts of HR managers, during the HR devolution process, it is increasingly challenging for them to obtain adequate support from line managers in the implementation of desired SHRM practices due to reasons such as line managers' lack of people management skills and competencies, and adherence to the traditional expectations of HRM practices.

Achieving external and internal fit – sporadic or widely practised?

Few resorts have formally integrated HRM into their management philosophies. However, the vision, mission and values statements of some resorts reflect the importance of their human resources. For example, the following core values from resort A are closely related to the employees:

We display fairness and integrity, and foster mutual trust and care in our dealings with our employees, our business partners and clients; we foster the development of all our employees ...

(Company profile, Resort A)

Some government officials interviewed reported that resorts with written vision and mission statements are more likely to adopt more progressive HRM practices than others. Although there are no written business strategies in some resorts, their activities are linked to achieve business objectives, such as reducing costs or improving the quality of service delivery. HR practices such as stringent qualifications, experience-based recruitment and selection, and an emphasis on training and development show the emphasis on quality enhancement in service delivery. Similarly flexible workplace practices are linked to offering flexible and personalised services to their guests. These resorts adopt a quality enhancement strategy focused on the improvement of guest services (Schuler and Jackson, 1987).

High-end international resorts adopt a systematic approach to integrate HRM strategies and practices into business and other functional strategies. For example, in Resort A, HRM practices are integrated with each other and with other business and functional strategies through a 360 degree performance evaluation and feedback system. Similarly, in both Resorts A and G, succession planning is linked to their corporate social responsibility strategies. The top management of these resorts regard the employment and empowerment of local employees as a corporate responsibility. Hence, they try to ensure that, at least, the second-in-charge of every department is a local. Using such strategies, these resorts differentiate themselves from their competitors (Cooper, 2005). Other resorts also attempt to adopt and implement these highly progressive SHRM practices, such as human capital development programmes. However, these programmes are often not well-sustained as managers in some of these resorts still view HR as a cost. With regard to the implementation of HRM practices, decoupling – the actual practice differs from the policy – is a norm in resorts. There are two explanations for decoupling. First, despite the HR managers' rhetoric that employees are the most important resources in resorts, in some resorts such as D, HRM is still seen as an expense or a cost. Second, resorts operate in a very unstable and uncertain environment that drives changes in HRM practices, reflecting external fit. Faced with this uncertainty, resort managers used decoupling as a coping strategy.

Resorts' HRM practices are not only linked to Schuler and Jackson's (1987) quality enhancement strategy, but also are affected by the cost minimisation strategy. The latter strategy is evident in all resorts in general, and highly visible in Resorts C, D and E. The cost minimisation strategy is having a significant impact on practices such as staffing as well as compensation and benefits:

> I am looking after the accounts and I know how much profit the resort is making. In spite of the high profit the resort makes, our salaries remain the same.
>
> **(NME38, Resort A)**

Employees report that they often become victims of a resort's cost-reduction efforts. Many employees are of the view that resorts are making super profits and that there is therefore no basis for not providing them with a reasonable salary and benefits.

In summary, resort managers largely try to achieve external and internal fit. HRM practices at many resorts are not only linked to organisational strategies, such as quality enhancement, differentiation and cost minimisation (Schuler and Jackson, 1987), but are also linked with each other and with other functional strategies. These strategic efforts are driven by market orientation and the nature of the industry.

DISCUSSION

This study reports the findings from a qualitative study focused on the shaping of HRM practices from a sample of (mainly) resort managers and employees in seven tourist resorts in the Maldives. This study analysed the nature and roles of HRM as highlighted in contemporary SHRM literature. The study reveals that the interviewees' perception of HRM in part reflects the different interests and positions of the respondents within the resort or industry. This is consistent with Janssens and Steayaert's (2009) findings that the views on HRM could vary among stakeholders. Their perspectives also reflect the unique settings of resorts, the service philosophy they adopt and the strategic challenges they face. However, further analysis into the themes presented in the findings shows that there is a mismatch between the managerial view of HRM and the actual HRM situation in resorts.

The analysis depicts a mixed picture with regard to the roles of the HR managers. Strategic, administrative, welfare and employee advocacy roles are part of the HR department's remit in resorts (Boxall and Purcell, 2011; Ulrich, 1997, 1998). Various contextual factors are responsible for these roles. First, the self-contained setting of the resorts causes HR managers to play a more welfare-oriented role. Second, the perception of general managers of HRM leads HR managers to play a more strategic HR role as they provide HR legitimacy, leadership and resources and link organisational strategies with HR strategies (Stanton et al., 2010). Case studies (A, C, D, F and G) confirmed top-management support, involvement and commitment to HRM. Third, the market-orientation and competitive conditions drive strategic HR roles, as the delivery of quality services is often regarded as the number one priority in luxury resorts, which can only be achieved through the effective management of their human resources (Taylor and Finley, 2008). Fourth, the perception of HRM by line managers and employees leads HR managers to play administrative, consultative and employee advocacy roles, often simultaneously. Although HR managers are highly regarded and better positioned in resorts to execute HR, the perception of senior and line managers and employees impacting on HR managers' roles suggests that the HR department's role is established in the context of the role preference of other actors (van Gestel and Nyberg, 2009). The administrative roles of HR departments that arise from other actors' perceptions of HR hinder the implementation of SHRM. As particularly evident in Resorts A and C, only limited time is available for HR managers to engage in strategic issues. Therefore, these actors' views and perceptions of HRM are critical in the effective implementation of SHRM in these kinds of organisations.

The study demonstrates that most of the seven resorts (A, B and C in particular) are in the process of devolving HR responsibilities to line managers. In the process of shifting HR responsibilities to line managers, HR managers play a key role, not only by proposing the change, but also by leading the change (Peters and Heusinkveld, 2010). As line managers' performance of both management and leadership components of the HR function is substantially weak (Purcell and Kinnie, 2007), HR managers increasingly interact with line managers in the implementation of HRM practices, which characterises partnership in managing people in resorts

(Marchington and Wilkinson, 2012). Despite the best efforts of HR managers, line managers still play a limited role in the implementation of HRM practices. The tension created in the change process is often resolved through the corporate culture of sharing and collaboration, as in the case of Resort A. Hence, corporate culture plays an enabling role in managing change in resorts.

The analysis shows that resort managers try to achieve both internal and external fit in order to achieve competitive advantage. There are conscious efforts to integrate HRM practices with each other and with business strategies such as quality and differentiation (Schuler and Jackson, 1987), as in Resorts A and E. All resorts, including those that serve the high-end market, are also cost conscious, leading to decoupling and sometimes failing to sustain progressive HRM practices. A plausible explanation for this behaviour is that resorts are operating in a volatile, vulnerable and seasonal industry where future revenues are highly unpredictable and are continuously under the dual pressures of ensuring a return for owners and maintaining brand recognition (Davidson et al., 2011). In the case of international hotel chains, their profits may have to be split in many ways. Hence, resort managers need to adopt a strategic HRM approach that maximises employee motivation concurrently with reducing the cost of managing employees.

Besides HRM roles, the study also identifies context-specific HRM competencies needed for resort managers to effectively perform HRM roles that enhance organisational effectiveness. For example, in general, competencies such as leading, guiding and maintaining fairness and equality are needed to perform HRM roles in resorts. Competencies such as business acumen, networking and team work, social skills, credibility, and building and maintaining relationships (business partners) are required to perform a change agent role, as evident in devolving HR roles to line managers and managing human resources through partnerships (Marchington and Wilkinson, 2012). Similarly, coping with uncertainty and analytical skills are required as resorts operate in a changing and unstable environment and/or in a highly volatile and unpredictable industry (Davidson et al., 2011).

Finally, the study suggests that resorts in the Maldives are increasingly adopting a strategic role. These findings are consistent with those of other studies conducted in Asian and/or small-island developing countries, such as in Australia and Singapore (Nankervis and Debrah, 1995), India (Ananthram and Nankervis, 2013), Jordan (Al-Taee and Alwaely, 2012), Tonga and Samoa (Naidu and Chand, 2014) and Barbados (Alleyne et al., 2008). Although there are no marked differences between SHRM roles and practices in resorts, the findings show that those that serve high-end markets and are involved in highly personalised services, such as A and G, adopt more progressive HRM practices, reflecting spending on service quality and investments in HRM. Hence, the variation in SHRM roles and practices are attributed to market orientation and level of services rather than ownership type.

HRM and organisational effectiveness

The findings of this research need to be interpreted within the context of the organisations it examined. The study used resorts – strategic business units (sub-units) of their respective organisations – as the central unit of analysis, which is consistent with the claim that SHRM analysis is typically conducted at the business–unit level (Kramar, 2014). It analysed the nature and roles of HRM largely from an implementation perspective, which is as strategic as the design and development of HRM systems (Guest, 2011; Rupidara and McGraw, 2011). With regard to the context, the findings from Resort A highlighted that HR managers' welfare role in resorts can be considered as strategic due to the self-contained settings of resorts. Managers need to take into consideration the unique context of resorts when managing employees. The findings have implications for the contextual paradigm of SHRM which suggests that, depending on the context within which organisations operate, HRM roles may differ. Hence, an administrative role in one context may be considered a strategic role in another (Brewster and Mayrhofer, 2012; Lengnick-Hall et al., 2009; Naidu and Chand, 2014).

The study highlighted the importance of a proactive role of HRM for resorts, and international hotel chains in particular, operating in complex and dynamic business environments in order to achieve competitive advantage (Ananthram and Nankervis, 2013). It is critical for managers to understand that the performance of hotels is determined by the quality of its workforce and that what differentiates great companies from their competitors is their ability to manage human resources effectively (Cooper, 2005).

This study found that line managers' performance is substantially weak in the implementation of HRM in resorts due to the lack of leadership and management competencies required to perform HRM roles. This implies that as human resources are managed through partnerships in resorts it is important that not only HR managers but also all HR partners (senior, HR and line managers) should have leadership, management and social skills (Gilbert et al., 2011; Purcell and Kinnie, 2007) to implement SHRM effectively. While the objective of the HRM devolution programmes in resorts is to completely shift some of the HR responsibilities to line managers (the current status), a moderate level of HR devolution to line management should be viewed positively as this would minimise the risk of ill-equipped managers taking charge of HR functions completely. The study also highlights that in the HRM devolution process, there is no clear distinction of HRM roles between HR and line managers, leading to potential tensions. In such situations, the high level of social capital of managers helps to resolve their differences and to enhance the effectiveness of HRM implementation, thus enhancing overall organisational effectiveness.

CONCLUSION

In summary, the study suggests that driven by service and competitive and market conditions, tourist resorts in the Maldives are increasingly adopting universalistic SHRM roles and practices. However, these roles and practices are modified or influenced by contextual factors, principally the self-contained setting of resorts. Besides adopting strategic roles and SHRM practices, the SHRM characteristics embraced by resorts include: having a highly regarded HR department, managing HR through partnerships, HR managers' participation in strategy formulation and implementation, having a strong corporate culture to shape HRM practices, aligning HRM practices with each other and with organisational strategies and securing top-management support and involvement for HRM. The study also identified context-specific competencies needed to perform HRM effectively, and found that although HRM roles and practices are largely similar across resorts, international high-end resorts tend to adopt more strategic roles and SHRM practices than the rest.

The main contribution of the study is that it applied SHRM concepts from contemporary literature to explore SHRM roles in depth from a broader stakeholder perspective in an unstable environment and a context which thus far has been seldom explored. The empirical data generated by this research and the findings help to distinguish SHRM in luxury tourist resorts from other sectors within the hospitality industry, while previous studies have largely treated the industry as a generic unit (Knox, 2002).

However, the findings from this study have limitations. First, this research is a qualitative study based on interviews, field observations and other documentary sources. Data used in this study are clustered at the sub-unit level (resorts). The study is also limited to a single sector/industry. This presents limitations to generalising the findings. Future studies might focus on other sectors and compare it with this study. Second, this is a cross-sectional study.

A longitudinal study can be better-suited to capture the dynamics of micro-politics of HR actors in the implementation of SHRM in resorts and how the HRM roles of these actors in resorts change over time. Third, as only comparative empirical research can help illuminate whether similar patterns exist in other countries (Björkman et al., 2007), future research could study SHRM roles and practices in other countries with different characteristics. Finally, extant SHRM research explicitly linked HRM practices to organisational performance, particularly to financial and market outcomes that reflect shareholders' interests, ignoring other stakeholders such as employee interests (Kramar, 2014). Therefore, future SHRM research needs to consider the impact of SHRM practices on employees.

REFERENCES

Alleyne, P.A., Greenidge, D., Corbin, A., Alleyne, P., Devonish, D., 2008. The practice of HRM and SHRM in the Barbados Hotel Sector. Journal of Human Resources in Hospitality and Tourism 7 (2), 219–240.

Al-Taee, H., Alwaely, D.F.J., 2012. Examining the relationships among human resources roles, professional competencies and emotional intelligence (an empirical study). Global Journal of Management and Business Research 12 (23), 1–10.

Altarawneh, I.I., Aldehayyat, J.S., 2011. Strategic human resource management (SHRM) in Jordanian hotels. International Journal of Business and Management 6 (10), 242–254.

Ananthram, S., Nankervis, A., 2013. Strategic agility and the role of HR as a strategic business partner: an Indian perspective. Asia-Pacific Journal of Human Resources 52 (4), 454–470.

Antoine, R.L., 2015. HR as a business partner. In: Ulrich, D., Schiemann, W.A., Sartain, L. (Eds.), The Rise of HR: Wisdom from 73 Thought Leaders. HR Certification Institute, Alexandria, VA, pp. 461–464.

Baptiste, R., Bailey, V., 2003. The status of strategic human resource management in Trinidad and Tobago. Journal of Eastern Caribbean Studies 28 (1), 1–16.

Baum, T., 2007. Human resource in tourism: still waiting for change. Tourism Management 28 (6), 1383–1399.

Baum, T., 2012. Human resource management in tourism: a small island perspective. International Journal of Culture, Tourism and Hospitality Research 6 (2), 124–132.

Björkman, I., Lervik, E.J., 2007. Transferring HR practices with multinational corporations. Human Resource Management Journal 17 (4), 320–335.

Boxall, P., Purcell, J., 2011. Strategy and Human Resource Management, 3rd edn. Palgrave Macmillan, Basingstoke and New York.

Brewster, C., Mayrhofr, W., Moreley, M. (Eds.), 2004. Human Resource Management in Europe. Evidence of Convergence? Oxford, Elsevier/Butterworth-Heinemann.

Brewster, C., Mayrhofer, W., 2012. Comparative human resource management: an introduction. In: Brewster, C., Mayrhofer, W. (Eds.), Handbook of Research on Comparative Human Resource Management. Edward Elgar, Cheltenham, pp. 1–23.

Chow, I.H., 2004. The impact of institutional context on human resource management in three Chinese societies. Employee Relations 26 (6), 626–642.

Cooper, K., 2005. The missing link in people strategies. Customer Inter@section Solutions 24 (5), 48–50.

Darvish, H., Moogali, A., Moosavi, M., Panahi, B., 2012. Survey relationship between human resources roles and human resource competencies. International Journal of Academic Research in Business and Social Science 2 (9), 254–265.

Davidson, M.C.G., McPhail, R., Barry, S., 2011. Hospitality HRM: past, present and the future. International Journal of Contemporary Hospitality Management 23 (4), 498–516.

DNP, 2014. Statistical Year Book of Maldives 2014. Department of National Planning. Retrieved from: http://planning.gov.mv/yearbook2014/ (accessed 7 June 2015).

Eisenhardt, K., 1989. Building theories from case study research. Academy of Management Review 14 (4), 532–550.

Gilbert, C., De Winne, S., Sels, L., 2011. The influence of line managers and HR department on employees' affective commitment. International Journal of Human Resource Management 22 (8), 1618–1637.

Guest, D., 2011. Human resource management and performance: still searching for some answers. Human Resource Management Journal 21, 3–13.

Hamid, I.H., 2015. "1.4 million figure for 2014 tourist arrivals incorrect", says Tourism Minister. Retrieved from: http://minivannewsarchive.com/business/1-4-million-figure-for-2014-tourist-arrivals-incorrect-says-tourism-minister-91961#sthash.mmPPW6o8.dpbs (accessed 27 September 2015).

Jackson, S., Seo, J., 2010. The greening of strategic HRM scholarship. Organisation Management Journal 7 (4), 278–290.

Janssens, M., Steyaert, C., 2009. HRM and Performance: A Plea for Reflexivity in HRM Studies. Journal of Management Studies 46, 143–155.

Knox, A., 2002. HRM in the Australian luxury hotel industry: signs of innovation? Employment Relations Record 2 (2), 59–68.

Kohont, A., Brewster, C., 2014. The roles and competencies of HR managers in Slovenian multinational companies. Baltic Journal of Management 9 (3), 294–313.

Kramar, R., 2014. Beyond strategic human resource management: is sustainable human resource management the next approach? International Journal of Human Resource Management 25 (8), 1069–1089.

Lawler, E., Mohrman, S., 2003. HR as a strategic partner: what does it take to make it happen? Human Resource Planning 26 (3), 15–30.

Lengnick-Hall, M.L., Lengnick-Hall, C.A., Andrade, L.S., Drake, S., 2009. Strategic human resource management: the evolution of the field. Human Resource Management Review 19 (2), 64–85.

Marchington, M., Wilkinson, A., 2012. Human Resource Management at Work, 5th edn. Chartered Institute of Personnel Development, London.

Maxwell, G.A., Watson, S., 2006. Perspectives on line managers in human resource management: Hilton International's UK hotels. International Journal of Human Resource Management 17 (6), 1152–1170.

Miles, M.B., Huberman, A.M., 1994. Qualitative Data Analysis. Sage, Newbury Park, CA.

Ministry of Tourism, Arts and Culture (MTAC), 2014. Tourism Year Book 2014. Ministry of Tourism, Arts and Culture. Available at: *http://www.tourism.gov.mv/pubs/yearbook2014.pdf* (accessed 21 July 2015).

Naidu, S., Chand, A., 2014. A comparative analysis of best human resource management practices in the hotel sector of Samoa and Tonga. Personnel Review 43 (5), 798–815.

Najeeb, A., 2011. HRM in paradise: similar or different? A study of tourist resorts in the Maldives. Employment Relations Record 11 (1), 1–18.

Najeeb, A., 2013. The role of HR actors in designing and implementing HRM in resorts in the Maldives. Employee Relations 35 (6), 593–612.

Najeeb, A., 2014. "Not for us, but for them": hospitality industry stakeholder views on design and implementation challenges of Maldivian employment legislation. Labour and Industry 24 (2), 124–145.

Nankervis, A., Debrah, Y., 1995. Human resource management in hotels: a comparative study. Tourism Management 16 (7), 507–513.

Nankervis, A.R., Stanton, P., Foley, P., 2012. Exploring the rhetoric and reality of performance management systems and organisational effectiveness – evidence from Australia. Research and Practice in Human Resource Management 20 (1), 40–56.

Peters, P., Heusinkveld, S., 2010. Institutional explanations for managers' attitudes towards telehomeworking. Human Relations 63 (1), 107–135.

Purcell, J., Kinnie, N., 2007. HRM and business performance. In: Boxall, P., Purcell, J. (Eds.), The Oxford Handbook of Human Resource Management. Oxford University Press, Oxford, pp. 533–551.

Ramlall, S.J., 2006. Identifying and understanding HR competencies and their relationship to organizational practices. Applied Human Resource Management Research 11 (1), 27–38.

Rowley, C., Warner, M., 2013. Strategic challenges and issues for Chinese managers and management in the global economy. Asia Pacific Business Review 19 (4), 617–624.

Rupidara, N.S., McGraw, P., 2011. The role of actors in configuring HR systems within multinational subsidiaries. Human Resource Management Review 21 (3), 174–185.

Schuler, R., Jackson, S., 1987. Linking competitive strategies with the human resource management practices. Academy of Management Executive 1, 207–219.

Schuler, R.S., Budhwar, P., Florkowski, G.W., 2002. International human resource management: review and critique. International Journal of Management Reviews 4 (1), 41–70.

Stanton, P., Young, S., Bartram, T., Leggat, S.G., 2010. Singing the same song: translating HRM messages across management hierarchies in Australian hospitals. International Journal of Human Resource Management 21 (4), 567–581.

Steers, R.M., Nordon, L., Sanchez-Runde, C.J., 2013. Management Across Cultures: Developing Global Competencies. Cambridge University Press, Cambridge.

Storey, J., 1992. Developments in the Management of Human Resources: An Analytical Review. Blackwell, London.

Taylor, M., Finley, D., 2008. Strategic human resource management in U.S. luxury resorts – a case study. Journal of Human Resources in Hospitality and Tourism 8 (1), 82–95.

Tompkins, J., 2002. Strategic human resources management in government: unresolved issues. Public Personnel Management 31 (1), 95–110.

Ulrich, D., 1997. Human Resource Champions: The Next Agenda for Adding Value and Delivering Results. Harvard Business Press, Boston, MA.

Ulrich, D., 1998. A new mandate for human resources. Harvard Business Review 76 (1), 124–134.

Ulrich, D., Brockbank, W., Ulrich, M., Younger, J., 2013. Global HR Competencies: Mastering Competitive Value from the Outside In. McGraw-Hill, Boston, USA.

Ulrich, D., Younger, J., Brockbank, W., Ulrich, M., 2012. The New HR Competencies – Business Partnering from the Outside In. RBL Group, Boston, MA.

Van Gestel, N., Nyberg, D., 2009. Translating national policy changes into local HRM practices. Personnel Review 38 (5), 544–559.

Wright, P.M., McMahan, G.C., 1992. Theoretical perspectives for strategic human resource management. Journal of Management 18 (2), 295–320.

Yin, R., 1994. Case Study Research. Sage, Newbury Park, CA.

CHAPTER 8

The quality of working Australia and its relevance for HRM and organisational effectiveness in the Asia Pacific

J. Connell, J. Burgess

INTRODUCTION

This chapter draws from a Quality of Work project in Australia that was conducted in 2013 (Burgess et al., 2013). The purpose of this chapter is to consider the job quality (JQ) framework that was developed for the project and assess the project findings within the context of strategic human resource management (HRM), particularly in terms of employee well-being as an important component of organisational performance and effectiveness. While there is existing literature addressing how strategic HRM approaches can potentially improve employee performance and well-being (Birdi et al., 2008; Clarke and Hill, 2012) there is a lack of Australian data that considers quality work and HRM across a number of sectors using a JQ framework. The project was focused at the firm-level and it aimed to:

> *Identify practical strategies to improve organisational effectiveness (OE) through closer links between JQ and other work-related factors.*

The chapter begins by outlining key concepts related to understanding the quality of work, strategic HRM and employee well-being. A JQ framework is presented as a basis for analysis of the linkages between these concepts. The case studies and the research methods are then outlined. The following sections discuss the findings from the project and then compare and contrast the findings of the case-study organisations with the JQ framework. Next, the conclusions and implications for research and for HRM practice are presented before, finally, the application of JQ analysis to HRM and OE in Asia is considered.

*Asia Pacific Human Resource Management
and Organisational Effectiveness*
ISBN 978-0-08-100643-6

LITERATURE REVIEW

What is job quality and why does it matter?

The 'quality of work' is a nebulous concept which can be viewed from many perspectives and disciplines. However, following an extensive literature review, it was determined that JQ is associated with a focus on employee well-being as a critical contributor to organisational effectiveness. This approach is consistent with that followed by other researchers who maintain that 'the quality of work life or job quality is constituted by the set of work features which foster the well-being of the worker' (Green, 2006: 9).

The rationale for this perspective is that it is through work that the material and psychological benefits and costs of employment are allocated. Green (2006) applied Amartya Sen's 'capability' approach to the assessment of job quality. Sen developed a notion of well-being based upon '… a general approach that concentrates on the capabilities of people to do things – and the freedom to lead lives – that they have reason to value' (Sen, 1999: 85). The focus on capabilities and freedoms partly circumvents problems of differences in preferences, value judgments and interpersonal comparisons that beset attempts to measure well-being for different people. More recently, this has been explained as a demand for a 'holistic' management style, in Indian and Chinese workplaces in particular, 'which allows strategies, processes and techniques that energize people and aligns resources to emerging opportunities and challenges. The holistic imagination offers the possibility for the first time for corporate leaders to enhance the performance of their human and other resources, but through extensive employee participation' (Nankervis, Cooke, Chatterjee and Warner, 2013: 20).

Work quality relates to the extent to which a job offers workers a high capability to achieve the things they value. This may include the ability to exercise influence over their work, to pursue their personal and work-related goals, and variations between workers as to the needs they choose to prioritise (Eurofound, 2012: 10). When reviewing JQ in Europe, Holman (2012: 476) similarly defined JQ as the extent to which a job fosters beneficial outcomes for the employee, noting in particular the importance of psychological well-being, physical well-being and positive attitudes such as job satisfaction. In Asian workplaces, spiritual and identity characteristics may also be of significance (Chatterjee, 2009a, 2009b; Nankervis et al., 2013). The Eurofound (2012: 10) project builds on these ideas to develop a potential framework for isolating a limited number of key job characteristics that are linked to well-being in the world of work.

JQ is important at a number of levels. First, it impacts on worker well-being and the well-being of their family member, for example through the quality of workers' relationships and the health and well-being of their children and others within their relationships and households (see, for example, Bardoel et al., 2008). These aspects, including the perceived social responsibility of employers to extended families and local communities, are often crucial in many Asian workplaces. Such consequences have been observed in Australia (Knox et al., 2011; Pocock et al., 2008). A 2002 OECD report which focused on work–family reconciliation in Australia, Denmark and the Netherlands is cited by Pocock et al. (2008), who noted that a good work–family balance is conducive to, among other things, resilience in the face of the stresses of modern life, better child development outcomes and notably significant savings in health costs (2008: 6). Contributions in the psychological literature from the likes of Bandura (1982), Jahoda (1982) and Warr (1987) have proposed that one's work is an important source of the factors that promote psychological well-being, such as a sense of purpose, connectedness, self-identity, self-esteem and self-efficacy, and these factors also appear in research conducted within Asian organisations (see, for example, Chatterjee 2001; Chatterjee and Pearson, 2006; Chatterjee, 2009b). Self-determination theory offers a further approach that considers the psychological needs that promote an individual's inherent personal growth tendencies and motivation. Specifically, three basic needs relating to competence, relatedness and autonomy have been identified that underlie positive personal and social development and, in turn, personal well-being (Ryan and Deci, 2000: 68).

Within the organisational context, JQ impacts upon worker performance and, in turn, organisational performance and effectiveness. There is evidence that the job quality/well-being relationships outlined here may act as significant mediators in the job quality/productivity nexus. In their study of HR practices, operational practices and the impacts on productivity, Birdi et al. (2008) investigated the practices of 308 organisations over more than twenty years. They identified that the practice most likely to affect organisational productivity was employee empowerment, indicating that, not only does empowerment promote an improved quality of work life, but it also has economic value. In developing a JQ framework it is important to indicate not only why and how JQ is important for employee well-being but also how JQ may be linked to employee and organisational performance and effectiveness. This provides a context for developing a JQ agenda as part of an organisation's strategic HRM

programme which encompasses both employee and organisational effectiveness objectives.

Job quality and strategic HRM

Beer et al. (2015: 427) pointed out that human resource management as a
discipline is now more than 30 years old. The emergence of strategic human
resource management (SHRM) in the latter decades of the twentieth century (Wright and MacMahan, 1992) focused on empirically testing the link
between HRM and long-term organisational effectiveness. However, economic measures of firm performance largely neglected employee well-
being and societal well-being (with some exceptions such as Pfeffer, 1994,
1998). Moreover, Beer et al. (2015) argued against the view that the only
purpose of the firm is to maximise shareholder value, claiming that HRM
needs to have a broader focus if it is to 'catch up with leading-edge CEOs
and their companies, who are redefining the purpose of the firm and consequently their HRM practice in a way first articulated 30 years ago by Beer
et al. (1984)' (p. 427).

One 'leading edge CEO' who transformed his business is Vineet Nayar,
CEO of HCL Technologies and author of *Employees First, Customers Second*
(2010a). His transformational change strategy led him to invert the traditional organisational pyramid, making support functions and executives
accountable to frontline workers rather than the other way around. He also
recast the CEO's role, transferring the ownership of change from the CEO's
office to employees. As a result Nayar stated that when the global downturn
began, 'Rather than engage in layoffs or restructuring, I asked employees for
ways to help us get through the bad times. They offered many suggestions.
Some of them related to cost-cutting, but most of them focused on how to
increase revenues' (2010b: 113). Thus, when other IT businesses that did not
take an employee-inclusive approach collapsed, HCL grew its business by
20 per cent during the worst year of the global recession. Other Asian companies such as the Tata Group, Reliance and Infosys in India, and Alibaba,
Lenovo and Huawei in China, have adopted similar participative employee
strategies reflecting their cultural traditions, resulting in similarly positive
outcomes.

Beer et al.'s (1984) Harvard model acknowledges a range of organisational stakeholders, not just shareholders but also employees, trade unions,
management, community and government. Many other HRM models
followed, such as the Michigan model of HRM (1984) which focuses on
the role of personnel departments and processes, using a short-term focus

and cost minimisation as the key evaluation criteria (see Guest, 1987). Guest's 'human resource systems' (1987) builds on the Harvard model with an additional three categories: policy formulation and the management of change, employee appraisal, training and development and communication systems (Cakar et al., 2003). The Warwick model of HRM (1992) also built on the Harvard model but has a stronger focus on strategy.

In this chapter, we apply the Harvard framework as it can be more closely associated with the quality of work. Beer et al. (2015) claimed that it applies a social systems perspective acknowledging the influence and relevance of multiple stakeholders (internal and external), their social interactions and their influence on HRM policy choices (p. 427).

Consequently, there is support for the notion that SHRM, and more specifically HR managers, have a key role to play in supporting employee well-being (Brown et al., 2009) and in the design of quality jobs. One of the core principles of SHRM is that organisational performance is heavily influenced by the way in which employees are managed. Thus failure to pay attention to well-being in the workplace can have a negative effect on the sustainability of organisational performance at a number of levels (Hope-Hailey et al., 2005). From an HRM perspective, well-being has also been associated with a combination of structural factors such as work organisation and job design, and social and environmental factors (such as supervisor/peer support and work relationships). While not unequivocal, the majority of studies have reported a positive relationship between HRM practices and overall corporate performance (Richard and Johnson, 2001; Jensen, 2005).

There is evidence of the need to develop innovative and flexible HRM practices that are designed to increase levels of employee engagement, reduce turnover and maximise skill utilisation when endeavouring to meet both organisational and employee workplace needs (Clarke and Hill, 2012; Dorio et al., 2008). Specifically, extensive recruitment, selection and training procedures; formal information sharing, attitude assessment, job design, grievance procedures and labour-management participation programmes; and performance appraisal, promotion and incentive compensation systems that recognise and reward employee merit have all been widely linked with organisational effectiveness (Huselid, 2005).

In recent years many studies have focused on the relationship between HRM practices and organisational performance and effectiveness, with a view to identifying practices that will ensure excellence and high performance at the strategic business level (Guest et al., 2003, 2004). Strategic HRM practices have been associated with improvements in key indicators such as employee turnover, job satisfaction, productivity and financial performance (Richard and Johnson, 2001).

Recent literature (Boxall, 2012) has focused on high performance work systems (HPWS) constituting a bundle of HRM practices intended to enhance firm performance by improving employee attitudes and behaviours. HPWS have been associated with positive employee and workplace outcomes including diversity, family-friendly workplaces and job security, among other factors (Gooderham et al., 2008; Richard and Johnson, 2001). Overall, there appears to be some agreement that these practices include attention to selection, training, mentoring, incentives and knowledge-sharing mechanisms.

The SHRM literature suggests that employee well-being counts not only for the individual employee but also fits into an integrated programme that links employee well-being to organisational effectiveness. As such, it is important to understand JQ and its determinants and evaluate how a JQ programme can be developed within the organisation.

DEVELOPING A JQ FRAMEWORK IN AUSTRALIA

The growing focus on work quality as a policy issue in Europe has seen the emergence of an extensive suite of measures and indicators of JQ being systematically applied across Europe on a regular basis (Burgess et al., 2013). The methodology around JQ involves the identification of those factors that contribute to JQ, the assignment of indicators to the identified attributes and the grouping of the attributes into broad groupings of strategic factors supporting JQ. The purpose behind the evaluation of JQ is to develop a holistic interpretation of JQ (Connell and Burgess, 2014) that incorporates many different aspects of well-being from pay through to safety and job satisfaction.

The European Working Conditions Survey (EWCS) and the European Job Quality Index are two of the main instruments used to assess job quality in EU organisations. The EWCS is conducted every five years, covering 34 countries and 40,000 participants. The regular JQ assessments provide a systematic data set that reports on the progress of JQ within the EU as a whole as well as differences by country, sector, employee and organisational profiles. The systematic data set provides a link to HRM policy development concerning important issues such as training, occupational health and safety, equal employment opportunity (EEO), minimum pay and the employment contract.

This extensive database is used to explore the quality of work and employment, its impact on health and well-being at work, work organisation, the provision of sustainable work for an aging population, working conditions profiles for different sectors, employability and security, working hours and work–life balance, and gender differences (Eurofound, 2012). The EWCS forms part of the European Observatory on Working Conditions (EOWC) which aims to provide regular updates and information on the quality of work and working conditions in European member states (Burgess et al., 2013).

The Australian study conducted in 2013 (Burgess et al., 2013) utilised the EU JQ framework to the extent that key groupings or attributes of JQ were identified. It was an exploratory study and the analysis was limited to a small number of organisations and a limited number of participants. The purpose was to identify the extent to which employees saw JQ attributes as linked to their well-being.

Following an extensive review of the job quality/quality work literature, a quality of work framework was constructed for the study reported here based on the Eurofound 2012 surveys (p. 20). The generic dimensions of the JQ framework that were considered as being relevant to Australia were as follows:

- *Dimension 1 – Job prospects*: job security, recognition (being given credit for effective work, etc.) and career progression (potential for advancement).
- *Dimension 2 – Extrinsic job quality*: comprised earnings (satisfaction with earnings), a good physical environment: safety aspects, a pleasant work environment, level of physical and posture-related hazards.
- *Dimension 3 – Intrinsic job quality*: work itself, meaningfulness of work, interesting work, skills and discretion, skills and autonomy (ability to influence decisions, use full range of skills, apply own ideas), training access (skill development and training can influence job prospects), work intensity, pace of work and work pressures, emotional/value conflict demands, dealing with angry clients/job requires 'emotional labour', good social environment, relations at work, direct supervision (manager helps and supports you), level of consultation, organisational support (positive work environment).

- *Dimension 4: Working time quality/work–life balance/fit*: impact of work on home/family life; duration/work scheduling discretion/flexibility, working hours, shift patterns, flexible work arrangements, impact of technology on working time arrangements (blurring of work/life boundaries).

METHODOLOGY

Case-study protocol

For the purpose of the case studies, the protocol adopted was exploratory with the aim of covering organisations that differed in size, sector, ownership and location. In total, nine organisations were analysed for the case studies. The selection of the case studies involved purposeful and convenience criteria. The purposeful criteria were to ensure that the cases included large and small businesses, were distributed across sectors and in particular included sectors that have large numbers of employees. The purposeful criteria were determined by time and resources (see Table 8.1 below for the case-study details). The purpose of the case studies was to examine whether the JQ typology had relevance and application across the range of different organisations that participated in the study.

The case studies

The case-study stage of the research project concerned the examination of a number of workplaces in order to identify the JQ issues that were relevant at each and to consider how specific JQ issues were being addressed. Although case-study research can be illustrative and purposeful it is not necessarily representative. However, it can assist in identifying issues and challenges that are likely to apply across workplaces in Australia. Case-study research has a number of advantages that include the reduced time and costs associated with research, the ability to target cases towards either representative or extreme example cases, the multiple levels of data collection that can be employed and the depth of analysis it supports (Eisenhardt, 1989; Yin, 2009).

In this instance, the case studies were used to inform and develop practice and policy recommendations. The principles driving case-study selection concerned the diversity of the organisations across a range of characteristics.

Table 8.1 outlines the case studies, locations, sector, industry and total number of employees, indicating diversity by location, size, sector and industry.

Table 8.1 Participating case study organisations

Case study identifier	Workplace location	Sector	Industry	No. of employees
ResourceCo	Western Australia	Private	Resources	12,000
MiningCo	Western Australia	Private	Mining	1,108
ConstructionSvsCo	Western Australia	Private	Construction services	35
ManufactureCo	Western Australia	Private	Manufacturing	100
LocGov	Sydney, New South Wales	Public	Local government	1,000
TAFE	Melbourne, Victoria	Public	Vocational education and training	2,000
AgedCareCo	Melbourne, Victoria	Private	Health – aged care	100
EnergyCo	Gladstone, Queensland	Private	Energy	270
ConsultCo	Perth, Western Australia and Sydney, NSW	Private	Professional services/ consulting	500

Case-study analysis

The information collected from each case study was assimilated and analysed. Organisational documents were reviewed, and interviews and focus groups were conducted to identify relevant key themes and issues. In total, 42 interviews and nine focus groups were conducted across the case studies. As can be determined, most of the participants were male, between the ages of 25 and 44 years and in possession of formal qualifications (vocational qualifications or a degree). Participant positions were divided between 48 per cent managers and supervisors, and 52 per cent non-managers. Non-managers included professional services, administrators, trades workers, labourers and other similar positions. The majority of participants were full-time permanent staff (90 per cent) and (51 per cent) had worked with the case-study organisation for more than five years. Around one-third of participants worked between 40 and 50 hours per week, 33 per cent said that they usually work weekends and the same proportion indicated that they did some work from home. (See Table 8.2 for details.)

Although the case studies were not representative of Australian organisations nor the workforce (across age, gender, occupation, industry, working

Table 8.2 Quality work case-study participant demographics (n = 69)

Gender	N and (%)	Tenure (organisation)	N and (%)
Male	40 (58%)	1–5 years	34 (49%)
Female	29 (42%)	≥5 years	35 (51%)
Age (years)		**Highest education level**	
≤24	2 (1%)	Not completed year 12	10 (15%)
25–44	28 (42%)	Completed year 12	13 (19%)
45–54	20 (29%)	Skilled vocational	5 (7%)
≥55	19 (28%)	Qualifications diploma/degree/ postgraduate	41 (59%)
Occupation level		**Hours worked per week**	
Manager/ supervisor	33 (48%)	20–35 hours	9 (13%)
		35–40 hours	24 (33%)
Non-manager	36 (52%)	40–50 hours	23 (32%)
		≥55 hours	13 (22%)
Employment status		**Work weekends/from home**	
Full time Permanent	62 (90%)	Weekends **Yes**	23 (33%)
		Weekends **No**	46 (69%)
Part time	4 (6%)	Work from Home **Yes**	23 (33%)
Casual/other	3 (4%)	Work from Home **No**	46 (69%)

hours, tenure), the purpose of the study was to scope the relevance of the JQ framework to employee well-being as an important component of overall organisational effectiveness.

RESEARCH FINDINGS

The broad findings from across the case studies are as follows. Firstly, the JQ framework developed for the study was found to resonate with all participants involved in this study (both managers and non-managers) in identifying factors that influenced their quality of work and motivation, suggesting that it is a useful framework and process for identifying job quality issues within specific workplaces.

Secondly, the case-study findings showed that employees who participated in the case studies were satisfied with the attributes of JQ as identified within the JQ framework. During many of the case-study interviews and focus groups, participants expressed the passion they had for their work and their strong commitment to their organisation and clients. This was especially the case for the Aged Care, TAFE, Local Government and Consulting case studies. Notwithstanding the biases and preliminary nature of the research, it was able to identify what the participants involved in this study saw as being important in their work satisfaction.

Apart from positive findings, the analysis indicated that JQ is important in developing commitment and reducing employee turnover, factors which are both closely associated with organisational performance and effectiveness. That is, there are important aspects of JQ that require ongoing monitoring and development. For example, HR managers can help to improve employee commitment and retention rates, thus increasing productivity and reducing costs. In several organisations participants indicated that their pay was below what they could earn elsewhere in the industry/region, but that their current quality of work was a key factor in retaining them – this was evident for EnergyCo, LocGov, TAFE, ResourceCo and ConsultCo. This is important in those sectors where pay is constrained by public sector wage caps or in underpaid care work. Here, important issues for employees included the work rosters, the quality of management and their levels of job satisfaction, lifestyle and social relations at work. There were differences across workplaces, industries and occupations as JQ issues and challenges are contextually dependent.

Another important contextual factor is the state of the business cycle: a period of strong economic growth is usually associated with improving JQ as job security increases and organisations attempt to retain staff. Changing external market conditions and changes to public sector funding had an impact at ResourceCo, EnergyCo, TAFE and LocGov, making employees feel that job insecurity was increasing. Another mechanism where these external conditions manifest themselves was through increasing job intensity and extended working hours. Two senior managers at MiningCo stated that their responses to the case-study questions would probably change according to the business lifecycle and/or their particular career stage. At the time of the research, the business was healthy and they had a great order book which influenced its employees' perceptions of job security. There were also differences that were generated by local labour conditions, the age of employees and the region in which the workplace is located. What this suggests is that even where business cycle conditions are deteriorating, HR can address JQ through measures associated with the development of intrinsic JQ through particular programmes and initiatives as outlined in the next section with regard to ConsultCo and other organisations.

In all cases, there were generally high levels of job satisfaction, trust in management, a commitment to the organisation and a good working environment. Once again, this is clearly not the case across all organisations.

Career development, or a lack of an evident career path, was evident at TAFE and AgedCareCo as factors undermining JQ. At MiningCo a key challenge was developing the skills of line managers to carry through programmes aimed at increasing employee commitment, job autonomy and employee skill development. Work–life balance and working hours (schedules and shift patterns) emerged as issues in several case studies (LocGov, ConstructionSvsCo, TAFE and ManufactureCo). In some of the cases, workplace health and safety concerns (WH&S) were ongoing issues that were linked to the sector – mining, aged care, construction – but appeared to be generally taken seriously by HR managers in terms of the development of comprehensive organisational programmes. The main job quality issues identified in the specific case studies are summarised in Table 8.2. As discussed earlier, this study set out to (1) identify strategies to improve job quality and (2) examine associations between job quality and other work-related factors. The key factors related to both are outlined in Table 8.3 and indicate that the JQ issues are sector, industry and organisationally dependent.

Each dimension and factor of the JQ framework was considered important by some participants, although the intrinsic JQ dimensions were consistently ranked as being more important overall. Intrinsic JQ conditions can be developed through effectively designed and implemented HRM programmes. There is a key contribution that HRM can play in employee well-being and organisational effectiveness. Here, there appears to be some resonance with Herzberg's two-factor motivational theory (Herzberg, 1967), whereby hygiene factors such as job security, earnings and work conditions do not give positive satisfaction, but dissatisfaction results from their absence. Conversely, the 'motivators' (the intrinsic work factors) were considered to motivate our case-study participants and lead to greater organisational effectiveness. Specifically, a good work environment and reasonable earnings were expected by our sample group. It was the other factors such as job prospects, recognition, and the meaningfulness of their work, the quality of supervision and the ability to balance their work and life at different stages of their lifecycles that were considered important. These are conditions that can be developed within the organisation and are not dependent on external environmental factors.

Some of the case-study organisations in the resources sector utilise mobile workforces, specifically fly-in-fly-out workers (FIFO) who reside in capital cities and fly to work sites for extended employment shifts (Rainnie et al., 2014). MiningCo and ResourceCo had endeavoured to improve their

Table 8.3 The main job quality topics identified from the case studies

Case study	Job quality challenges
MiningCo	OH&S; the quality of workplace supervision and its impact on consultation, communication and workforce autonomy. MiningCo has been awarded due to specialist recruitment/ training developed specifically for the hiring of Indigenous employees, widespread health programme aimed at preventative care and Family Support programme in place for carers.
ResourceCo	Leadership and communication was the single most important factor influencing the quality of work and biggest lever for employee engagement. Direct employee engagement advocated and practised – shift coordinators enable supervisors to spend time out in the field with the staff on site rather than sitting behind a desk. The ability for employees to develop, change jobs/sites considered key for employee retention.
EnergyCo	The ageing workforce will impact over next five years. Approach to attracting, recruiting, retaining apprentices/ trainees and engineering graduates a stand-out activity, also the nine-day fortnight due to work–life balance. All participants said earnings were adequate, but when compared to those offered in competing industries they were not as high. Satisfaction expressed with other conditions, leadership and workplace culture.
AgedCareCo	Most participants felt that their salary/benefits were inadequate for the work undertaken. Almost all considered their work meaningful/interesting, their skills crucial, and that they have adequate job autonomy. Main concern is the 'intensity of the work' and projected future workload consequent on the transition towards more high care places.
TAFE	Challenges are linked to structural and funding changes in the sector impacting on job security and career opportunities. Another challenge is increased work intensity and growing administrative burdens. Earnings regarded as low compared to comparable jobs elsewhere but recognition of high job satisfaction, good social environment and opportunities for skill development and job autonomy.
LocGov	Challenges concerned scheduling of work/shift patterns, and resolving different demands (from the organisation and clients). Perceived lack of job security was also an issue. Some respondents also mentioned the lack of work flexibility and work–life balance, the pace of work/work pressures, lack of autonomy and opportunities to use their skills as other challenges.

Continued

Table 8.3 The main job quality topics identified from the case studies—cont'd

Case study	Job quality challenges
Construction SvsCo	'Shop floor' employees identified earnings and recognition as key issues. Managers recognised the importance of leadership and communication and that the latter required greater attention in their workplace. Work–life balance also recognised as important concerning the manner in which the company allows individuals to balance work with family commitments.
ConsultCo	Low pay, relative to elsewhere, was offset by high job satisfaction through challenging work, high levels of autonomy, career advancement, teamwork and being associated with a prestigious organisation. These JQ aspects provided employees with high levels of intrinsic job quality which contributed to the encouragement of innovation and productivity.
ManufactureCo	Job prospects, the work itself, meaningfulness of work, organisational support, skills/autonomy and good relations with colleagues were key issues identified as being important to retention and employee commitment. Some employees regarded work–life balance as an important factor.

remote worksites as well as working towards improving worker health and well-being. There were issues related to job security in some cases, but they were also linked to changes and challenges facing the sector. There were also differences indicated by age group and occupation. No one factor stood out as being a challenge related to all cases, but issues identified in the literature such as work–life balance, working time (especially rosters), job security and career path development were prominent in many of the case studies. Skill use and training and development were also identified as important aspects of career development and contributed to participants' perceptions of job prospects. In some case-study organisations, there was a need for clearer succession planning and identification of talent pipelines.

In comparison with earlier surveys of job quality in Australia, the findings presented here have some resonance. The majority of case-study participants enjoyed their job and were committed to their work and their organisation, a finding from an earlier survey on job quality (Considine and Callus, 2001). There are apparently bundles or attributes of jobs linked to JQ that are important in attracting and retaining employees, and facilitating commitment. While JQ is important, it is also apparent that the quality of management is an important factor that influences all of its dimensions, especially intrinsic JQ. Moreover, intrinsic job features are an important factor in terms of organisational effectiveness. However, context does matter in terms of location, interactions with clients, the industry, the business cycle and the age of the employee (Considine and Callus, 2001; Morehead et al., 1997).

DISCUSSION

Job quality and strategic HRM

Due to the perceived centrality of intrinsic JQ conditions the quality of leadership and management is implicated as being a critical factor influencing JQ. However, there is a lack of current literature linking the two factors. Instead, extant research tends to focus on aspects such as leadership and employee commitment (Wallace et al., 2013), job satisfaction (Voon et al., 2011) and employee performance (Carter et al., 2013). The case-study findings revealed in particular that 'direct supervision' is important due to the supervisor's influence on employees' daily work. Several senior managers in our sample group also discussed the importance of employees being able to communicate directly with their supervisors as being an important element of JQ and an important contributor to organisational performance and effectiveness. Leadership and management are pivotal since they also impact upon other factors identified in shaping JQ. Studies conducted in China and India have reported similar findings (Chatterjee, 2001, 2009a, 2009b).

An association with JQ and employee well-being (Holman, 2012) was also supported, indicating that HR managers would be well-advised to work with leaders and managers to ensure that they seek to discuss employees' expectations and aim to provide appropriate career paths according to lifecycles and other circumstances, and to assess job design and workplace systems in order to identify areas where flexibility may be offered.

Nurturing ownership and autonomy within work teams also stood out from the case-study analysis as an important strategy for the promotion of job quality. An example was the 'Just Do It' programme (see LocGov case study) which encourages employees to implement small changes without having to seek approval from higher up the organisation. This programme was cited as a highly positive initiative that empowers employees and makes them proud of the organisation – resonating with the research conducted by Ryan and Deci (2000) relating positive personal and social development to well-being. This finding also reflects the results obtained from studies conducted in several Asian countries (Chatterjee and Pearson, 2006).

These findings also resonate with the Australian Institute of Management (AIM) surveys of Australian business leaders and managers conducted for the past three years (2010–12). The (AIM, 2012) survey comprised 1,700 respondents. In common with the previous surveys, many AIM respondents reported that their greatest skills gap was in 'middle management' (40 per cent) with the main problem area being 'leadership' (45 per cent). Some organisations managed to avoid these gaps, attributing this to their 'strong commitment to training and development' (69 per cent), 'promoting internal job candidates' (58 per cent) and 'using internal resources to boost training' (52 per cent) indicating a commitment to talent management. Others reported that they do not have succession planning in place (43 per cent), had poorly defined job roles and unclear employee expectations (32 per cent) and only 14 per cent were retaining older workers indicating an urgent need for talent management strategies.

The case-study findings and analysis highlight a number of benefits in relation to both employees and organisations of ensuring that various job quality factors, especially intrinsic JQ, are being recognised and addressed. These benefits include:

- attracting and retaining employees (see Clarke et al., 2012);
- capitalising on employees' skills and abilities (Sen, 1999; Guest; 2002, Guest et al., 2006);
- improving employee engagement/passion for the job (Birdi et al., 2008);
- creating a pleasant/supportive work environment conducive to employee well-being (Holman, 2012).

Many of the case-study participants were acutely aware of the work quality and commitment nexus. Some employers/managers were consciously utilising aspects of job quality as a way of motivating workers and striving to match the requirements of jobs to worker preferences, a process that often commences with attraction, recruitment and corporate branding.

To operationalise aspects of the JQ framework it is proposed that a number of factors need to be considered at the organisational level to improve JQ. HR, leaders and managers would be advised to consider the provision of appropriate career paths and training and development according to life-cycles and discuss employer/employee expectations, promote a supportive workplace culture; encourage open communication/contribution of ideas, check job design/workplace systems to identify areas where flexibility may be offered, and nurture ownership and autonomy in the workplace. Some of these factors would also seem appropriate in Asian organisations.

As identified by Birdi et al. (2008), Boxall (2012) and Connell and Burgess (2014), there are bundles or attributes of jobs (such as those discussed here) that are associated with job quality and are important in attracting and retaining employees and facilitating commitment.

Perhaps the HR 'theory' that is closest to the job quality framework presented here is that created by Guest (1987) who proposed four human resource goals (discussed earlier) that 'provide a framework for identifying areas of human resource policy' that was intended to influence employee/organisational outcomes. However, 24 years after his 1987 article, Guest (2011) stated that 'after over two decades of extensive research, we are still unable to answer core questions about the relationship between human resource management and performance' (p. 3). Guest (2011) maintained that part of the problem is that most of the research on HRM and performance makes it difficult to be confident about cause and effect, suggesting that more longitudinal studies are recommended. Perhaps one recommendation for future research could therefore include a longitudinal study using the JQ framework in order to assist in the search to close the knowledge gap between HRM and performance.

CONCLUSION

In the Asian context, the challenges of linking HRM practices associated with JQ to organisational effectiveness are likely to be similar to those faced in Australia. These include: population ageing and changing demographics, the global financial crisis and organisational adjustment, skill development and skill shortages, employee attraction and retention, leadership development and talent management, and the need for more effective utilisation of groups that are under-represented in the workforce such as the young, ageing workers and women (ILO, 1997; Asian Development Bank, 2002; Chan and Burgess, 2011; McDonnell et al., 2012; Burgess and Connell, 2013).

However, there is much diversity among the various countries that constitute Asia. Notably, South Korea, Hong Kong and Singapore have the highest incomes and growth rates. Despite the plethora of studies on the determinants of Asian growth, there has been little work conducted to date to consider how this growth has affected the quality of work in the region (Seguino, 2010). Seguino (2010) commented that, while the rapid growth in some Asian economies has raised absolute levels of living standards, measured by a wide array of indicators (such as women's access to jobs, education and workforce share), poverty and inequality persist.

Thus, improving the quality of jobs remains a challenge in developing Asia as approximately half of all employment is either of a vulnerable nature or takes place on an informal basis (Sziraczki et al., 2011). Globalisation can contribute to employment growth but open markets alone are unlikely to create enough good quality jobs. For example, many new jobs in the service sector are low skilled and offer low pay, while sometimes technology replaces workers. Moreover, the service sector has been a significant engine of growth that needs different skills and talents than those required in the traditional primary and secondary sectors. Hence, there is a need to consider changes in human resource development strategies as well as education and training systems across countries and regions. These need to take into account the realities of the different stages of economic and social development of various countries, demographic issues and the industrial direction taken by each country (Chatterjee et al., 2013).

So what do these factors mean for the quality of work and strategic HRM in Asia? Changing global demographics have led to what is often referred to as a 'demographic dividend' where there are considerably younger populations and workforces in some countries (such as India and Indonesia) compared with countries such as China, the US and Australia. However, such dividends exist alongside skill shortages and skills gaps amounting to large unemployed populations (Baum and Kabst, 2013). Skill imbalances lead to sub-optimal production and, depending on the technology, may substantially inhibit production. Such shortages may also make a country less competitive in a fast-moving global economy (Shah and Burke, 2005). With developing Asia having made a rapid recovery from the global economic crisis, policy-makers now need to create policies to ensure that high growth rates are sustained and, importantly, that this growth results in not just more jobs, but better quality jobs.

Evidently Asia is home to some of the world's fastest-growing emerging economies – China and India are two that are currently significantly contributing to the world's economic growth in relation to global manufacturing (China) and services (India) (Cooke and Budhwar, 2015; Nankervis et al., 2013). However, as Cooke and Budhwar (2015) point out, in order to sustain this growth both countries are facing a number of challenges to their human resource management systems for a variety of reasons. In China HR competence is low and the HR capacity of the country as a whole is under-developed (p. 338), while in India the history of HR is longer but it is currently in a state of rapid transition (p. 342). The authors argue that existing studies on China and India indicate a number of challenges relating to people management, identifying three of the largest challenges as: skill and talent shortages; labour discontent; and lack of HR competence (Cooke and Budhwar, 2015: 344). In other Asia Pacific countries, including Indonesia, Malaysia, Thailand and even Singapore, these challenges are also more (or less) evident, impacting on both employees' quality of work and relative organisational effectiveness.

In summary, having a good quality job is generally thought to result in higher productivity and enhanced organisational effectiveness (European Foundation for the Improvement of Living and Working Conditions (Eurofound), 2012; Green, 2006; Knox et al., 2011). This may materialise through a range of channels, including lower rates of employee turnover, absenteeism and tardiness (Clarke and Hill, 2012; Eurofound, 2012; Warr, 1987) and improved employee well-being (Holman, 2012). Hence, the proposition to continue research in this area is a strong one for both organisations and their employees. In particular, and despite the limitations of the case-study research presented here, intrinsic JQ is important as it is has resonance with the development of effective SHRM programmes within the organisation.

Despite the limited number of cases and their possible biases (i.e. more managers and supervisors represented than workers), the JQ framework highlighted the importance of developing the intrinsic dimensions of JQ (such as the meaningfulness of work, using one's skills and discretion, having the ability to influence decisions, access to training and more). At the organisational level, formal JQ assessment programmes are not required; however, recognising the nexus between JQ and organisational performance is important, as is the role of those important work and workplace issues linked to intrinsic JQ that organisations can develop through strategic HRM programmes.

ACKNOWLEDGEMENT

This research study represents part of a larger study contracted by the Australian Workplace and Productivity Agency.

REFERENCES

Asian Development Bank, 2002. Key Developments in Developing and Asian Pacific Countries. ADB, Bangkok.

Australian Institute of Management, 2012. 'Australia's "Skill Gap"', Australian Institute of Management, Idria Pty Ltd. Available at: http://www.aimvic.com.au/pdf/AIM-skillsgap-2012.pdf.

Bandura, A., 1982. Self-efficacy mechanism in human agency. American Psychologist 37, 122–147.

Bardoel, E.A., De Cieri, H.L., Santos, C., 2008. A review of work-life research in Australia and New Zealand. Asia Pacific Journal of Human Resources 46 (3), 316–333.

Baum, M., Kabst, R., 2013. How to attract applicants in the Atlantic versus the Asia-Pacific region? A cross-national analysis on China, India, Germany and Hungary. Journal of World Business (Special Issue) 48 (2), 175–185.

Beer, M., Boselie, P., Brewster, C., 2015. Back to the future: implications for the field of HRM of the multistakeholder perspective proposed 30 years ago. Human Resource Management 54 (3), 427–438.

Beer, M., Spector, B., Lawrence, P.R., Mills, D.Q., Walton, R.E., 1984. A Conceptual View of HRM in Managing Human Assets. Free Press, New York.

Birdi, K., Clegg, C., Patterson, M., Robinson, A., Stride, C.B., Wall, T.D., Wood, S.J., 2008. The impact of human resource and operational management practices on company productivity: a longitudinal study. Personnel Psychology 61 (3), 467–501.

Boxall, P., 2012. High-performance work systems: what, why, how and for whom? Asia Pacific Journal of Human Resources 50 (2), 169–186.

Brown, M., Metz, I., Cregan, C., Kulik, C.T., 2009. Irreconcilable differences? Strategic human resource management and employee well-being. Asia Pacific Journal of Human Resources 47 (3), 270–294.

Burgess, J., Connell, J., 2013. Asia and the Pacific Region: change and workforce adjustments post GFC. Asia Pacific Business Review 19 (2), 279–285.

Burgess, J., Connell, J., Dockery, M., 2013. Quality of Work Research Project Report Report commissioned by the Australian Workplace and Productivity Agency. Curtin Business School, Perth.

Cakar, F., Bititci, U.S., MacBryde, J., 2003. A business process approach to human resource management. Business Process Management Journal 9 (2), 190–207.

Carter, M.Z., Armenakis, A.A., Feild, H.S., Mossholder, K.W., 2013. Transformational leadership, relationship quality, and employee performance during continuous incremental organizational change. Journal of Organizational Behavior 34 (7), 942–958.

Chan, J., Burgess, J., 2011. Challenges for the professional and continuous education of human resource managers in Hong Kong. International Journal of Learning 17 (12), 45–57.

Chatterjee, S., 2001. Relevance of traditional value frameworks in contemporary Chinese work organizations: implications for managerial transition. Journal of Human Values 7 (1), 21–32.

Chatterjee, S., 2009a. Managerial ethos of the Indian tradition: relevance of a Wisdom Model. Journal of Indian Business Research 1 (2/3), 136–162.

Chatterjee, S., 2009b. From Sreni Dharma to global cross-vergence: Journey of Human Resource Practices in India. International Journal of Indian Culture and Business Management 2 (3), 268–280.

Chatterjee, S., Pearson, C., 2006. Changing work goals of Asian managers: a comparative empirical study in ten Asian countries. Journal of Asia Pacific Business 7 (4), 5–33.

Chatterjee, S.R., Nankervis, A.R., Connell, J., 2013. Talent shortages in China and India: nature, antecedents and challenges. In: Srivastava, B., Mohapatra, M. (Eds.), Capability Building for Cutting-edge Organizations. Excel Books, New Delhi, pp. 40–49.

Clarke, M., Rao Hill, S., 2012. Promoting employee wellbeing and quality service outcomes: the role of HRM practices, Journal of Management & Organization, 18 (05), pp. 702–713.

Connell, J., Burgess, J., 2014. Do holistic human resource management practices make a difference to fly-in fly-out workers' job quality? An exploratory investigation. Australian Bulletin of Labour 40 (2), 159.

Considine, G., Callus, R., 2001. The Quality of Work Life of Australian Employees – The Development of an Index. Australian Centre for Industrial Relations Research and Teaching Series/Report no. 73. ACIRRT Working Paper. University of Sydney. Accessed September 5, 2015 http://ses.library.usyd.edu.au//bitstream/2123/13404/1/WP73.pdf.

Cooke, F.L., Budhwar, P., 2015. Human resource management in China and India. in Horwitz and Budhwar (Eds.), Handbook of Human Resource Management in Emerging Markets, Edward Elgar, Glos: UK. p. 337.

Dorio, J.M., Bryant, R.H., Allen, T.D., 2008. Work-related outcomes of the work-family interface: why organizations should care. In: Korabik, K., Leroy, D., Whitehead, D. (Eds.), Handbook of Work-Family Integration. Academic Press, Amsterdam, pp. 157–176.

Eisenhardt, K.M., 1989. Building theories from case study research. Academy of Management Review 14 (4), 532–550.

European Foundation for the Improvement of Living and Working Conditions (Eurofound), 2012. Trends in Job Quality in Europe: 5th European Working Conditions Survey. Publications Office of the European Union, Luxembourg.

European Foundation for the Improvement of Living and Working Conditions (Eurofound), 2013. 'Employment polarisation and job quality in crisis', European Jobs Monitor 2013. Eurofound, Dublin.

Gooderham, P., Parry, E., Ringdal, K., 2008. The impact of bundles of strategic human resource management practices on the performance of European firms. International Journal of Human Resource Management 19 (11), 2041–2056.

Green, F., 2006. Demanding Work: The Paradox of Job Quality in the Affluent Economy. Princeton University Press, Princeton, NJ.

Guest, D.E., 1987. Human resource management and industrial relations [1]. Journal of management Studies 24 (5), 503–521.

Guest, D., 2002. Human resource management, corporate performance and employee well-being: Building the worker into HRM. Journal of Industrial relations, 44 (3), 335–358.

Guest, D.E., Oakley, P., Clinton, M. and Budjanovcanin, A., 2006. Free or precarious? A comparison of the attitudes of workers in flexible and traditional employment contracts. Human Resource Management Review, 16 (2), 107–124.

Guest, D.E., 2011. Human resource management and performance: still searching for some answers. Human Resource Management Journal 21 (1), 3–13.

Guest, D.E., Michie, J., Conway, N., Sheehan, M., 2003. Human resource management and corporate performance in the UK. British Journal of Industrial Relations 41 (2), 291–314.

Guest, D., Conway, N., Dewe, P., 2004. Using sequential tree analysis to search for "bundles" of HR practices. Human Resource Management Journal 14 (1), 79–96.

Herzberg, F., Mausner, B., Snyderman, B.B., 1967. The Motivation to Work, 2nd edn. Wiley, New York.

Holman, D., 2012. Job types and job quality in Europe. Human Relations 66 (4), 475–502.

Hope-Hailey, V., Farndale, E., Truss, C., 2005. The HR department's role in organisational performance. Human Resource Management Journal 15 (3), 49–66.

Huselid, M.A., Beatty, R.W., Becker, B.E., 2005. "A players" or "A positions"? The strategic logic of workforce management. Harvard Business Review 83 (12), 110–117.

International Labour Organisation, 1997. Human Resource Development in the Asia Pacific in the 21st Century. ILO Workshop. Italy, May, Turin.

Jahoda, M., 1982. Employment and Unemployment: A Social Psychological Analysis. Cambridge University Press, Cambridge.

Jensen, E., 2005. HRs role in helping companies achieve high performance. Employment Relations Today 32 (2), 39–52.

Knox, A., Warhurst, C., Pocock, B., 2011. Job quality matters. Journal of Industrial Relations 53 (1), 5–11.

McDonnell, A., Collings, D., Burgess, J., 2012. Talent management in the Asia Pacific. Asia Pacific Journal of Human Resources 50 (4), 391–398.

Morehead, A., Steele, M., Alexander, M., Stephen, K., Duffin, L., 1997. Changes at Work – The 1995 Australian Industrial Relations Survey. Longman, Melbourne.

Nayar, V., 2010a. Employees First, Customers Second: Turning Conventional Management Upside Down. Harvard Business School Press. Cambridge, MA.

Nayar, V., 2010b. A maverick CEO explains how he persuaded his team to leap into the future. Harvard Business Review, June 110–113.

Nankervis, A.R., Cooke, F.L., Chatterjee, S.R., Warner, M., 2013. New models of human resource management in China and India. Routledge.

Pfeffer, J., 1998. The Human Equation. Harvard Business School Press, Cambridge, MA.

Pocock, B., Skinner, N., Williams, P., 2008. Measuring work-life interaction: the Australian Work and Life Index (AWALI) 2007. Labour and Industry 18 (3), 19–43.

Rainnie, A., Michelson, G., Goods, C., Burgess, J., 2014. Guest editors' introduction to the special issue on FIFO work. Australian Bulletin of Labour 40 (2), 92.

Richard, O.C., Johnson, N.B., 2001. Strategic human resource management effectiveness and firm performance. International Journal of Human Resource Management 12 (2), 299–310.

Ryan, R., Deci, E., 2000. Self-determination theory and the facilitation of intrinsic motivation, social development, and well-being. American Psychologist 55 (1), 68–78.

Seguino, S., 2010. Gender, distribution, and balance of payments constrained growth in developing countries. Review of Political Economy 22 (3), 373–404.

Sen, A., 1999. Development as Freedom. Oxford University Press, Oxford.

Shah, C., Burke, G., 2005. Skills shortages: concepts, measurement and policy responses. Australian Bulletin of Labour 31 (1), 44.

Sziraczki, G., Kim, K.B., Bhattacharyya, N., Dasgupta, S., Schmitt-Diabate, V., 2011. Recovery, job quality and policy priorities in developing Asia, The global crisis: causes, responses and challenges. International Labour Organisation, Geneva, pp. 35–49. Downloaded 5 September, 2015, file:///C:/Users/104609/Documents/Research%20Admin/Global%20financial%20crisis.pdf.

Voon, M.L., Lo, M.C., Ngui, K.S., Ayob, N.B., 2011. The influence of leadership styles on employees' job satisfaction in public sector organizations in Malaysia. International Journal of Business, Management and Social Sciences 2 (1), 24–32.

Wallace, E., de Chernatony, L., Buil, I., 2013. Building bank brands: how leadership behavior influences employee commitment. Journal of Business Research 66 (2), 165–171.

Warr, P.B., 1987. Work, Unemployment and Mental Health. Clarendon Press, Oxford.

Wright, P., McMahon, G., 1992. Theoretical perspectives for strategic human resource management. Journal of Management 18 (2), 295–320.

Yin, R.K., 2009. Case Study Research: Design and Methods. Sage, Newbury Park, CA.

Employment relations and Islamic perspectives

CHAPTER 9

Collective voice and union effectiveness: is relational capital the missing link?

**N.M. Salleh, A.K. Rosline, J.K.S. Len,
K.Ag. Budin**

INTRODUCTION

Trade unions in Malaysia, like those in other countries, are formed to improve members' working conditions and economic well-being, as well as to ensure that their rights and social benefits are protected (Aminuddin, 2003). Workers, employers and the government have important roles to play in ensuring that the objectives of unions are achieved and that relevant rules and regulations governing the working conditions of employees are observed. Currently, trade unions in Malaysia and other Asian countries face a number of challenges, particularly in the decline in union membership among workers (union density). The result is that trade unions are losing the standing and influence that they once held (Rose et al., 2011; Kuruvilla et al., 2002). Among the reasons for this decline is the tendency for employers to encourage 'union-free' workforces (Aminuddin, 2003; Gall and McKay, 2001). The curbing of trade unionism by employers is imposed through threats of dismissal and redundancy; workers feel intimidated and are thus discouraged from being active union members. Temporary workers, contract workers and foreign workers are often deterred from union membership through fears of their contract or work permit not being renewed. From the legal perspective, all Malaysian workers have the right to form or join a trade union. At the same time, however, unions are subject to various restrictions under the Trade Unions Act 1959 (TUA) and the Industrial Relations Act 1967 (IRA), with their movements falling under the purview of the Trade Unions Affairs Department in the Ministry of Human Resources. For example, the Malaysian government has the absolute right to withhold registration of a trade union at its discretion

*Asia Pacific Human Resource Management
and Organisational Effectiveness*
ISBN 978-0-08-100643-6

(Ramasamy, 2008; Aminuddin, 2003). As such, enhancement of the standing of trade unions in Malaysia, and positive changes in the manner in which they operate and interact with their members would improve workers' perception of trade union membership.

Although the Relational Capital Theory in socio-economics has been well researched, its relevance and application in trade unionism have not been adequately investigated. Most of the previous studies on relational capital focused on relationships between customers and suppliers, employers and employees, or suppliers and retailers in mainly profit-oriented industries. On the other hand, the present study sought to analyse the impact of relational capital (the key components of which are communication, commitment and trust) on the relationship between a trade union and its members. The study further examined how the underlying relational capital could serve to mediate between workers' needs and their perception of the effectiveness of their trade unions. While trade unions in Malaysia are commonly immersed in issues such as the collective bargaining process and the laws governing trade union activities, what is often sidelined are the interactions among union members and between members and union leaders. Indeed, the relational capital components of communication, participation, commitment and trust are key to the foundation upon which rests the success of the trade union. These often neglected elements of solidarity are, in fact, vital to the union's strength.

Malaysian industrial relations

The Malaysian industrial relations system in Malaysia is a tripartite set-up consisting of the employer, the employees and the government. There are three broad approaches to the decision-making process in manpower relations, namely unilateral, bilateral or as a tripartite consensus. In deliberations between the parties, the Ministry of Human Resources chairs the discussion and appoints government representatives. Workers are represented by the Malaysian Trade Union Congress (MTUC) and the Congress of Unions of Employees in the Public and Civil Services (CUEPECS), while employers are represented by the Malaysian Employers Federation (MEF). These bodies are members of the National Labour Advisory Council (NLAC) that meet at least twice a year, or whenever it is deemed necessary. In 1957, Malaysia joined the International Labour Organisation (ILO), an agency of the United Nations which plays a role in the Malaysian industrial relation system. The agency provides an international forum pertaining to labour issues. The key statutes governing the industrial relations framework in Malaysia include the Trade Union Act 1959, the Industrial Relations Act

1967 and the Public Services Tribunal Act 1977. These laws protect and regulate relations between employers, workers and their unions to ensure fairness, justice and amicable working relations (Aminuddin, 2003).

The Malaysian manufacturing industry

The Malaysian manufacturing sector provides jobs to nearly 40 per cent of the country's total workforce, generating an income of more than RM65 billion a year in the second quarter of 2015. The total number of employees engaged in the sector in the same year reached more than 2.2 million, making it the highest contributor of employment in Malaysia. It is the second highest contributor to the country's gross domestic product (GDP) after the services sector. Manufacturing contributed RM254 (23 per cent) of the total Malaysian GDP of RM1,107 billion in 2014 and continues to be the second largest contributor to the national GDP, with its share growing by 5.4 per cent in 2014 (Department of Statistics, Malaysia). Most of the employment opportunities created in manufacturing are in the electric and electronic subsector, followed by basic metal products and transport equipment sectors. The recent issue of note in the manufacturing industry was the implementation of a minimum wage for workers, an enactment directly impacting employers, employees and the government. The law, implemented in January 2013, was aimed at achieving a high-income economy for the country by the year 2020. However, manufacturers were concerned that they would lose out in export competitiveness, especially if output did not match the higher overheads resulting from increased wages. Unskilled and semi-skilled workers were the main beneficiaries, with the wage increments helping to defray the high costs of living among the lower income group.

The Malaysian government pursues an industrialisation strategy primarily focused on low-cost labour, export-oriented industries and capital injections from foreign multinational corporations (MNCs). Most employers would prefer a union-free labour force, but where trade unions are in place, leaders representing the trade union and the employer need to be sincere and skilful at maintaining harmony in the workplace.

RESEARCH OBJECTIVES

To help understand why the proportion of unionised workers (trade union density) in Malaysia is the lowest in the Asia Pacific region (Kuruvilla et al., 2002), this study investigated the application of the Relational

Capital Theory that has been researched extensively in the institution of marriage and family (Dollahite and Rommel, 1993). The theory identifies and characterizes the criteria for creating strong bonds between the parties involved, i.e. between the husband, the wife and the children. According to the rationale of the theory, it takes three main factors, namely commitment, communication and trust, to make a marriage successful (Kelley, 2013). In an analogous situation, the same triad of factors might lay the foundation for the success of a trade union by acting as the glue that binds the union leaders to the rest of the union members. It is the present authors' belief that solidarity between workers and their union, cultivated through the interplay of commitment, communication and trust, is important for maintaining and sustaining organisational effectiveness and success.

Accordingly, the research objectives in this study were:

1. To investigate the role of the Relational Capital Theory in explaining the sustenance and success of a trade union.
2. To examine the Relational Capital Theory (focusing on communication, participation, commitment and trust) as a mediator between the collective voice of workers and their perception of union effectiveness.

Trade union effectiveness

Low union density is an indication of weak union power (Hayter et al., 2011; Kuruvilla et al., 2002), and this is very much the situation in Malaysia where union density is reported to be the lowest in the Asia Pacific region (Kuruvilla et al., 2002). Low union density is mostly due to ineffectiveness in protecting members' well-being (Blackett and Sheppard, 2003; Strunk and Grissom, 2010), loss of the membership's confidence in union leaders because of negative perceptions (Cregan, 2013; Tetrick et al., 2007), the long process of bargaining and settlement (Aminuddin, 2003; Strunk and Grissom, 2010) and, finally, pressures and constraints from employers due to union laws and work regulations (Rose et al., 2011; Wad, 2013). Among the suggestions that might enable unions to function effectively are creating an effective communication system to engender commitment and trust (Brewster et al., 2007; Goslinga and Sverke, 2003), changing workers' perceptions and demonstrating that the union can be trusted in managing and safeguarding their well-being (Fuller and Hester, 2001; Rhoades and Eisenberger, 2002). A common denominator in achieving union effectiveness lies in the interplay of the three main factors in relational capital, namely communication, commitment and trust (Brewster et al., 2007; Tetrick et al., 2007).

Workers' collective voice

Abraham Maslow's theory on the 'Hierarchy of Needs' has been widely applied in the past to explain the needs of employees (Mitchell and Moudgill, 1976) that is termed the 'collective voice' in this study. By transposing the worker and his working environment into the context of the theory, the needs of employees can be explained in five stages. The first stage concerns basic physiological needs; this refers to the need for a source of income for sustenance. In the case of an employee, this would be a job with a fair salary to enable a comfortable livelihood. The second stage covers safety needs; each worker desires a safe job with fringe benefits and job security. The third stage is the need for belongingness; this reflects the desire for a good relationship with co-workers, participation in work groups and a positive relationship with supervisors and other superiors. The fourth stage covers esteem or the need for the recognition of work performance, responsibility, status and credit for contributions to the organisation. Finally, the fifth stage relates to self-actualisation needs, i.e. employees need to be provided with opportunities to grow, be creative, be given challenging assignments and to achieve success career-wise. The Hierarchy of Needs theory, as adapted to explain the expectations of workers, posits that each of these needs have to be periodically satisfied to enable sustained high performance from the worker. In this context, it is the role of the trade union to provide assistance and assurance that their members' varied needs (their 'collective voice') are met and honoured by their employers. In view of the burden of expectation of trade unions to satisfy the workers' needs as discussed above, it is necessary to determine whether this expectation has been met. Thus the first hypothesis was constructed as follows:

H1: *The collective voice has a positive and significant effect on union effectiveness*

Relational capital: communication, trust and commitment

Sustaining and maintaining non-profit organisations require effective communication, trust and the commitment of its members (Brewster et al., 2007). The absence of any one of the triad will affect the success of collective bargaining negotiations (Hayter et al., 2011; Johari and Ghazali, 2011). The factors were further tested in different fields and were found to have a positive relationship with organisational effectiveness in marketing, management, accounting and marriage institutions (Gall, 2005; Morgan and Hunt, 1994; Zeffane et al., 2011). Drawing from Kelley (1979), when communication, commitment and trust are present in trade unions, they help to strengthen the unions' internal functioning. The triad's presence is also important for a sustainable long-term relationship, and this contributes to positive organisational performance (Loke et al., 2009; Sambasivan et al., 2011).

Effective communication is the key to creating commitment and trust among members of an organisation (Tapia, 2013). In the present study, communication between union leaders and members is explored in terms of communication quality (i.e. timeliness, accuracy, adequacy, completeness and credibility of information) and information sharing (i.e. the extent to which critical, often proprietary, information is communicated to union members).

Commitment pertains to attachment to an ongoing relationship that is sufficiently important to warrant concerted effort to maintain it. In other words, the committed party believes the relationship is worth working on to ensure that it endures; it is maintained as a valued relationship (Moorman et al., 1993; Morgan and Hunt, 1994). One way in which a trade union member can demonstrate his or her commitment is through active participation in union activities. Participation is defined here as the extent to which members play active roles in the goal setting, planning, forecasting and decision-making of the union. There cannot be participation without committed members. Participation may be considered one aspect of commitment.

It is unlikely that commitment alone is enough to ensure the union's success. Another key factor, namely trust, plays an important role as well. Trust can be defined as a willingness to rely on an exchange partner in whom one has placed confidence (Moorman et al., 1993). As such, efficacy of communication leads to trust and possibly engenders commitment. Accordingly, Hypotheses 2 and 3 can be written as follows:

H2: The collective voice has a positive and significant effect on relational capital.

H3: Relational capital has a positive and significant effect on union effectiveness.

Relational capital mediating between worker needs and union effectiveness

Garbarino and Johnson (1999) found that communication, trust and commitment acted as mediators between satisfaction, attitudes and future intentions of attending a non-profit theatre. These three elements of relational capital also act as mediators between supply chain partners and strategic alliances (Sambasivan et al., 2011). A study which investigated customers' trust and commitment found that the interplay between these two elements

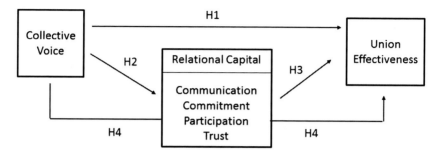

Figure 9.1 Framework of hypothesised relationships between the study constructs

influenced customer intentions to remain in a relationship (De Ruyter et al., 2001). A study in Australia found that trust, commitment and communication were able to bring about a strong bond and strengthened the relationship between management and employees (Zeffane et al., 2011).

A postulation in this study was that if efficacy between the interplay of the triad of communication, commitment and trust (with member participation being an integral characteristic of commitment) was achieved, organisational objectives of the trade union in heeding the members' collective voice would follow. In this regard, the study tested the mediating effects of relational capital through the following hypothesis:

H4: Relational capital mediates the relationship between collective voice and union effectiveness.

The hypothesised relationships between the variables investigated in this study are summarised in Figure 9.1.

RESEARCH METHODOLOGY

The methods adopted in this study were based on those from previous reports. Data for the analyses were obtained from 443 randomly selected trade union members in a cross-section of organisations across the country. The list of workers earning a minimum wage of RM800 from each organisation was obtained from selected union leaders. To conduct the survey, a stratified random sampling was carried out, with a provision to include union leaders. Each participant was given a questionnaire to complete at his or her own pace. The Confirmatory Factor Analysis (CFA) was used to validate unidimensionality, validity and reliability of the constructs prior to their use in Structural Equation Modelling (SEM) (Zainudin, 2012, 2014).

Abraham Maslow's theory of employees' needs formed the basis for the following to be used as correlation variables: (a) the collective voice of trade union members; (b) union effectiveness; and(c) relational capital as suggested by Daft and Marcic (2006) and Mitchell and Moudgill (1976). A fourth variable, participation, which is integral to commitment, was treated separately in this analysis because of its distinctive attributes (refer to the appendix at the end of the chapter for the definitions). The scale employed in this study was the five-point Likert Scale (1 = strongly disagree to 5 = strongly agree). The collective voice of members' needs was measured by five items (Mitchell and Moudgill, 1976) while the relational capital items consisted of communication, information sharing and quality (five items), participation (nine items), trust (four items) and commitment (three items). The combined items used were measured as suggested by Sambasivam et al. (2011) while trust measurements were calculated according to Yong-Ybarra and Wiersema (1999). The seven items of perceived union effectiveness followed those adopted by Mellor et al. (1999). A summary of definitions of the variables analysed appears in the appendix at the end of the chapter.

RESEARCH FINDINGS AND DISCUSSION

Profile of respondents

From a total of 443 usable questionnaires (88.6 per cent response rate), 327 (73.8 per cent) were from personnel in the manufacturing industry, with the remaining 116 (26 per cent) from staff in the banking and retailing industries. The demographic breakdown of the respondents is shown in Table 9.1. Most of the respondents were male (261 or 58.9 per cent) and 182 were female (41.1 per cent). Those between the ages of 31 and 40 (30.9 per cent) and 21 and 30 (30.2 per cent) formed the major proportion (60.1 per cent) of the respondents. The majority of respondents (82.4 per cent) were ordinary members while the remaining 17.6 per cent were executive members of trade unions. They included ten presidents, four chairpersons or vice-chairpersons, 14 secretaries, 15 treasurers, one internal auditor and 34 committee members. A large majority (76.7 per cent) of the respondents were married and 276 (62 per cent) of them had been working for more than ten years.

Confirmatory factor analysis (CFA)

Structural Equation Modelling (SEM) is a comprehensive means to validate measurement models of latent constructs (Zainudin, 2012, 2014). In

Table 9.1 Demographic profile of respondents

Manufacturing	327 (73.8)	Ordinary union	365 (82.4)
Banking and	116 (26.1)	members	78 (17.6)
retailing		Union leaders★	
Male	261 (58.9)	Married	340 (76.7)
Female	182 (41.1)	Single	97 (21.9)
		Other★★	6 (1.4)
Age above 61	Age above 61	Tenure	22 (5)
51–60	3 (0.7)	Below 3 years	88 (19.9)
41–50	43 (9.7)	3–5 years	276 (62.3)
31–40	119 (25.9)	Above 10 years	
21–30	137 (30.9)		
Below 21	134 (30.2)		
	7 (1.6)		

Percentages shown in brackets
★Presidents, chairpersons, vice-chairpersons, secretaries, treasurers, auditors, committee members
★★Divorced, widowed

the validating procedure, Confirmatory Factor Analysis (CFA) is used to verify the measurement model of all constructs for unidimensionality, validity and reliability prior to modelling these constructs into SEM for hypothesis testing. Unidimensionality is achieved when all measuring items have an acceptable factor loading (Zainudin, 2012, 2014). As for validity, the measurement model of a construct has to achieve convergent validity, construct validity and discriminant validity. According to Zainudin (2014), convergent validity is achieved when Average Variance Extracted (AVE) for the construct exceeds the threshold value of 0.5. Construct validity is achieved when the Fitness Indices meet the minimum threshold values for three fitness categories, namely Absolute Fit (RMSEA < 0.08), Incremental Fit (CFI > 0.90), and Parsimonious Fit (Chi-square/df < 3.0).

Discriminant validity of the construct is achieved when the square root of the AVE is greater than the correlation between the constructs (Zainudin, 2012, 2014). Composite Reliability (CR) of a construct has to exceed the threshold value of 0.6. The factor loading for components and items were obtained from Figure 9.2 and the computed values for AVE and CR for the constructs pertaining to collective voice (CV), relational capital (RC) and union effectiveness (EFFECT) are tabulated in Table 9.2.

Table 9.2 shows that all AVE exceeded the threshold value of 0.5 and all CR exceeded the threshold value of 0.6. The results indicated that the

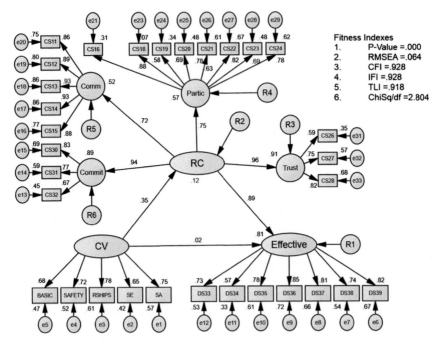

Figure 9.2 Standardised path coefficients of the model

Table 9.2 AVE, CR and correlations for the measurement model

Questionnaire item	Collective voice (CV)	Relational capital (RC)	Union effectiveness (effect)
1	0.68	0.94	0.73
2	0.72	0.72	0.57
3	0.78	0.75	0.78
4	0.65	0.96	0.85
5	0.75		0.81
6			0.74
7			0.82
AVE	**0.515**	**0.826**	**0.581**
CR	**0.841**	**0.950**	**0.905**

constructs achieved convergent validity and reliability. Table 9.3 gives the square roots (in bold) of the Average Variances Extracted (AVEs) of the three constructs, CV (Collective Voice), RC (Relational Capital) and Effect (Union Effectiveness). They are greater than their corresponding correlation coefficients presented in the rows and columns, indicating that the

Table 9.3 Discriminant validity index summary

	CV	RC	Effect
CV	**0.72**		
RC	0.35	**0.91**	
EFFECT	0.33	0.90	**0.76**

Table 9.4 Fitness indices for the measurement model

Name of category	Name of index	Index value	Comments
Absolute fit	RMSEA	0.064	The required level is achieved (RMSEA < 0.08)
Incremental fit	CFI	0.928	The required level is achieved (CFI > 0.9)
Parsimonious fit	Chisq/df	2.332	The required level is achieved (Chisq/df < 3.0)

constructs had achieved discriminant validity among them (Hair et al., 2006; Zainudin 2012, 2014).

Another validity assessment is construct validity, which is the validity that is achieved when all fitness indexes for the constructs reached the required level. Table 9.4 gives the fitness indexes for the model showing that all fitness index requirements were satisfied.

The results in Figure 9.2 indicate that the construct CV estimates only 12 per cent of RC while CV and RC estimate about 81 per cent of Effective. Hence RC was shown to be a mediator linking the relationship between CV and Effective. Nevertheless, formal testing for mediation would be required.

Causal influence of collective voice and relational capital on union effectiveness

As indicated by the regression path coefficient, when **CV** went up by 1, **RC** increased by 0.41 (Figure 9.3 and Table 9.5). The probability of arriving at a critical ratio as large as 6.104 in absolute value was less than 0.001. In other words, the regression weight for **CV** in the prediction of **RC** was significantly different from zero at the 0.001 level (Table 9.5). Again, when **RC** rose by 1, **Effective** increased by 1.06, with the probability of less than 0.001 to arrive at a critical ratio as large as 15.556. This showed that the regression weight for **RC** in the prediction of **Effective** was significantly different from zero at the 0.001 level. On the other hand, **Effective** increased

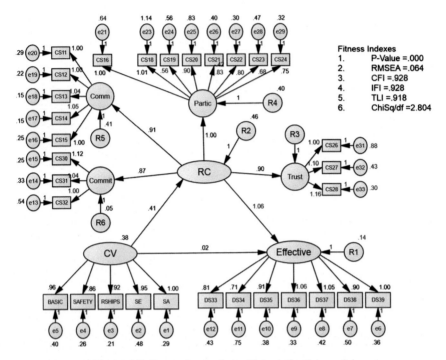

Figure 9.3 Regression path coefficients for the model

Table 9.5 Regression path coefficient and its significance

			Estimate	SE	CR	p	Result	Result on hypothesis
RC	<---	CV	0.408	0.067	6.104	***	Significant	Supported
Effective	<---	CV	0.024	0.049	0.499	0.618	Not significant	Not supported
Effective	<---	RC	1.060	0.068	15.556	***	Significant	Supported

by only 0.024 when **CV** went up by 1. The critical ratio of 0.499 was not statistically significant (p = 0.618.)

DETERMINING THE MEDIATION MODEL EFFECT

The method of Zainudin (2012, 2014) was adopted to test the role of Relational Capital (RC) as a mediating variable between the Collective Voice (CV) of workers' needs and their perceived union effectiveness. The standardised path coefficients were extracted from the model (Figure 9.2) and positioned in the triangle as shown in Figure 9.4.

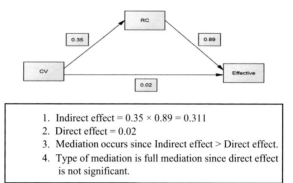

1. Indirect effect = 0.35 × 0.89 = 0.311
2. Direct effect = 0.02
3. Mediation occurs since Indirect effect > Direct effect.
4. Type of mediation is full mediation since direct effect is not significant.

Figure 9.4 Procedure for testing the mediator in a model

Table 9.6 Bootstrapping to determine the significance of direct and indirect effects

	Indirect effect p-value	Direct effect p-value
Bootstrapping p-value	0.002	0.705
Results	Significant	Not significant
Type of mediation	Full mediation since direct effect is not significant	

CONFIRMING THE RESULTS THROUGH BOOTSTRAPPING

The results of the mediation tests were confirmed using the re-sampling procedure, bootstrapping (Zainudin, 2014), that is used especially to test an indirect effect. In this procedure, sampling with replacement was performed with the algorithm instructed to take the sample of size n from the existing data set to obtain a sampling distribution for the estimates. The result shown in Table 9.6 was obtained using 1,000 samples with a percentile confidence interval of 0.95 and a bias corrected confidence interval of 0.95. We also ran Harman's test to identify the common method bias and found that a single factor only explained 42 per cent of the variance. Although there is a lot variance to be explained by a single factor, it is not a majority and it is accepted.

DISCUSSION

Long-term concerns over declining union membership and persistent claims of organisations being poorly run have become crucial issues in maintaining and sustaining the existence of trade unions in Malaysia. Despite the declining density of trade unions, most union members in this study expressed confidence that their unions were committed to playing their roles. Most of the union members perceived their unions as being successful in bringing about valued procedures or outcomes. The appendix at the end of the chapter shows the questionnaire scores relating to union effectiveness that were mostly high (between 3.6 and 3.9), indicating agreement with the statements.

As such, it is important to investigate why some union leaders are more committed and effective than others. In the absence of empirical evidence that explain this situation, this chapter seeks to understand trade union members' attitudes, perceptions and behaviour. Relevant findings from the study could contribute to the effectiveness of trade unions.

CONCLUSION

It is suggested from the results of this study that commitment, participation, communication and trust are powerful tools that can be utilised by trade unions to highlight their relevance to workers and, indeed, ensure their own survival. The main players in a union are its members and to showcase the purpose and function of the organisation, union leaders should strive to improve communication, cultivate trust and commitment, and encourage participation by members. The Relational Capital Theory proposed by Kelley (2013) was tested to determine if these four elements mediated the collective voice of union members vis-à-vis the perceived effectiveness of their unions. From the regression path coefficient (Table 9.5), it was evident that the. second hypothesis, that *the collective voice has a positive and significant effect on relational capital*, was supported.

The ability to achieve trade union effectiveness in bringing about valued procedures or outcomes is dependent on the strength of its members' voice. When union members voice out their needs, awareness of those needs is created and negotiations should commence. In particular, the strong voice that is channelled through communication, commitment, participation and trust builds a stable and robust long-term relationship that contributes to a positive organisational performance (Loke et al., 2009; Sambasivan et al., 2011). This finding also shows support for the third hypothesis i.e. *the relational capital has a positive and significant effect on union effectiveness*.

Frequent communication and information sharing between members and the union leadership encourage commitment to the union and participation in its activities. From there, trust often follows (Tapia, 2013). When there is a good relationship between members and the leadership, it enables union activities to be undertaken with the full backing of the members, leading to union effectiveness. This finding echoes the study by Brewster et al. (2007) who found that in order to sustain and maintain non-profit organisations, effective communication, trust and commitment were prerequisites. However, it is important to note that members' voice alone does not affect union effectiveness directly as shown in the analysis that rejected Hypothesis 1, i.e. *the collective voice has a positive and significant effect on union effectiveness.*

While union members have a plethora of needs and aspirations, many of these concerns may remain unheard by the union leadership. This suggests that union leaders could not effectively carry out their roles without proper communication, commitment, participation and trust among members. Previous studies have found that the absence of any one of these entities would affect effectiveness in collective bargaining negotiations (Hayter et al., 2011; Johari and Ghazali, 2011). It is here that the fourth hypothesis, *relational capital mediates the relationship between collective voice and union effectiveness*, shows the importance of relational capital in bridging the gap between collective voice and union effectiveness. The findings suggested that the four factors were the missing link between the voice of members and trade union effectiveness. Communication, commitment, participation and trust are proven to be important factors in dealing with declining union density and other challenges to trade unions, particularly those dealing with trade liberalisation and deregulation, technology effects, trade union rights violation and the impediment of labour laws. The four main factors are also important for the retention of union membership. Active communication between the union leaders and members encourages union activities such as participation at meetings or industrial action such as pickets or strikes. This would increase union members' trust in their leaders to improve their well-being and protect their rights (Kelley, 1979).

One limitation in this analysis stems from the fact that the study population comprised a mixture of union leaders (17.6 per cent) and ordinary members (82.4 per cent), even though responses to the same statements in the questionnaires were likely to be influenced by whether the respondents were committee members or ordinary members. The needs and expectations of the latter (the collective voice in the general union membership) might not be similar to those of the union leaders. At the same time, union leaders may not be relied on to give objective opinions on union effectiveness. Although this study has attempted to provide an in-depth view of the collective voice of trade union members, workers' needs tend to be varied and complex. A closer look at specific needs is therefore worthwhile. Members' perception of the effectiveness of their unions and the importance of the role they play would be enhanced if union leaders paid more attraction to relational capital.

In future studies, attention might be accorded to how improvements in the way union activities are run so that they would meet members' expectations. Such improvements would instil confidence among members in having the union protect their rights and represent them in negotiations and disputes.

APPENDIX

See Table A9.1.

Table A9.1 Questionnaire item responses

Questions	Mean	SD
Basic	4.46	0.86
Safety	4.56	0.74
Relationships	4.52	0.73
Security	4.25	0.91
Self-actualisation	4.39	0.82
Information quality and information sharing	3.68	1.06
The union shares information with me	3.72	1.02
The union shares accurate information with me	3.68	1.03
The union shares adequate information with me	3.67	1.03
The union shares complete information with me	3.76	1.04
The union shares credible information with me	3.73	0.95
I actively communicate with my union for advice and information	3.46	1.04
The union participates in my planning and goal-setting activities that are relevant to the union's goal	3.44	1.11
I appreciate any suggestion from my union for improvement	4.04	0.93

Continued

Table A9.1 Questionnaire item responses—cont'd

Questions	Mean	SD
The union shares exclusive information with me	3.30	1.25
I, beforehand, inform my union about any changes regarding my needs	3.60	1.02
The relationship between my union and I obliges each party to share any important information with the other	3.82	0.94
The union and I are expected to keep each other informed about any changes or events that may affect the other	3.86	0.95
The union and I are expected to provide each other only with the pre-specified information.	3.69	0.91
I am fully updated by my union on the issues affecting my interest	3.60	1.03
When we encounter difficulties or new situations, the union will take care of it	3.47	1.15
The union is familiar with the patterns of behaviour our partner firms have established and we can rely on them to behave in certain ways	3.53	0.99
I have found that my union is dependable	3.84	0.96
I rarely feel distrust in my union	3.40	1.23
We are committed to the relationship with union members	3.72	0.89
The relationship between us is something that we intend to maintain indefinitely	4.00	0.92
The relationship that we have deserves our union's maximum effort to maintain	3.86	0.99
The trade union has helped me improve my work quality	**3.71**	**0.95**
I have gained additional benefits because I am a union member	**3.81**	**1.05**
I feel my job is secure because of the union's efforts	**3.92**	**0.99**
The trade union helped me acquire a better pension plan than what I supposedly should have been given	**3.68**	**1.07**
The trade union protected me from unfairness in performance appraisal	**3.66**	**1.10**
The trade union carried out its roles effectively in handling disagreements and complaints, and I have freedom to express my opinions	**3.68**	**1.04**
The trade union played crucial roles in improving the safety level at the workplace	**3.85**	**1.04**

ACKNOWLEDGEMENTS

The research reported in this paper is sponsored by the Research Acculturation Grant Scheme (RAGS), Ministry of Higher Education (Malaysia).

We would like to express our gratitude towards Professor T. Ramayah for his valuable comments.

REFERENCES

Aminuddin, M., 2003. Malaysian Industrial Relations and Employment Law. McGraw-Hill (Malaysia) Sdn Bhd.

Blackett, A., Sheppard, C., 2003. Collective bargaining and equality: Making connections. International Labour Review, 142 (4), pp. 419–457.

Brewster, C., Wood, G., Croucher, R., Brookes, M., 2007. Are works councils and joint consultative committees a threat to trade unions? A comparative analysis. Economic and Industrial Democracy 28 (1), 49–77.

Cregan, C., 2013. Does workplace industrial action increase trade union membership? An exchange relationship approach to union joining and leaving behaviour. International Journal of Human Resource Management 1–15.

Daft, R.L., Marcic, D., 2006. Understanding Management. Available at: CengageBrain. com.

De Ruyter, K., Moorman, L., Lemmink, J., 2001. Antecedents of commitment and trust in customer–supplier relationships in high technology markets. Industrial Marketing Management 30 (3), 271–286.

Dollahite, D.C., Rommel, J.I., 1993. Individual and relationship capital: implications for theory and research on families. Journal of Family and Economic Issues 14, 27–48.

Fuller Jr., J.B., Hester, K., 2001. A closer look at the relationship between justice perceptions and union participation. Journal of Applied Psychology 86 (6), 1096.

Gall, G., 2005. Organizing non-union workers as trade unionists in the "new economy" in Britain. Economic and Industrial Democracy 26 (1), 41–63.

Gall, G., McKay, S., 2001. Facing "fairness at work": union perception of employer opposition and response to union recognition. Industrial Relations Journal 32 (2), 94–113.

Garbarino, E., Johnson, M.S., 1999. The different roles of satisfaction, trust, and commitment in customer relationships. Journal of Marketing 70–87.

Goslinga, S., Sverke, M., 2003. Atypical work and trade union membership: union attitudes and union turnover among traditional vs atypically employed union members. Economic and Industrial Democracy 24 (2), 290–312.

Hair, J.F., Black, W.C., Babin, B.J., Anderson, R.E., Tatham, R.L., 2006. SEM: confirmatory factor analysis. Multivariate data analysis. Pearson Prentice Hall, Upper Saddle River, pp. 770–842.

Hayter, S., Fashoyin, T., Kochan, T.A., 2011. Review essay: collective bargaining for the 21st century. Journal of Industrial Relations 53 (2), 225–247.

Johari, H., Ghazali, S., 2011. Exploring Commitment among union members: perspective and direction. International Review of Business Research Papers 7 (4), 104–117.

Kelley, H.H., 1979. Personal Relationships. Lawrence Erlbaum, Hilsdale.

Kelley, H.H., 2013. Personal Relationships: Their Structures and Processes. Psychology Press.

Kuruvilla, S., Das, S., Kwon, H., Kwon, S., 2002. Trade union growth and decline in Asia. British Journal of Industrial Relations 40 (3), 431–461.

Loke, S.P., Sambasivan, M., Downe, A.G., 2009. Strategic alliances outcomes in supply chain environments: Malaysian case studies. European Journal of Social Sciences 9, 371–386.

Mellor, S., Barnes-Farrell, J.L., Stanton, J.M., 1999. Unions as justice-promoting organisations: the interactive effect of ethnicity, gender, and perceived union effectiveness. Sex Roles 40 (5–6), 331–346.

Mitchell, V.F., Moudgill, P., 1976. Measurement of Maslow's need hierarchy. Organisational Behavior and Human Performance 16 (2), 334–349.

Moorman, C., Deshpande, R., Zaltman, G., 1993. Factors affecting trust in market research relationships. Journal of Marketing 81–101.

Morgan, R.M., Hunt, S.D., 1994. The commitment-trust theory of relationship marketing. Journal of Marketing 20–38.

Ramasamy, N., 2008. The Future of the Trade Union Movement in Malaysia. Paper presented at the MTUC/American Council for Labour Solidarity National Workshop on 'MTUC – The Way Forward'.

Rhoades, L., Eisenberger, R., 2002. Perceived organisational support: a review of the literature. Journal of Applied Psychology 87 (4), 698.

Rose, R.C., Kumar, N., Ramasamy, N., 2011. Trade unions in Malaysia: perspectives of employers and employees of unionized companies. Indian Journal of Industrial Relations 46 (3), 384–395.

Sambasivan, M., Siew-Phaik, L., Mohamed, Z.A., Leong, Y.C., 2011. Impact of interdependence between supply chain partners on strategic alliance outcomes: role of relational capital as a mediating construct. Management Decision 49 (4), 548–569.

Strunk, K.O., Grissom, J.A., 2010. Do strong unions shape district policies? Collective bargaining, teacher contract restrictiveness, and the political power of teachers' unions. Educational Evaluation and Policy Analysis 32 (3), 389–406.

Tapia, M., 2013. Marching to different tunes: commitment and culture as mobilizing mechanisms of trade unions and community organisations. British Journal of Industrial Relations 51 (4), 666–688.

Tetrick, L.E., Shore, L.M., McClurg, L.N., Vandenberg, R.J., 2007. A model of union participation: the impact of perceived union support, union instrumentality, and union loyalty. Journal of Applied Psychology 92 (3), 820.

Wad, P., 2013. Getting international labour rights right at a foreign controlled company in Malaysia: a global labour network perspective. Geoforum 44, 52–61.

Young-Ybarra, C., Wiersema, M., 1999. Strategic flexibility in information technology alliances: the influence of transaction cost economics and social exchange theory. Organisation Science, 10 (4), 439–459.

Zainudin, A., 2012. Structural Equation Modelling Using AmosGraphic. UiTM Press, Shah Alam, Malaysia.

Zainudin, A., 2014. A Handbook on SEM for Academicians and Practitioners. MPWS Publisher, Bangi, Malaysia.

Zeffane, R., Tipu, S.A., Ryan, J.C., 2011. Communication, commitment and trust: exploring the triad. International Journal of Business and Management 6 (6), 77.

CHAPTER 10

A study on the determinants of job satisfaction from an Islamic perspective: Indonesia, Brunei Darussalam and Malaysia

A.M. Noor, R.U. Mohammed

INTRODUCTION

Employees often ask what they will get after completing certain jobs given to them by their management. In normal situations, they will receive rewards, especially financial rewards, in the forms of bonus, overtime and allowances. According to Jurgensen (1978), money is one of the most commonly cited reasons to perform a task. However, rewards can be in both extrinsic and intrinsic forms. The importance of rewards themselves have significant impacts on the positive growth of an organisation. In Malaysia, only a few researchers have attempted to identify the uniqueness of Islamic management, and in particular human resource management (HRM). Azmi (2010), for example, claimed that even though the practice of Islamic human resource management is only 'moderate' in Malaysia, the result in terms of enhancing job satisfaction is acceptable. There might be two main reasons behind these findings. The first is the concept of Islamic moderation (*wasatiyyah*). This concept concentrates on a moderate, just and 'best' approach. Its objective is to moderate between two extreme aspects in every part of a person's life. This does not mean that the *wasatiyyah* concept takes a 50:50 position, for example between rich and poor or being wise and unwise. Based on the concept, one can become rich, but at the same time help the poor (Hanapi, 2014). The second reason is due to Malaysian organisations' emphases on competency-based performance, organisational and career development. Previous research has focused on these components of human resource management, but less emphasis has been placed on job satisfaction and reward systems.

Asia Pacific Human Resource Management and Organisational Effectiveness
ISBN 978-0-08-100643-6

Azmi (2010) concluded that Islamic HRM systems should be internalised in all Islamic-based organisations (IBOs) since they are preferable to conventional Western systems in Islamic contexts. The latter generally concentrate on extrinsic rewards including higher position, pay, status, job security and working facilities. A study by Ahmad et al. (2010) found that those who are motivated intrinsically with their jobs are more satisfied in their organisations, and therefore contribute more significantly to organisational effectiveness. This study highlights the intrinsic motivation in the forms of workplace environment, organisational support, employee engagement, training and development, and proficiency in Islam as the key determinants of job satisfaction and hence organisational effectiveness. The chapter does not attempt to explore the holistic view of Islamic HRM, but rather the use of intrinsic elements as the motivational tools to achieve job satisfaction in IBOs. It uses existing literature to develop a conceptual framework with which to analyse the intrinsic motivation–job satisfaction link in IBOs in Islamic regional countries such as Brunei Darussalam, Indonesia and Malaysia.

LITERATURE REVIEW

Job satisfaction can be defined as a positive emotional state resulting from the pleasure an employee derives from doing a job (Locke, 1976; Spector, 1997), or as the affective and cognitive attitudes held by an employee about various aspects of their work (Kalleberg, 1977; Wong et al., 1998). Job satisfaction is a result derived from both extrinsic and intrinsic motivation. Extrinsic motivation is driven by the goal of obtaining additional resources (Lindenberg, 2001). According to Brief and Aldag (1977), extrinsic working rewards are in the forms of money, power and recognition. Based on the study conducted by Gottschalg and Zollo (2004), the performance impact of intrinsic motivation is much more powerful than that of extrinsic motivation. However, if the employees are able to perform tasks even without receiving any forms of payment, their willingness to complete a task with extra responsibility and working hours is called proficiency (or *ihsan* in Malay language).

Beekun and Badawi (1999) defined proficient employees as those who push themselves beyond the call of duty with energy and willingness to make sacrifices in the performance of their task. This demonstrates that an employee is a human being who does not only do things for themselves but also takes actions which positively affect the lives of others (e.g. family, siblings, neighbours, fellow employees and close friends) in order to defend and protect the *sha'aer* (signs) of Allah). In the case of management, someone who has proficiency works tirelessly to carry out their responsibilities, doing it as a religious duty (*ibadah*) (ISCC, 2000). The question is whether many employees are willing to work more without asking for extra rewards? If they are, is it because they are loyal to the company or perceive their work as *ibadah*? This is the question that this chapter explores in the Islamic context, as well as how it can be related to intrinsic motivation towards job satisfaction in IBOs.

Islam proposes that humans are dual in nature, constituting both physical and spiritual dimensions. It is argued that the spiritual dimension has been substantially neglected in the Western literature. Islamic teaching suggests that it is this core element of employees that needs to be motivated. The material rewards that one gets can be disappointing sometimes. However, the non-material rewards can be more satisfying, exciting and lasting. In other words, it is the spiritual dimension that needs to be continually motivated and inspired in order to develop that passion for excellence or feeling to excel. While this aspect is included in Western motivational theories, its importance has seldom been researched and may be the real key to excellence, especially in Islamic contexts (Alhabshi, 1998), and may contribute significantly to enhanced organisational effectiveness.

We have seen a dramatic increase in the growth of IBOs in banking institutions in Malaysia. Even though, the demand for the Islamic banking products and services in Malaysia is considered encouraging, the corresponding development of Islamic HRM for all banks in Malaysia is quite disappointing. Breaches of trust among employees, especially in the Islamic banking industry, is a very big issue to be taken seriously by the management. Positive public perceptions of Islamic banks are important because they believe that such institutions should apply Islamic values in their daily work. In Indonesia for instance, the work ethics of job satisfaction of its Islamic banking staff were discussed extensively by the local researchers in order to examine the association between Islamic values and job satisfaction (Komari and Djafar, 2013). Although the result of this study showed that the factors are not necessarily related to one another and depend on the types of institutions studied, doubtless the employees' behaviours in performing their jobs are likely to contribute towards organisational effectiveness (Ali and Azim, 1995; Valentine and Barnett, 2007). Thus supporting job satisfaction among employees of an organisation, in particular IBOs, is considered crucial.

A study, which was undertaken by Basir (2001) in the Islamic country of Brunei Darussalam, found that high intrinsic motivation will increase one's job satisfaction, together with job-related knowledge or technical know-how. The study also supports other Muslim scholars (Altalib and Aiyah, 1991; Tayeb, 1997; Ali, 2005; Hashim, 2009) who have long advocated that effective Islamic principles and compliance and guidelines in HRM practices would positively reinforce the workforce and create a synergy of commitment, quality, productivity and overall organisational effectiveness in workplaces. In Islamic countries, the employer has a major responsibility which he must perform to ensure the necessary rights acquired by employees, meaning that employers have a responsibility to make sure that people who work with them are treated fairly and with respect, and to provide them with a safe and secure workplace. The manager also needs to understand some common Islamic practices such as daily prayers, observance of Ramadan, wearing the hijab and *halal* requirements. *Halal* is an Arabic word which means lawful or permitted. It is the standard of conduct for Muslims, prescribed in the Al-Qur'an. Thus acknowledging different religions and cultures can help managers to meet their legal obligations and at the same time will be able to attract and retain the best possible employees regardless of their background (Ab Rahman, 2006). This can require flexibility to accommodate people of different religions and beliefs. The employer–employee relationship, according to Islamic principles, is based on kinship relations, not on a master–slave relationship. Therefore the employer–employee relationship should meet the characteristics of the services of a person and their brother or sister. The Prophet Muhammad (*pbuh*) said:

> *Your brothers are your responsibility. Allah has made them under your hands. So whosoever has a brother under his hand, let him give him food as he eats and dress as he dresses. Do not give them work that will overburden them and if you give them such task, then provide them assistance.*
>
> ***(Al-Bukhari)***

Sharia (Islamic Law) allows everyone the right to undertake any lawful activities. Employees should be treated with self-respect. An employer does not have any right to degrade others' jobs. As mentioned earlier, the employer–employee relationship should be based on kinship. Hence, any relevant questions pertaining to job descriptions, salary, top-down relationships, career development and promotional programmes need to be addressed effectively by both parties. Based on these aspects, the following section proposes a conceptual framework for establishing the link between intrinsic motivation and job satisfaction, with implications for HRM practices and organisational effectiveness.

PROPOSED CONCEPTUAL FRAMEWORK

In the proposed framework, five determinants of intrinsic motivation are suggested as a set of tools to measure the components of job satisfaction, and indirectly to find out the inner drive of the employees to perform jobs as a religious duty. Each of the proposed determinants is supported by quotations from the primary sources of *Sharia*. The five determinants are workplace environment, training and development, employee engagement in the workforce, organisational support and proficiency in Islam. Each of these determinants is initially derived from the components under Maslow's Hierarchy of Needs. As a result, for adequate workplace motivation, it is important that leaders understand which needs are most important for individual employee motivation. In this regard, Abraham Maslow's model indicates that basic, low-level needs such as physiological requirements and safety must be satisfied before higher-level needs are pursued. The related determinants were chosen in the first place based on the needs of intrinsic values at the IBOs (see Figure 10.1).

The proposed framework of the intrinsic determinants that contribute towards job satisfaction in the IBOs is further illustrated in Figure 10.2. Justifications for their selection are further explained in the next few paragraphs.

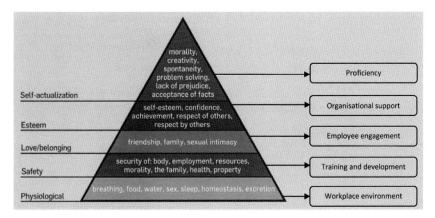

Figure 10.1 Intrinsic values of IBOs, as derived from Maslow's Hierarchy of Needs
Source: *Maslow (1943)*.

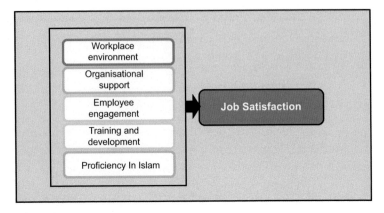

Figure 10.2 The intrinsic determinants of job satisfaction in Islamic contexts

Workplace environment

If houses for dwelling use are a must for humans, workplaces are the same for employees. From the management's perspective, the physical workplace and its environment play a vigorous role in motivating employees to perform their work better. Ab Rahman (2006) considered the workplace environment as a working space with a set of positive characteristics, including safety, health, cleanliness, less hazards, a convenient physical layout and an adequate emergency system. According to Chandrasekar (2011), money is not a sufficient motivator in encouraging the workplace performance required in today's competitive business environment. Job satisfaction begins by first providing a positive workplace environment. A positive working environment will boost employees' productivity and therefore their collective contributions to organisational effectiveness. Furthermore, when the environment is positive, the problems faced by employees who may have contributed to the decline in productivity, such as accidents at work, absenteeism, sick leave, loss of focus and loyalty to the company, can be overcome (Whitmore, 2015). In Islam, being a responsible employer even to their employees at the workplace is very important. The prophet said:

> It is the responsibility of the master (employer), giving the work to his employees, what is easily made by him. They should not be given a job which causes their health to be affected.

> **(Narrated by Ibn Majah)**

As was included in Maslow's Hierarchy, safety also needs to be fulfilled before one can achieve job satisfaction. Therefore, the responsibility of an employer to provide better workplaces for their employees is also required in Islam, as is to boost the 'inner drive' of the employees directly through intrinsic motivation and overall satisfaction with what they are doing. The examples of good working environments may include a conducive workplace, clean and fresh air, suitable layout of office arrangement, safety requirements, sport room facilities, prayer room and less hazards in the workplace. Gensler (2005) confirmed the impact of the workplace environment on improving productivity by 19 per cent, and 79 per cent of his respondents linked their environment to their job satisfaction. The research was based on a survey of 200 middle and senior managers in the legal, media and financial sectors in the UK. A prior study done by a group of researchers showed the same result as the previous study mentioned where the majority of the employees of Bank Islam Malaysia Berhad (BIMB) agreed that workplace environment was one of the main contributors to their job satisfaction (Mohd Noor et al., 2013).

Organisational support

Organisational factors also impact on job satisfaction. The facilities and support provided make the employees more comfortable in the organisation and reduce complaints, as organisational commitment is communicated by such components as insurance, medical assistance, training, educational support, recognition, recreation and study leave. The Value Attained Model (VAM), studied by Kreitner and Kinicki (2007) is based on the belief that satisfaction comes from the perception that one's job fulfils an individual work value. Employers can improve their employees' job satisfaction by encouraging them to take their holidays and have appropriate work–life balance (Westover et al., 2010). The concept of the Islamic paradigm of management has its origin in Al-Qur'an and the sayings and practices of the Prophet Muhammad (*pbuh*), who suggested that:

> Those working with or under you are your brothers. Those who serve you have been made by God, subservient to you. So, whoever has his brother under his control should feed him from what he eats and give him clothes the like of which he wears; and do not impose on them a task which should be too hard for them, and if you impose on them such task, then help them.

In addition, Islam speaks about honesty, flexibility, justice, responsibility, accountability and fair work systems, and encourages acquiring skill and technology for excellence and continuous improvement in performance and job satisfaction of the team (Abbassi et al., 2010). Prophet Muhammad (*pbuh*) said,

> When you hire, compensate the workers and treat them fairly.

> Compensate the worker before the sweat dries.

Employee engagement

Employee engagement is an assessment of an employee's emotional commitment to an organisation. It serves both employees and their employers well. Research conducted by Trenouth (2009) shows that employees who are committed in their work are likely to be more ethical, loyal, progressive in their careers and happier in their personal life. The employer gains significantly through a reduction in layoffs and an increase in competitive advantage among their employees that contributes to organisational effectiveness. Employees are more committed and have higher levels of their engagement when there is a process for them to contribute their ideas and suggestions. This gives them a sense of ownership and pride in their work. Capturing employees' suggestions and ideas engages and improves employee motivation, creating a more productive satisfying work environment.

An Equity Model asserts that satisfaction is based on the perception of how fairly an individual is treated at work. This is largely based on how one's own work outcome, relative to their input and effort, is compared to the input or output of others in the workplace (Kreitner and Kinicki, 2007). Islam is a religion that believes in freedom, justice and equality. Islam is an Arabic term meaning 'peace and submission to the Will of Allah (God)'. Islam is a way of life that encompasses every aspect of a Muslim's life at home and abroad, at all times. Fairness and equity are a part of that way of life. Allah said in the Al-Qur'an:

> Give full measure when you measure out and weigh with a fair balance. This is fair and better in the end.
>
> **(17:35)**

If one sees that another is receiving equal or greater rewards for doing less work, the employer's duty is to make an effort to seek their employees' understanding, and to try to interact with the employees in a way that could help them to feel that they are being treated fairly (Westover et al., 2010). Today's managers have to change their style of functioning in order to bring about effective changes in these aspects. They have to spend more time facilitating engagement with their employees rather than micro-managing them (Chandrasekar, 2011). This requires the delegation of adequate authority to employees, the clarification of job responsibilities, increased accountability and the encouragement of teamwork.

To meet the standard, goal-oriented individual work consistently and effectively as a team, they share a common purpose and present with patience to perform consistently at a high level. The Islamic paradigm of team management promotes consistent excellence in meeting job satisfaction standards both in personal and collective efforts, and encourages improvement in all related fields. It also focuses on strengthening intrinsic ethical value, for example honesty, decency, truth and justice among the team members. Prophet Muhammad (*pbuh*) was also stern about Muslim employees working together as a team. In a *hadith*, he once said:

> Faithful believers are to each other as the bricks of a wall, supporting and reinforcing each other. So saying, the Prophet Muhammad clasped his hands by interlocking his fingers.

(Al-Bukhari)

According to Zain (2015), the 'interlocking fingers' image represents how close *ummah* (believers) can stick to each other and how much stronger they can be, without allowing anything to fall through the 'net'. Islam has always looked highly upon leadership as the head of teamwork, reminding *ummah* to select the best leaders, according to leadership qualities, and also to be good followers of such a leader. Criticising leaders is also allowed in Islam as long as it is conducted in a dignified manner. A leader is a human like everyone else. They have their own flaws and fears, no matter how intelligent they may be. Thus a good follower is also someone who can advise their leader when they see them doing wrong things. This can be done without insults and violence. In management, *shura* (consultation) is one of the Islamic principles of leadership, which instils brotherhood and also the fear of God. *Shura* will not allow a leader to make decisions based on their personal interests. Basically, *shura* comprises learned representatives from the community and acts as the consultative panels. By doing this, any disputes will be discussed in *shura* in order to ensure that all levels of the community are well-taken care of. Hence, leadership is a responsibility and not a luxury. Thus *shura* can be viewed as a tool to keep a leader on the right track in their leadership for the benefits of all nations.

Ahmed et al. (2010) observed a significant relationship between intrinsic motivation and job satisfaction. When an individual works based on Islamic ethics, the motivation, which comes from inside the individual seems to be better and more satisfying. It may be the intrinsic motivation which also results in the satisfaction (Haroon et al., 2012; Zaman et al., 2013). On the other hand, satisfied employees show more motivation than their colleagues. Employees satisfied with their job are often motivated at work (Machado et al., 2011). However, keeping employees happy in their workplace is hard, because happiness comes from within. Happy employees are satisfied and feel a sense of accomplishment in their work. They like themselves and what they do, and they find satisfaction from their work, a sense that what they do is important and meaningful. Such feelings reduce stress, which is a major harmful factor for productivity. This strength of inner character in the team member guides them to the strong commitment to meet their objective (Abbasi et al., 2010). That is why IBOs are the most suitable platform to implement the above framework, which derives from the Islamic perspective:

> O you who believe, Stand out firmly for justice, as witnesses to Allah, as against yourselves, or your parents, or your kin; and whether it be against rich or poor: For Allah can best protect both. Follow not the lusts (of your hearts), lest you swerve, and if you distort justice or decline to do justice, verily Allah is well-acquainted with all that you do.
>
> *(4:135)*

Training and development

Training and development refer to the process of increasing the knowledge, skill, attitude, ability, aptitude and potential of employees for better job performance and to accomplish the organisational goals (Flippo, 1984). Islamic training and development focus on purifying one's soul (tazkiyah al-nafs). The Al-Qur'an encourages human beings to acquire knowledge, skills and technology and highly praises those who strive in order to earn a living. Indeed, humans' basic qualification for being the representative of Allah on earth is to process knowledge. Allah said:

> Are those who know equal to those who know not? But only they who are endowed with understanding, keep this in mind.
>
> *(58:11)*

Many organisations today are modelling their training towards the fulfilment of individualised needs in order to enhance job performance (Smith, 2006). A combination of training and development with proper execution and monitoring inculcate progressively the wealth of human capital consisting of skills, knowledge, innovative ideas and positive attitude. The outcome is not merely a capable workforce or quality human capital, but also a wide spectrum of career enhancement opportunities. In the case of Malaysia, the formation of the Islamic Banking and Finance Institute (IBFIM), the International Centre for Education in Islamic Finance (INCEIF) and the Malaysian International Islamic Centre (MIFC) are indicators as well as initiatives toward realising and supporting the importance of training and development for the growth of Islamic financial management. The fast growth of Islamic-based financing and the diligent actions of government in supporting financial institutions to adopt and practise banking services divisions on Islamic principles sees the role of training becoming more critical in familiarising and understanding Islamic concepts and practices.

Thus training and development are considered essential ways for organisations to help their employees gain both generic or specialised knowledge and skills (Goldstein and Gilliam, 1990; Rosow and Zager, 1988). Training and development motivate people and make them more productive and innovative. Well-trained employees are more capable and willing to assume more control over their job. The amount and perceived helpfulness of training are both positively correlated with job satisfaction and affective commitment (Ismail, 2012). In contrast, it has a negative correlation in employees' intentions to leave their organisations (Saks, 1996). In Islam, *ummah* are required to learn and teach.

Daniels (2003) suggested that training should not be regarded as a luxury to be undertaken when time and budgets allow. Nor is it wise to think of training as remedial, as a matter of shoring up weak employees or fixing problems. Many organisations have already changed their mindset about the training function. They have seen for themselves that training is where skills are developed, attitudes are transformed, ideas evolved and the organisation reinvented. In the course of learning, skills will indirectly increase sales, build effective teams and improve quality, innovativeness and creativity. Thus employees create a new dimension of organisational culture. Islam places the emphasis on using wisdom and translating the theoretical into behaviours rather than solely relying on one's theory.

Proficiency in Islam

Proficiency is commonly understood as doing more than the minimum requirement or what has only been asked (Abbasi et al., 2010). Alhabshi and Ghazali (1994) defined performance as proficiency. Proficiency, among other outcomes, means efficiency, which suggests greater productivity of goods and services. Employees who have performed in doing their job show high satisfaction and productivity as compared to those who do not. There are two types of people, one who performs their duties scrupulously but does not demonstrate any additional commitment, and others who push themselves beyond the call of duty. It is not enough for a person to be good at their work. They need to give it their every effort. They excel in showing care in its finishing touches and in how it is presented. According to Ahmad (2008), the term proficiency signifies the beauty or perfection of one's behaviour. Proficiency relates to *ihsan*, which means doing a good job or doing a task in a proficient manner. As an Islamic concept, *ihsan* denotes the divine presence, as indicated by the following *hadith* when the holy prophet was asked by the Allah about *ihsan* and he said:

> That you worship Allah as if you see Him; for if you see Him not, surely He sees you.
> **(Narrated by Bukhari)**

Ihsan is closely related to faith in God (*iman*) and fear of God (*taqwa*). In fact, it has been described as the beautification of faith and Islam. It indicates a state of sincerity in one's conviction and practice. It embodies both faith and Islam, since the former relates to the conviction and the latter is more related to practice. *Ihsan* has at least three shades of meaning. The dictionary meaning includes right action, goodness, charity, sincerity and the like. Do the right things and increase efficiency. If employees in an organisation show good proficiency, understand what they are doing (*fiqh*) and know the impact of their good performance. This will increase an organisation's profitability, reduce waste and build a good reputation for the entire organisation. As a result, the stakeholders will become more satisfied. The second signifies proficiency and is derived from the *hadith*:

> Verily Allah has prescribed proficiency in all things. Thus, if you kill, kill well; and if you slaughter, slaughter well. Let each one of you sharpen his blade and let them spare suffering to the animal he slaughters.
> **(Narrated by Muslim)**

The proposed framework is considered timely in identifying factors which contribute towards job satisfaction, with a modification of Maslow's Hierarchy (1943) in order to make it suitable for the Islamic way of management. Besides, the framework also can determine the level of job satisfaction of employees in IBOs based on empirical study. The importance of developing the inner drive of all employees is in no doubt. This is because most of the conventional approaches to motivation will only lead people to ask more from the management in fulfilling their ultimate desire (self-actualisation), which is normally translated into extrinsic rewards. For example, having a big house and a luxury car. Fail to fulfill one's desire will lead to the discretion of dissatisfaction of unlimited tangible human needs and wants. On the other hand, Islam emphasises commitment and dedication to work and intrinsic ethical values relate more closely to team commitment than extrinsic measures. Intrinsic motivation implies the intangible factors including the relationship between God and human (hablu minallah), and the relationship between human beings (hablu minannas). Both relations are extremely important to ensure long lasting satisfaction in life. This type of motivation results from the pleasure of work or the satisfaction of taking an action or even simply work itself (Zamani and Talatapeh, 2014). Starting with fulfilling the need for a better workplace and giving knowledge pertaining to their work, the employees then are motivated to work eagerly at the workplace by engaging and seeking commitment between workers and employers in order to obtain internal satisfaction (Zaman et al., 2013). The last stage of intrinsic motivation refers to proficiency and it is intrinsically interesting and enjoyable, has a significant relationship with job satisfaction, and influences organisational commitment and effectiveness (Hayati and Caniago, 2012).

CONCLUSION

Intrinsic motivation is an inner drive which reflects the internal aspect of individuals, rooted inside them. This motivation has a permanent effect and it is the spirit which helps individuals to consider themselves in a higher position compared to all creatures. With this type of motivation, an individual enjoys internal satisfaction which has a more enduring and long-term effect compared to the material (extrinsic) type. As discussed before, doing work for life and for the benefits of others are considered a form of worship. From an Islamic perspective, employees who work with this idea know that God observes them in whatever they do and believe that they will achieve real success in their eternal life or life after death. Thus intrinsic motivation is at the top of the list for Muslims because only spiritual motivation can be a real force towards real success (Ghauri, 2009).

It is understood that there are difficulties in estimating or delivering new knowledge to academic researchers since it is intangible, and not many researchers have explored it in any depth. For this reason, exploring the way to ensure employee satisfaction in an organisation is very important because it leads to loyalty and ultimately organisational effectiveness. Employees are assets and resources of an organisation that are essential in achieving an organisation's targets. An employee who is satisfied with their job may remain loyal to the organisation. Similarly, dissatisfied employees may have an intention to leave the organisation (Ramly et al., 2010).

According to Freeland (2013), employee satisfaction and engagement have proven to be an effective way to motivate employees to be more productive, work harder and display more loyalty to their organisations. Hence, ensuring long-term employee satisfaction is a key to reduce the disruptive tendencies that could hamper organisational effectiveness such as low productivity and frequent turnover. However, in achieving organisational effectiveness (defined by Etzioni (1964) as 'the degree to which an organisation realises its goals') through HRM needs a wider framework that will take into consideration the external and internal approaches as suggested by

Bisig et al. (2007) in their study entitled *Improving Organizational Effectiveness – Theoretical Framework and Model*. Subsequent empirical research will look for representative data gathered from the local IBOs to identify the possible connection between intrinsic factors and job satisfaction as proposed in the framework presented earlier in this chapter.

REFERENCES

Abbasi, A.S., Hameed, I., Bibi, A., 2010. Team management: the Islamic paradigm. African Journal of Business Management 5, 1957–1982.

Ahmad, H., Ahmad, K., Shah, I.A., 2010. Relationship between job satisfaction, job performance attitude towards work and organizational commitment. European Journal of Social Sciences 18 (2), 257–267.

Ahmad, R.A., 2008. An Islamic perspective on organizational motivation, department of political science. American Journal of Islamic Social Science 2, 12–14.

Ahmed, I., Nawaz, M.M., Iqbal, N., Ali, I., Shaukat, Z., Usman, A., 2010. Effect of motivational factors on employees' job satisfaction: a case study of the University of the Punjab, Pakistan. International Journal of Business and Management 5 (3), 70–80.

Alhabshi, S.O., 1998. Values-based leadership: its significance to modern organizations. In: Hassan, M.N. (Ed.), Values-Based Management. Institute of Islamic Understanding Malaysia, Kuala Lumpur.

Alhabshi, S.O., Ghazali, A.H., 1994. Islamic Values and Management. Selangor: Institute of Islamic Understanding Malaysia.

Ali, A., 2005. Islamic Perspectives on Management and Organization. New Horizons in Management Series. Edward Elgar Publishing Limited, United Kingdom.

Ali, A.J., Azim, A., 1995. Work ethic and loyalty in Canada. Journal of Social Psychology 135 (1), 31–37.

Altalib, H., Aiyah, I.A., 1991. Training Guide for Islamic Workers. International Islamic Federation of Student Organizations, USA.

Azmi, I.A.G., 2010. Islamic human resource practices and organizational performance: a preliminary finding of Islamic organizations in Malaysia. Journal of Global Business and Economics 1 (1), 1–16.

Basir, N., 2001. A Study of Motivation and Job Satisfaction in the Brunei Civil Service Doctoral thesis. University of Leicester. Retrieved from ProQuest/UMI Dissertation Publishing (accession order no. U139756).

Beekun, R., Badawi, J., 1999. Leadership: An Islamic Perspective. Amana Publications, Beltsville, MD.

Bisig, E., Tresch, T.S., Seiler, S., 2007. Improving Organizational Effectiveness - Theoretical Framework and Model. Swiss Military Academy at the ETH, Zurich. Working Paper for the HFM-163/RTG Working Group. Available from http://www.vtg.admin.ch/internet/vtg/de/home/schweizerarmee/organisation/hkaneu/milak/militaerwissenschaftliche/militaersozioligie/publikationen.parsys.93405.downloadList.3336.DownloadFile.tmp/521theoreticalframeworkimprovingorganizationaleffectivenesstelaviv.pdf.

Brief, A.P., Aldag, R.J., 1977. The intrinsic-extrinsic dichotomy: towards conceptual clarity. Academy of Management Review 2 (3), 496.

Chandrasekar, K., 2011. Workplace environment and its impact on organizational performance in public sector organizations. International Journal of Enterprise Computing and Business Systems 1 (1), 1–20.

Daniels, S., 2003. Employee training: a strategic approach to better return on investment. Journal of Business Strategy 24 (5), 39–42.

Etzioni, A., 1964. Modern Organizations. Prentice-Hall, Englewood Cliffs, NJ.

Flippo, E.B., 1984. Personnel Management, 6th edn. McGraw-Hill, New York.

Freeland, D., 2013, April 24. Employee satisfaction leads to increased productivity. Loyalty Today. 24 April. Available from *http://loyalty360.org/loyalty-today/article/employee-satisfaction-leads-to-increased-productivity* (accessed 28.09.15).

Gensler.com, 2005. These Four Walls: The Real British Office. London. Retrieved 25 September 2015 from http://www.gensler.com/doc/survey-these-four-walls.

Ghauri, M.T., 2009. Religious motivation: a multiplying force. The Dialogue 6 (2), 103–123.

Goldstein, I.L., Gilliam, P., 1990. Training system issues in the year 2000. American Psychologist 45, 134–143.

Gottschalg, O., Zollo, M., 2004. Interest Alignment and Competitive Advantage. INSEAD Working Paper. Wharton Alliance Centre for Global Research & Development, University of Pennsylvania.

Hanapi, M.S., 2014. The wasatiyyah (moderation) concept in Islamic epistemology: a case study of its implementation in Malaysia. International Journal of Humanities and Social Science 4 (9), 51–62.

Haroon, M., Fakhar, M., Rehman, W., 2012. The relationship between Islamic work ethics and employee job satisfaction in the healthcare sector of Pakistan. International Journal of Contemporary Business Studies 3 (5), 6–12.

Hashim, J., 2009. Islamic revival in human resource management practices among selected Islamic organisations in Malaysia. International Journal of Islamic and Middle Eastern Finance and Management 2 (3), 251–267.

Hayati, K., Caniago, I., 2012. Islamic work ethic: the role of intrinsic motivation, job satisfaction, organizational commitment and job performance. Procedia – Social and Behavioral Sciences 65, 272–277.

ISCC, 2000. Unity of Muslim Ummah? Islamic Supreme Council of Canada. Retrieved 25 September from http://www.islamicsupremecouncil.com/unity-of-muslim-ummah/.

Ismail, N., 2012. Organizational Commitment and Job Satisfaction Among Staff of Higher Learning Education Institutions in Kelantan Master's thesis. Universiti Utara Malaysia.

Jurgensen, C.E., 1978. Job preferences: what makes a job good or bad? Journal of Applied Psychology 50, 479–487.

Kalleberg, A.L., 1977. Work values and job rewards: a theory of job satisfaction. American Sociological Review 42, 124–143.

Komari, N., Djafar, F., 2013. Work ethics, work satisfaction and organizational commitment at the Sharia Bank, Indonesia. International Business Research 6 (12), 107–117.

Kreitner, R., Kinicki, A., 2007. Organizational Behavior. McGraw-Hill, Irwin, Boston.

Lindenberg, S., 2001. Intrinsic motivation in a new light. Kyklos 54 (2), 317–342.

Locke, E., 1976. The nature and causes of job satisfaction. In: Dunnette, M.D. (Ed.), Handbook of Industrial and Organizational Psychology. Rand McNally, Chicago, pp. 1297–1349.

Machado, M.L., Soaresb, V.M., Britesc, R., Ferreirad, J.B., Gouveiae, O.M.R., 2011. A look to academics job satisfaction and motivation in Portuguese higher education institutions. Procedia - Social and Behavioral Sciences 29, 1715–1724.

Maslow, A.H., 1943. A theory of human motivation. Psychological Review 50 (4), 370–396.

Mohd Noor, A., Johan, A., Abok, I., Mohammed, R.U., 2013. Does Intrinsic Motivation Influence the Level of Job Satisfaction? A Case Study on Staff of BIMB in Kota Kinabalu Master's Thesis. Universiti Teknologi MARA.

Rahman, Ab, 2006. Protection of safety, health and welfare of employees at workplace under Islamic law. IIUM Journal 14 (1), 51–66.

Ramly, Z., Majdi, H., Rashid, A., 2010. Critical review of literature on corporate governance and the cost of capital: the value creation perspective. African Journal of Business Management 4 (11), 2198–2204.

Rosow, J.M., Zager, R., 1988. Training: The Competitive Edge. Jossey-Bass, San Francisco.

Saks, A.M., 1996. The relationship between the amount and helpfulness of entry training and work outcomes. Human Relations 49, 429–451.

Smith, A., 2006. The development of employer training in Australia. Education and Training Journal 48 (4), 95–108.

Spector, P., 1997. Application. Assessment, Causes and Consequences. Sage Publications, Inc., California.

Tayeb, M., 1997. Islamic revival in Asia and human resource management. Employee Relations 19 (4), 352–364.

Trenouth, S., 2009. in OPCA, Employee Satisfaction versus Employee Engagement. Oregon Primary Care Association. Retrieved from http://www.oregon.gov/oha/OHPR/PCO/Documents/Employee%20Engagement%20vs%20Satisfaction.pdf (accessed 06.09.15).

Valentine, S., Barnett, T., 2007. Perceived organizational ethics and the ethical decisions of sales and marketing personnel. Journal of Personal Selling and Sales Management 27 (4), 373–388.

Westover, J.H., Westover, A.R., Westover, L.A., 2010. Enhancing long-term worker productivity and performance: the connection of key work domains to job satisfaction and organizational commitment. International Journal of Productivity and Performance Management 59 (4), 372–387.

Whitmore, J., 2015. Boost Productivity by Optimizing Your Work Environment. Entrepreneur Media, 25 February. Retrieved from http://www.entrepreneur.com/article/243201 (accessed 25.09.15).

Wong, C.S., Hui, C., Law, K.S., 1998. A longitudinal study of the job perception–job satisfaction relationship: a test of the three alternative specifications. Journal of Occupational and Organisational Psychology 71, 127–146.

Zain, M., 2015. Teamwork in Islam: Living in a Muslim Team. OnIslam, 17 March. Retrieved from http://www.onislam.net/english/reading-islam/living-islam/islam-day-to-day/society/463665-teamwork-in-islam-living-in-a-muslim-team.html (accessed 17.09.15).

Zaman, H.M.F., Nas, Z., Ahmed, M., Raja, Y.M., Marri, M.Y.Kh, 2013. The mediating role of intrinsic motivation between Islamic work ethics and employee job satisfaction. Journal of Business Studies Quarterly 5 (1), 93–102.

Zamani, A., Talatapeh, B.B., 2014. Discussion of the motivation in the Islamic and non-Islamic worlds. Journal of Applied Environmental and Biological Sciences 4 (4), 68–73.

CHAPTER 11

Conclusion: the human resource management–organisational effectiveness link: overview and the role of HR practitioners

C. Rowley, A. Nankervis, N.M. Salleh

INTRODUCTION

As we stated in Chapter 1, the contributions of human resource (HR) functions and practitioners and HR management (HRM) systems and processes to organisational effectiveness has been less focused on Asia. Our book explores this subject and region both conceptually and empirically. Accordingly, our book adds to the literature and strategic HRM (SHRM) on this important topic and the differences and similarities between these linkages in Asian and Western contexts using diverse countries, sectors and organisations, including multinational companies (MNCs).

This chapter has twin aims. First we reiterate our individual contributions, before exploring HRM more broadly and the developmental role of HR practitioners on organisational effectiveness more specifically.

OVERVIEW OF CONTENT

A quick reminder of the logic and content of our book follows. We divided the chapters into three parts. The first part comprised two conceptual chapters and explored broad contextual issues impacting on the HRM and organisational effectiveness relationship in different regions and organisations. Chapter 2 overviewed the challenges and opportunities associated with the formation of the new Asian Economic Community (AEC) to reveal 'winner' and 'loser' economies. Thus Singapore had significant attraction and retention opportunities relative to Malaysia, Thailand, Indonesia and the Phillipines, but possibly struggled to retain its advantages against Australia and New Zealand due to their attractive employment conditions

*Asia Pacific Human Resource Management
and Organisational Effectiveness*
ISBN 978-0-08-100643-6

and lifestyle issues. The HRM and organisational effectiveness relationship will be a crucial factor in the projected increases in labour mobility envisaged by the AEC.

Chapter 3 presented a different macro-perspective on HRM and organisational effectiveness. Through an intra-psychic lens it examined the transference of Western theories of emotional intelligence (EI), mindfulness and neurobiological science to Asian cultures and HRM practices given the significant cultural differences in emotional expression between them. It considered the application of these concepts to teamwork, job performance, productivity, leadership and overall organisational performance and found EI enabled better assessment and moderation of contingencies while making decisions.

The second part had five chapters on HRM roles and competencies and organisational effectiveness in Asian countries. Chapter 4 took a broader approach, and analysed corporate social responsibility and unethical practices during and after the 2008 global financial crisis in the Australian banking sector. This showed how unethical behaviours eroded stakeholders' (employees' and customers') commitment and engagement, with consequences for organisational effectiveness and how HRM practices could be enhanced through attention to and reinforcement of ethical behaviours.

The next three chapters focused more on the relationship between HRM roles and competencies and organisational effectiveness. Chapter 5 explored the HRM 'strategic business partner' (SBP) role in Indian MNCs. It argued that SHRM was most productive when it encompassed the three key components of 'strategic agility' (external fit), 'knowledge management' and 'management development' (internal fit). It concluded that the SBP role was especially critical for MNCs operating in complex and dynamic business environments.

Chapter 6 analysed HRM's 'evolution' in stages from an administrative to a more strategic role and the associated contributions to organisational effectiveness in three Asian economies. It found that while there were differences in the forms and applications of SHRM across diverse ownership and sector types, overall most HR roles remained primarily the 'functional HRM specialist', having progressed from purely 'administrative expert' roles but not yet developed fully as SBPs. It identified differences between countries, sectors and organisational types and concluded that HRM is in a transitional phase.

Chapter 7 analysed the application of concepts of HRM devolution and social capital to the links between HRM, line managers and organisational effectiveness. Using the example of hospitality resorts in the Maldives, this chapter explored how these managerial relationships enhanced HRM practices and organisational effectiveness. It concluded that there was an 'interaction effect' between HR professionals and line managers.

Chapter 8 focused on the relationships between SHRM and work quality in Australian organisations. Using a four-dimensional analytical framework of job prospects, intrinsic job quality, extrinsic job quality and working time quality, it demonstrated that organisational effectiveness had both qualitative and quantitative components and associated work quality with well-being from the employee perspective. Good work quality (on all four dimensions) was likely to result in higher productivity and organisational effectiveness, as seen in lower rates of employee turnover, absenteeism and tardiness and improved well-being.

The third part contained two complementary chapters which analysed the influences of Asian employee relations and Islamic traditions on the HRM and organisational effectiveness link. Chapter 9 explored trade union relationships with members and the government in Malaysia. To determine if trade union strength could be developed through its members relationship capital theory was used to identify if it could create a strong bond with members. It analysed the effectiveness of unions in relation to their representation of the collective 'voice' of members needs, particularly in negotiations over salary, security and safety and whether they assisted in the satisfaction of employees' self-esteem and self-actualisation needs. It questioned whether unions could be strengthened through the facilitation of expressions of member 'voice'.

Chapter 10 provided a conceptual framework for the analysis of job satisfaction from an Islamic perspective. Using Western notions of extrinsic and intrinsic job satisfaction determinants the chapter explored how they were applied in Islamic organisations. Intrinsic determinants were the motivation to actively engage in learning activities out of curiosity, interest or enjoyment in order to achieve intellectual and personal goals. Intrinsic factors focused on the non-materialistic goals. Examples of Islamic concepts and principles demonstrated the differences and similarities with Western counterparts within and outside these countries. It concluded that Islamic organisations were more likely to favour intrinsic rather than extrinsic approaches towards job satisfaction, with emphases on religious values and personal and community services.

Overall, our chapters indicated several important points in the HRM–organisational effectiveness relationship. One is the key issue of the role of HR practitioners themselves. We now locate this in its HRM context.

OVERVIEW OF THE ROLE OF HRM AND HR PRACTITIONERS

Marchington (2008) argued that HRM's key role was to 'balance the competing needs of different constituents … and to solve problems' (p. 4). He provided a categorisation of broad HRM competencies as 'a sound understanding of how institutions and markets shape people management and organisations; very strong technical knowledge of HR practice and processes' (p. 16). Hall and Fourie (2007) similarly summarised overall HRM roles as 'creators or drivers of the business' which required an 'understanding of the internal and external stakeholders' (p. 54).

Challenges to HRM include strategic decision-making, culture management, fast change and market-driven connectivity (Brockbank and Ulrich, 2003) as well as clearly and robustly 'proving' the added-value of HRM practices and HR practitioners. Much HRM research focuses on establishing linkages between HRM and organisational performance, a key driver in competitive advantage. Competitive advantage can derive from the optimal utilisation of internal organisational resources (Wright et al., 2001), notably HR or human capital, ensured through the alignment of HRM strategies and processes and overall business strategies (Brockbank and Ulrich, 2003; Boudreau and Ramstad, 2003). This is the key assumption underlying taxonomies of HR roles and competencies, which together facilitate such successful alignments.

However, not all organisational stakeholders are equally important in this pursuit and, therefore, diverse HR approaches and competencies may be required, not only for different countries, industries and organisations, but also for the 'lifecycle' stage within them. It might also be inferred that not all HR professionals will possess or require all of the designated competencies and that sector and business development stages will demand different sets of HRM skills and competencies.

VARIATIONS IN HR PRACTICE AND PROFESSIONALS

One key variable in the policies and practice of HRM is business strategy and its obvious organisational variations (see Rowley, 2003; Rowley and

Harry, 2011; Rowley and Jackson, 2011). Many taxonomies have been distinguished. These include those in so-called lifecycle models (such as Kochan and Barocci, 1985), with 'Start-Up', 'Growth', 'Maturity' and 'Decline' phases. Porter (1985) had 'Cost Reduction', 'Quality Enhancement' and 'Innovation' strategies. The earlier strategies of 'Defender' and 'Prospector' (Miles and Snow, 1978) were developed into 'Internal' and 'Market Type' employment systems (Delery and Doty, 1996). Grubman (1998) aligned HRM practices to strategic styles labelled 'Products', 'Operations' and 'Customers'. Each of these strategy types have radically different implications for HRM and HR practitioners.

HRM theorists have identified the key roles and competencies which define their strategic, policy and operational functions (Brockbank et al., 1997; Boudreau and Ramstad, 2003; Carroll, 1990; Tyson and Fell, 1986; Wright et al., 2001). It can be seen that, on the one hand, HRM strategies and processes should represent an amalgam of responses to the challenges of the external business environment and internal company imperatives, while on the other that all HRM functions should be integrated with each other (horizontally) and with HRM strategies (vertically).

However, labels often cover a myriad of meanings and practices. In the area of people management and HRM this is certainly the case. So, what has often emerged are a range of titles and names to capture the radically different roles and jobs HR practitioners do. For example, Renwick (2003) suggested three HR manager roles of 'Policy Makers', 'Advice Providers' and 'Administrators'. One useful early schema to recall is the framework developed by Tyson and Fell (1986) of different types of 'people manager'. Using variations in simple variables such as 'discretion' (low to high) and 'planning horizon' (short to long term), a trio of practitioner types each with distinctly different roles were distinguished. These were 'Clerk of the Works' (services junior line managers; administrative support; follows routines; looks for leadership from others), 'Contracts Manager' (services and advises middle managers; provides knowledge of systems/practice; follows systems but modifies to some extent; gives leadership within existing structures) and 'Architect' (consultant to senior managers; conceptualiser, inventiveness, problem-solver; changes routines/systems as necessary; copes rapidly with change; leads/participates with top management).

Another example is Ulrich (1997), whose HRM roles were 'Strategic Partner', 'Change Agent', 'Employee Champion' and 'Administrative

Expert'. Iterations of his study, conducted in 2002, 2007 and 2012, led to extensive revisions. One study (2012) canvassed 20,000 respondents (HR and non-HR managers) in ten countries and resulted in HR roles of 'Strategic Business Partner', 'Capability Builder', 'Change Champion', 'Technology Proponent', 'HR Innovator and Integrator' and 'Credible Activist' (Ulrich et al., 2013: 24).

We can add to this analysis of HR practitioner types by recalling and applying to HRM the seminal work of Katz (1955) with its useful 3 × 4 matrix/grid of skill requirements. This had three broad, general skills labelled 'Technical', 'Human' and 'Conceptual' and four job levels of 'Individual Producer', 'Supervisor', 'Middle Manager' and 'Senior Executive'. Of course, while skills were listed independently, they are interrelated when applied to managerial problems. Nevertheless, the relative importance of these skill groups shifted between job levels and with seniority came, roughly, the need for more human skills, taken as the ability to work cooperatively and be a team player, communicate effectively and resolve conflicts.

Variations in HR professionals may also occur due to the organisation's operational context. We can illustrate this point by considering and applying the underpinnings of the framework of leadership skills in Asia of Rowley and Ulrich (2012a, 2012b). They argued that being an effective leader was a mix of factors, the '3Cs' ('Context', 'Culture', 'Competence') (see Figure 11.1). Some HR practitioners, as detailed in the above typologies, will themselves be leaders of course, as well as, in the jargon, 'followers'.

The first factor, 'Context', is the philosophical country context that shapes how people think and act. Philosophical approaches which underlie behaviour and differences show up in Western versus Asian approaches to business (see Table 11.1). Those from the West assigned to work in Asian organisations need to be aware of their biases and to adapt to Asian philosophies. Similarly, those from Asia who only do things the 'Asian way' will be less able to respond to global pressures. Yet Asians who give into the 'Western way' will totally lose sight of their heritage and be inattentive to their cultural uniqueness.

The second factor, 'Culture', is the unique company culture challenges faced in a particular context. An organisation's culture can start with its strategic challenges. Organisations competing on price need to build cultures of efficiency and cost containment. Organisations competing on innovation need to build cultures of risk-taking and experimentation. Some Asian organisations are shifting from low-cost production of global goods

Figure 11.1 Factors affecting effective leadership. Source: *Rowley and Ulrich (2012b).*

to innovative products and services and face demographic trends impacting on labour force supply. Given this, cultural dimensions to consider include the following six.

1. *Paternalism* – Asian context and organisation cultures tend to be hierarchical and the leaders paternalistic, accepting personal responsibility for the well-being of employees. Asians need to balance hierarchical control through paternalism with employee autonomy that comes from independence.

2. *Time* – Asian mindsets focus more on long- rather than short-term goals. Partly because of financing through debt (convincing a few investors to support them) over equity (showing profits to convince many unknown investors to invest), Asians take longer-term views. HRM systems also need to reflect these imperatives.

3. *Benevolence* – Asian countries and companies have cultures of deference within the hierarchy and an emphasis on teamwork and conformity to shared behavioural expectations. Outspoken employees rarely challenge seniors and such behaviour is discouraged. Such traditions may restrict organisational effectiveness, especially with respect to innovation. Hence,

Table 11.1 Differences in Western and Asian business approaches

	Western	Asian
Time horizon	Short term – how	Long term – future
Strategy	Leading to allocation of resources today	Leading to positioning the firm for the future
Management philosophy	Management by objectives	Management by shared mindset
Decision-making	Fast to decide, longer to sell and implement	Slow to decide, quick to implement
Accountability	Personalised and focused on 'I'	Shared and focused on 'we'
Work	Linear and focused on the task at hand	Cyclical and focused on the context in which work is done
Career orientation	Generalist	Specialist
Rewards	High pay gap between senior executives and employees	Lower pay gap between senior executives and employees
	Pay often based on performance	Pay often based on tenure and position
Leadership philosophy	Hands on, walking ahead of people	Hands off, walking behind people
Philosophical schools	Christianity	Buddhism, Confucianism, Hinduism, Islam, Taoism, Han Fei

Adapted from Rowley and Ulrich (2012b).

managers will need to design internal communication mechanisms by means of which employees are encouraged to share their ideas without compromising manager–employee relationships.

4. *Collaboration* – Asian culture encourages collaboration, mutual support and banding together to achieve common goals. Differences of opinion are not encouraged and if voiced, are done so privately and respectfully. Public confrontations – including potentially constructive differences of opinion – are discouraged. Again, the advantages of these cultural features will need to be balanced with opportunities for individual endeavour and recognition.

5. *Relationships* – Asians learn the importance of 'good connections' (*guanxi*) as such relationships matter as much or more than technical expertise. Many of these relationships are forged through extended family ties, education or early in careers. In particular, relationships with government officials and agencies are crucial.

6. *Organisation* – the three archetypes with different requirements are as follows:

– *Private owned enterprises* – smaller start-ups commonly family run. Some have grown and shifted to professional management but they still have embedded family cultures.

– *State-owned enterprises* – large, government-owned and dominating the infrastructure (construction, telecommunication, education, utilities, finance). These need to adapt to changing conditions and make the bureaucracy more adaptable.

– *Multinational corporations* – large organisations headquartered outside of Asia and doing business in Asia and Asian organisations doing business globally. These face challenges of adapting practices from one Asian context to another.

The third factor, 'Competence', relates to personal characteristics. There have been numerous studies about whether leaders are 'born or bred'. These studies look at who leaders are, what they know and what they do as driven by their heritage versus their ability to learn. While some research implies leaders do have pre-dispositions that influence how they think and act, other research also implies leaders can learn to think and act differently if they consciously choose to do so. These findings give insights into what an individual needs to recognise to be effective in HRM. When people are self-aware of their predispositions, they are able to apply or adapt them to their required results. This can be applied to HR practitioners. This clearly indicates that even those managers with the same HR title may be radically different in what they do, what is expected and their skills.

CONCLUSION

Our focus on the HRM and organisational effectiveness link and relationships and the influences on them in the Asia Pacific region has yielded three key themes. First, there are the implications of ongoing global and regional transformation, including changing governmental policies, demographic profiles, economic shifts and social perspectives. These will inevitably affect Asia Pacific organisations with respect to both their changing measures of and criteria for 'effectiveness' and the associated HRM strategies, roles and competencies required to deliver them. The studies in our book suggest that the latter are dynamic and transitional in all of the countries studied and that there are significant variations between countries and between organisational types.

Second, organisational effectiveness is a complex concept that contains both quantitative and qualitative components which are inexorably intertwined and embrace multiple internal and external stakeholders. Hence, HRM researchers and professionals will need to develop more sophisticated modelling systems and measures which will enable more precise identification and subsequent justification of the links between HRM and organisational effectiveness.

The final theme is the importance of particular regional and country contexts on HRM theory and practice. It can no longer be assumed that US-biased and ethnocentric universalist HRM approaches are desirable or feasible in diverse economic, social, cultural or political environments. The debate over 'convergence versus divergence' in HRM has played an important part in reinforcing our understanding of this issue. However, we need to move further towards the recognition that HRM systems and practices need to be responsive to, and to be transformed by, local traditions as well as by global pressures and opportunities. Therefore, while we may use Western HRM models and frameworks to analyse HRM strategies, systems and roles in Asia Pacific countries, we should also be prepared to amend them according to practical experience and growing empirical evidence such as we have presented in this book.

REFERENCES

Boudreau, J., Ramstad, P., 2003. From Professional Business Partner to Strategic Talent Leader: What's Next for Human Resource Management? Cornell Center for Advanced Human Resource Studies, New York.

Brockbank, W., Ulrich, D., James, C., 1997. Trends in human resource competencies. Third Conference on HR Competencies, University of Michigan School of Business, Ann Arbor, MI.

Brockbank, W., Ulrich, D., 2003. The New HR Agenda: 2002 HRCS Executive Summary. University of Michigan Business School, Ann Arbor, MI.

Carroll, S.J., 1990. The new HRM roles, responsibilities and structures. In: Schuler, R.S. (Ed.), Managing Human Resources in the Information Age. Bureau of National Affairs, Washington, DC, pp. 204–226.

Delery, J., Doty, H., 1996. Modes of theorizing in strategic HRM: tests of universalistic, contingency and configurational performance predictions. Academy of Management Journal 39 (4), 802–835.

Grubman, E.L., 1998. The Talent Solution. McGraw-Hill, New York.

Hall, C., Fourie, L., 2007. Exploring the role of the human resource function in the South African IT industry. Journal of Human Resource Management 5 (1), 54–64.

Katz, R., 1955. Skills of an effective administrator. Harvard Business Review, January–February 33–42.

Kochan, T., Barocci, T., 1985. Human Resource Management and Industrial Relations. Little, Brown, Boston.

Marchington, M., 2008. Where Next for HRM? Rediscovering the Heart and Soul of People Management. Working Paper No 20. IES. Manchester Business School, University of Manchester.

Miles, R., Snow, C., 1978. Organizational Strategy, Structure and Process. McGraw-Hill, New York.

Porter, M., 1985. Competitive Advantage: Creating and Sustaining Superior Performance. Free Press, New York.

Renwick, D., 2003. Line manager involvement in HRM: an inside view. Employee Relations 25, 262–280.

Rowley, C., 2003. The Management of People: HRM in Context. Spiro, London.

Rowley, C., Harry, W., 2011. Managing People Globally: An Asia Perspective. Chandos, Oxford.

Rowley, C., Jackson, K., 2011. HRM: The Key Concepts. Routledge, London.

Rowley, C., Ulrich, D., 2012a. Setting the scene for leadership in Asia. Asia Pacific Business Review 18 (4), 451–464.

Rowley, C., Ulrich, D., 2012b. Lessons learned and insights derived from leadership in Asia. Asia Pacific Business Review 18 (4), 675–681.

Tyson, S., Fell, A., 1986. Evaluating the Personnel Function. Hutchinson, London.

Ulrich, D., 1997. Human Resource Champions: The Next Agenda for Adding Value to HR Practices. Harvard Business School Press, Boston.

Ulrich, D., Brockbank, W., Younger, J., Ulrich, M., 2013. Global HR Competencies: Mastering Competitive Value from the Outside In. McGraw-Hill, New York.

Wright, P.M., Dunford, B.B., Snell, S.A., 2001. Human resources and the resource-based view of the firm. Journal of Management 27, 701–721.

INDEX

'*Note*: Page numbers followed by "f" indicate figures and "t" indicate tables.'

Printed in the United States
By Bookmasters